D1472208

"New Hope for the Indians"

"New Hope for the Indians"

••••••••

The Grant Peace Policy and the Navajos in the 1870s

••••••••

Norman J. Bender

••••••••

Published in cooperation with
the Historical Society of New Mexico

••••••••

University of New Mexico Press
Albuquerque

Library of Congress Cataloging-in-Publication Data

Bender, Norman J., 1927–
New hope for the Indians : the Grant peace policy and the Navajos
in the 1870s / Norman J. Bender. — 1st ed.
p.   cm.
"Published in cooperation with the
Historical Society of New Mexico."
Bibliography: p.
Includes index.
ISBN 0-8263-1149-0. — ISBN 0-8263-1165-2 (pbk.)
1. Navajo Indians—Government relations. 2. Navajo Indians—
Missions. 3. Indians of North America—Southwest, New—Missions.
4. Indians of North America—Government relations—1869–1934.
I. Historical Society of New Mexico. II. Title. III. Title: Grant
peace policy and the Navajos in the 1870s.
E99.N3B44   1989   89-5491
979'.00497—dc19   CIP

For Eugenia

Contents

Illustrations viii

Foreword ix

Preface xi

1. Prelude: The Grant Peace Policy *1*

2. Presbyterians and Navajos: First Contacts *9*

3. The Peace Policy Enlarged, 1870 *27*

4. Trying to "Do Good" to the Navajos, 1871 *45*

5. A Martyr for the Cause, 1872 *73*

6. A Renewed Crusade to Cleanse the Temple, 1873 *93*

7. A Visit to the Great Father, 1874 *111*

8. A Fallen Idol, 1875 *131*

9. If at First You Don't Succeed, 1876 *151*

10. Where Do We Go from Here? 1877 *163*

11. Conclusion: "The Old, Sad Story" *181*

Epilogue 197

Notes 203

Bibliography 239

Index 247

Illustrations

Grant greeting an Indian delegation 61

Agent W. F. M. Arny and the Indian delegation 62

Ely Parker 63

President Ulysses S. Grant 63

James H. Carleton 64

Sheldon Jackson 64

John Lowrie 65

David F. McFarland 65

San Francisco Street in Santa Fe 66

Fort Defiance, Arizona 67

James M. Roberts 67

General Oliver O. Howard 68

John Menaul 69

Charity Ann Menaul 69

Grave of A. H. Donaldson 70

Map of the Navajo Reservation and Vicinity 71

Sketch of the Navajo Agency at Fort Defiance 72

Foreword

"New Hope for the Indians": The Grant Peace Policy and the Navajos in the 1870s discusses the application of a brief, but important, experiment in United States Indian policy. Under this policy, representatives of religious denominations were assigned to various Indian tribes as agents. In the case of the Navajos, these agents were from the Presbyterian denomination. In his study, Dr. Bender has detailed events in this experiment from optimistic start to its abject failure.

This is Dr. Bender's second contribution to the co-publication series between the Historical Society of New Mexico and the University of New Mexico Press. His first was *Missionaries, Outlaws, and Indians,* the story of another missionary effort by the Presbyterian Church. Both of these books add to the growing knowledge of American attitudes and policies toward the American Indian.

This volume is a thoroughly researched and documented story. The author has made extensive use of manuscript sources from the Presbyterian Church archives as well as other standard materials for the era and people involved. Selected aspects of the Grant Peace Policy have been treated in several publications, but very little has been published concerning that Peace Policy in Arizona and New Mexico; nowhere does an in-depth study such as this one exist.

The current officers and members of the Board of Directors of the Historical Society of New Mexico are: Spencer Wilson, president; Charles Bennett, first vice president; Michael L. Olsen, second vice president; John W. Grassham, secretary; M. M. Bloom, Jr., treasurer. The members of the Board are: John P. Conron, Thomas E. Chavez, Richard N. Ellis, Austin Hoover, John P. Wilson, Albert H. Schroeder, William J. Lock, Myra Ellen Jenkins, Susan Berry, Darlis Miller, Robert R. White, Robert J. Torrez, Elivs E. Fleming, Mary Jane Garcia, and David Townsend.

Preface

History has no record of any nation or people ever lifting
themselves out of barbarism into civilization and
Christianity by their own unaided efforts. Let us then
help these barbarians to the light of a higher life.
—Reverend William Truax to John Lowrie, Secretary,
Presbyterian Board of Foreign Missions
March 22, 1873

"With upright and benevolent men as Indian Agents; with the friendly influence of the Indian Department, fostering education and favouring missionary labors . . . , surely there is new hope for this people!"[1] This sanguine declaration appeared in a periodical published by the Presbyterian Church in October 1870.[2] The people who were to benefit from these great expectations were the Indians residing in the United States, and the new hope for their salvation and advancement was derived from a novel approach to administering that nebulous mechanism known as U.S. Indian policy. The new concept, labeled the Grant Peace Policy for the president who initiated the program, was a direct response to demands for reform in the Indian service following the Civil War. Reacting to these pressures, the administration agreed to a partnership of church and state that would, hopefully, provide ways and means to pacify, civilize, and Christianize the Indian tribes in the United States.

At the outset of the program, churchmen and statesmen alike believed that their close association in this noble venture could bring the long-awaited solution to the Indian problem. As part of the new policy, the Office of Indian Affairs permitted the churches to nominate Christian laymen for positions as Indian agents. In addition, the churches could assign, whenever possible, missionaries to preach and teach at the Indian agencies. Underlying the reasoning for this bilateral commitment was the assumption that agents and missionaries could work cordially together to uplift the Indians entrusted to their care. The churchmen, ordained and secular, who accepted these positions, approached their tasks intending to right the wrongs incurred when previous schemes to deal with the Indian problem had gone awry. If they had been accused at the time of harboring desires to destroy traditional tribal societies with methods that could only have been described as genocidal, the agents and missionaries would not have denied the charge. On the contrary, they would have argued that they were, in a sense, saving the Indians by destroying their cultures. Certainly the Indians would literally become extinct if unshielded from the rapacious greed of unprincipled whites who were determined to seize their lands. By first placing all of the tribes on protected reservations, and then civilizing and Christianizing them, the agents and missionaries could teach the surviving Indians to fend for themselves someday with reasonable hopes for successful assimilation into the white man's world.

Regrettably, the zealous churchmen blithely approached their tasks with the assumption that vigorous application of Christian axioms would overcome all obstacles. They soon discovered that their pious principles had little effect when directed, for example, to hard-headed negotiations for annual appropriations and to efforts to overcome opposition from Indians and whites who, quite simply, did not agree with their methods. When the agents perceived pressing needs requiring large expenditures from the public purse, they were invariably disappointed when a parsimonious Congress was not inclined to appropriate funds for a department of the government that had a dismal record of failure with previous programs directed, from the legislator's viewpoint, to hopeless attempts to uplift a degraded race. The agents were also distressed when they discovered that many westerners, who saw the Indians as bloodthirsty savages, looked with disdain at benevolent schemes derived by do-gooders in the East who had no appreciation of the harsh reality of life on the frontier. As for the Indians, some of the western tribes did have reputations as fiercely independent warriors, and it became an exercise in futility to try and convince them to turn to agricultural pursuits for their livelihood. Finally, agents and missionaries who were expected to work harmoniously together often found themselves at cross purposes when their approaches to problem solving were based on practical considerations on one hand and scriptural admonishments on the other. These and other dilemmas were faced by the Presbyterians who courageously left their comfortable and familiar surroundings in the East to aid the Indians in an area the churchmen regarded as a God-forsaken wilderness.

Focusing on events associated with application of the Peace Policy to the Navajo Indians in the Southwest in the 1870s, this study of the achievements, or lack thereof, of the dedicated churchmen and the representatives of the Great Father in the nation's capital is intended to draw conclusions, for the most part, from their own observations of their experiences. This added dimension of intimate personal commentary has been derived from extensive use of the collection of American Indian Correspondence at the Presbyterian Historical Society in Philadelphia, Pennsylvania. An examination of this large collection of letters from Indian agents and missionaries reveals much about the rigors of day-to-day existence at an Indian agency. The addition of this material to the records of the various government agencies associated with the post–Civil War Indian program presents a new and, perhaps, more objective understanding of the role played by the churchmen who at least brought honesty and good intentions to a system traditionally associated with corruption and callous disregard for the needs of the Indians.

I am indebted to many persons for their kind and generous assistance in making this work possible. Gerald Gillette and his staff at the Presbyterian Historical Society in Philadelphia were very helpful, as always, in providing pertinent documents from the society's collections. My visits to the Presbyterian Historical Society would not have been possible without the aid of a grant from the Council on Research and Creative Work of the University of Colorado. At the regional offices of the National Archives in the Federal Center, Denver, Colorado, Joel Barker guided me to the microfilm records of the Office of Indian Affairs. In Washington, Richard Crawford at the National Archives directed my attention to the collections pertaining to my topic.

Staff members of the library at the University of Colorado, Colorado Springs, devoted much time to acquiring materials needed for this study. Mrs. Jackie Nichols carefully researched microfilm copies of the Santa Fe *New Mexican* for items relevant to the Presbyterian involvement with the Grant Peace Policy in New Mexico. For newspaper accounts of the journey to Washington, D.C. by W. F. M. Arny and his delegation of Navajo chiefs, I am indebted to researchers at the Missouri State Historical Society, Columbia, Missouri; Illinois State Historical Society, Springfield, Illinois; Chicago Historical Society,

Chicago, Illinois; District of Columbia Public Library, Washington, D.C.; Columbia Historical Society, Washington, D.C.; Boston Public Library, Boston, Massachusetts; and the Providence Public Library, Providence, Rhode Island. Finally, my deepest thanks are extended to Elaine Schantz who provided indispensable typing services in the production of the manuscript.

1

Prelude

The Grant Peace Policy

A system which looks to the extinction of a race is too
horrible for a nation to adopt without entailing upon
itself the wrath of all Christendom and engendering in
the citizen a disregard for human life and the rights of
others, dangerous to society.
—Ulysses S. Grant, Address to the Congress
December 6, 1869

The origins of the so-called Grant Peace Policy of the 1870s can be
traced, in part, to rivalry between the legislative and executive branches
of the government for patronage appointments at Indian agencies.
However, a major impetus for the new and enlightened approach to
the Indian problem came from an elusive and hard to measure factor—
outraged public opinion. While the bloody struggles of the Civil War
held the attention of most Americans late in 1864, an incident occurred
at a remote and barren location in southeastern Colorado on November 29 that brought an outcry for reform of Indian policy. On that
date troops of the First and Third Colorado Cavalry led by Colonel
John Chivington, commanding officer of the military district of Colorado, attacked and destroyed a peaceful encampment of Cheyenne
and Arapahoe Indians.[1]

Stories of atrocities committed by the soldiers on the defenseless
Indians brought angry denunciations from many Americans who saw
the Sand Creek massacre as a glaring example of the failure of an
Indian policy that was, in the eyes of critics, ill defined at best. Admittedly, an Indian policy of sorts had evolved from the time prior
to the Civil War when some government officials began to call for a
program to locate all Indians on reservations. Writing in 1850, for
example, Commissioner of Indian Affairs Luke Lea had provided one
of the more succinct appraisals of the benefits anticipated from adoption of the new policy. In Lea's opinion, many tribes that still retained
passions for war and the chase would soon forget those bad habits
in the confined and controlled environment of a reservation where

1

they would have to resort to agricultural labor or starve. When each tribe was finally assigned to a permanent reservation with well-defined boundaries encompassing land suitable for agriculture, then surely a regeneration of the entire Indian race could be anticipated.[2]

In the fall of 1864, the Indians at Sand Creek may not have realized that they were being "regenerated" by their adoption of the white man's policy. Nevertheless, they did believe that they were residing peacefully on a reservation legitimately assigned to them in 1861 in a treaty signed at Fort Wise, Colorado. That treaty included the promise that the United States would "protect the said Arapahoes and Cheyennes in the quiet and peaceful possession of the said tract of land so reserved for their future home, and also their persons and property thereon, during good behavior on their part."[3]

Differences in interpretation of the incident at Sand Creek soon polarized into eastern and western viewpoints. Some easterners saw a shocking revelation of genocidal traits in many westerners whose bloodthirsty appetites could only be satisfied by the extermination of an inferior race. Indignant westerners, though, offended by a reaction from those far removed from the scene, argued that the military exercise carried out at Sand Creek was justified as a preventive measure against Indians who had certainly not exhibited "good behavior on their part." Many were the stories of the treacherous Indians taking advantage of the scarcity of troops in the West during the Civil War to plot depredations against white settlers. If the rules of civilized warfare had been ignored by some members of the punitive expedition, the westerners insisted that those rules hardly applied in a confrontation with a manifestly uncivilized enemy.

Although the complexity of the issues woven into the Sand Creek affair continues to inspire differing views from historians, most analysts would agree with Francis Paul Prucha who stated: "The Sand Creek Massacre became a *cause célèbre*, a never-to-be-forgotten symbol, of what was wrong with United States treatment of the Indians, which reformers would never let fade from view."[4] Indeed, reaction to the engagement at Sand Creek reached into areas of concern far removed from that battlefield. Those who had been agitating for reforms in Indian policy increased their demands for a new program that would reflect the interests of the great majority of right-thinking Americans who saw it as their Christian duty to help the Indians.[5]

The initial reaction in Congress to this pressure was to search out and condemn those who were responsible for the deplorable events in Colorado. The Joint Committee on the Conduct of the War conducted a formal investigation in Washington early in 1865. At the same time, a military commission held an inquiry in Denver, Colorado. The preponderance of evidence recorded in the reports of those investigative bodies identified the villains at Sand Creek as those Coloradans who, acting on their own initiative, had conspired to strike out ruthlessly at the supposed threat from their Indian enemies. Lest it appear that this apologia was designed to distract attention from the basic problem, the Congress then sought to calm the troubled waters with a joint resolution on March 3, 1865, authorizing a committee, chaired by Senator James R. Doolittle of Wisconsin, to inquire into the condition of the Indian tribes.[6]

The members of the committee agreed to tour the West in three subcommittees to obtain observations on the plight of the Indians. Knowing that these visitations would not reach all those who might wish to contribute information, the committee also sent a circular letter with twenty-three questions to regular army officers, Indian agents and superintendents, and others knowledgeable about Indian affairs. After the completion of their inspection tours, conducted during the summer of 1865, the roving members of the committee returned to Washington where they evaluated the results of their investigations. The testimony collected on the tours, along with twenty-seven responses to the questionnaire, appeared as a lengthy appendix to a report finally published on January 26, 1867.

The report of the Doolittle committee emphasized in particular the startling reduction in the numbers of Indians. The analysts attributed this attrition to several factors, including disease, intemperance, war among themselves and with white men, and loss of hunting grounds to the railroads and to those prospecting for precious metals. On the much discussed question of the proper home for the Office of Indian Affairs, the committee members agreed that it should stay where it was in the Interior Department, instead of being transferred back to the War Department from whence it came in 1849. The committee then concluded its general observations with a recommendation for passage of a bill to subdivide the Territories and States where the Indian tribes resided into five inspection districts. Five boards of distinguished civilians and army officers could then be appointed by the president to have broad supervisory powers over the administration of Indian affairs in their districts.[7]

To the dismay of many reformers, while timorous lawmakers hesitated to attempt drastic changes in the existing system, events in the West led to still another change of direction in Indian policy. In the summer of 1866, an outbreak of Indian attacks against forts along the Bozeman Trail in Wyoming and Montana raised again the spectre of widespread Indian warfare developing across the plains. Hoping to forestall this calamity, the Congress, on July 20, 1867, authorized creation of a Peace Commission of prominent military officers and civilians headed by Commissioner of Indian Affairs Nathaniel G. Taylor. The commissioners were empowered to secure treaties that would remove the just causes of complaints by the Indians. Beginning in the late summer of 1867, the commissioners, who all agreed that reservations must be selected that would become permanent homes for the Indians, worked diligently for almost a year to secure the treaties. When the last treaty was signed on July 3, 1868, agreements had been reached with representatives of the principal tribes in the high plains and eastern Rockies. Although the contents of the treaties varied somewhat to conform with the unique status of each tribe, the treaties all contained similar language pledging perpetual peace between the signatories. The government also promised to supply agency buildings, schoolhouses, teachers, seeds, farming implements, and various forms of gifts and annuities for the Indians on their new reservations.[8]

In the midst of this flurry of treaty making, the commissioners issued an interim report on January 7, 1868, summarizing their conclusions to date about the Indian problem. Their recommendations included a demand for thorough revision of existing legislation pertaining to Indian affairs, along with a sweeping restructuring of the Indian service. The commissioners clearly expressed their anger at the relative lack of concern by the Congress for the Indians. Members of Congress understood the Negro question, the commissioners noted, and they conducted learned discussions about political and financial problems, but, "when the progress of settlement reaches the Indian's home, the only question considred is 'how best to get his lands.' When they are obtained, the Indian is lost sight of." The report also criticized missionary societies and other benevolent institutions for excessive concern with civilizing the heathen in Asia and Africa, while "scarcely a dollar is expended or a thought bestowed on the civilization of Indians at our very door."[9]

Reformers in the East generally applauded the efforts of the Peace Commission. Surely these treaties, and the reservations that would be created therefrom, would be giant steps in the right direction toward a final solution of the Indian problem. News from the West once again thwarted these pleasing expectations. Even as the members of the Peace Commission completed their work, another outbreak of violence erupted across the plains. In August 1868, war parties of Cheyenne and Arapahoe Indians, angry at what they regarded as non-compliance with the terms of their treaty, raided settlements in western Kansas and eastern Colorado. The warfare spread across the southern plains, until a winter campaign by the army finally drove the rebellious Indians back to their reservations. Clearly, there was still much work to be done before the well-meaning intent of the great treaties could be translated into effective policy at the agency and reservation levels.

In the front ranks of those concerned about corrections of abuses at the lower levels of Indian policy administration were members of the Society of Friends, or Quakers, who had long been associated with programs for peaceful and humane treatment of the Indians. On January 25, 1869, a delegation of Quakers visited President-elect Ulysses S. Grant to discuss ways and means to improve the lot of the Indians. Soon after the meeting Grant, recalling the Quaker interest in this matter, authorized the presentation of a rather extraordinary proposal to the churchmen. Would the Quakers wish to recommend good men from their ranks to serve as Indian agents at selected agencies? The principal benefit anticipated from this action seemed obvious. The taint of corruption frequently associated with agency appointments would, of course, be eliminated when "good churchmen" carried out the responsibilities of these positions.[10]

As the Quakers carefully considered Grant's overture, the president touched briefly on the Indian problem in his concise inaugural address of March 4, 1869. "The proper treatment of the original occupants of this land—the Indians—is one deserving of careful study," he stated. "I will favor any course toward them which tends to their civilization and ultimate citizenship."[11] While hardly a clear and forceful statement of presidential policy, to the ears of his listeners who were concerned with Indian service reform, Grant's first presidential act in the area of Indian affairs could only have been regarded by the reformers as commendable. When the Quakers finally announced their willingness to accept his challenge, Grant permitted them to recommend appointees for agency positions in the Northern and Central Superintendencies, an area that included tribes in Kansas, Nebraska, and part of the Indian Territory. Grant then placed army officers as agents at the remaining agencies, reasoning that these officers would otherwise be obliged to resign their commission in the wake of continuing demands for postwar budget trimming in the military departments.[12]

While the president proceeded with implementation of the Quaker experiment, other leaders of the government finally responded to the many suggestions for creating boards of men who could be ever watchful for signs of corruption in the Indian service. On April 10, 1869, Congress authorized the president to appoint a Board of Indian Commissioners consisting of not more than ten men highly regarded for their intelligence and philanthropy. Without monetary compensation, these volunteers would strive to develop a policy of joint control with the Secretary of the Interior about the expenditure of funds appropriated for the Indians.[13]

Expressions of widespread approval in reform circles accompanied the announcement of the names of appointees to the new board. Drawn from the ranks of outstanding laymen of the great Protestant denominations, these men could well have been labeled a Blue Ribbon Commission. Their first problem was unanticipated and disruptive. The chairman, William Welsh, a wealthy merchant from Philadelphia, resigned soon after his appointment, angry at what he regarded as the very limited scope of the board's authority. Felix R. Brunot, part owner of a Pittsburgh steel mill, then accepted the chairmanship and the board members began their work with great determination. They arranged for creation of subcommittees of the board to conduct annual inspection tours at the Indian agencies. They also created a purchasing subcommittee to insure that procedures for purchasing supplies for the Indians would strictly adhere to requirements for awards to qualified low bidders. Provisions were also made for inspection of the quality of goods when delivered. The initial response of the commission members to their task was not particularly cheerful. In their first annual report of November 23, 1869, the commissioners characterized the deficiencies of previous Indian policy as "unjust and iniquitous beyond the power of words to express." They offered numerous recommendations, however, designed to right this injustice, including a call for the honest and prompt performance of all treaty obligations to the reservation Indians.[14]

As 1869 drew to a close, there was a noticeable air of optimism among those interested in advancing the cause of Indian policy reform. The administration's efforts to bring the spirit of Christian goodwill into the mainstream of Indian affairs administration, along with the attempt to experiment with using churchmen as Indian agents, became known collectively as the Grant Peace Policy. Approval for the introduction of these innovations was widespread in government circles in the East. In his annual report to the president, Secretary of the Interior Jacob D. Cox agreed that the sweeping changes were justified in response to the overwhelming demand for radical reorganization of the Indian service. The evidence of good work by the Quakers at their agencies was enough to make it certain that there had been no mistake in their selection. As for the record of achievement to date by the Board of Indian Commissioners, Cox believed their efforts could not fail "to stimulate the public conscience, and to give greater unity and vigor to the voluntary efforts made throughout the country in the cause of Indian civilization. . . ."[15]

Ely S. Parker, a Seneca Indian selected by the president as his Commissioner of Indian Affairs, offered comments in a similar vein. In his annual report, Parker expressed pleasure with the work of the Indian Commissioners following their first tours of inspection. Parker regarded suggestions offered by the commissioners for the welfare of the Indians important enough to receive careful consideration. The commissioner was also content with the results of the Quaker experiment during its trial period. As he saw it, the plan provided a positive benefit to the Indian service, "and the indications are that the interests of the government and the Indians will be subserved by an honest and faithful discharge of duty, fully answering the expectations entertained by those who regard the measure as wise and proper."[16]

In President Grant's annual report on the State of the Union dated December 6, 1869, his comments on the Indian problem exceeded by far his few remarks on this issue in his inaugural address. Since the embarrassment and expense associated with the previous management of the Indians could not be undone, the president reasoned that the problem must be considered as it then existed. He believed that his new policy toward the "wards of the nation" had exhibited commendable results so far. The Quaker experiment had certainly proved satisfying in its achievements. Reflecting upon his decision to select army officers for other agency positions, Grant justified this policy by explaining that army officers had a personal interest related to their trade in living harmoniously with the Indians and establishing a permanent peace. Looking to the future, the president declared: "A system which looks to the extinction of a race is too horrible for a nation to adopt without entailing upon itself the wrath of all Christendom and engendering in the citizen a disregard for human life and the rights of others, dangerous to society." The only reasonable alternative Grant offered to this untenable position was to place all Indians on large reservations and give them absolute protection there until they could farm their own lands and set up territorial governments for their own protection.[17]

This self-congratulation by government officials exuded a sense of unified purpose among those who were shaping the Peace Policy. If the legislative and executive branches of the government could only work together to carry out the intent of the lofty principles espoused by all, then perhaps the Indian problem could be solved. While the planners planned, many of the Indians in the West were concerned, as always, with the basic problems of day-to-day existence. Focusing on one of these distressed tribes, a group of reformers who wanted to expand the influence of the Presbyterian Church in New Mexico directed their attention to the terrible plight of the Navajos.

2

Presbyterians and Navajos

First Contacts

I think our church ought by all means to enter any door
amongst those poor Indians, as soon as practicable.
—John C. Lowrie, Secretary, Board of Foreign Missions,
Old School, Presbyterian Church
May 24, 1867

The movement of the Presbyterian Church into the Southwest after
the Civil War was not initially stimulated by intentions to do good
for the Indians. The Board of Domestic Missions, Old School, assigned
the first missionary to the area in response to reports of the evil
influences encountered by Christians in that notorious Sodom of the
Southwest—Santa Fe, New Mexico.[1] Many Anglo visitors to that city,
choosing to ignore its rich cultural heritage, viewed the society encountered there as a glaring example of the abandonment of civilized
codes of conduct by those residing in an isolated frontier community.
For example, a member of Senator James Doolittle's party investigating Indian conditions in the Southwest recorded his observations
of the ancient city. He saw a squalid frontier settlement with one-
story mud houses and narrow, filthy streets. Beggars appeared on
every corner, and gambling casinos stood open day and night. Perhaps worst of all, a lamentable disregard of the sanctity of the marriage
relationship was evident in the frequent introduction of courtesans
at parties and balls.[2]

Late in 1866, the observations of another Eastern visitor suggested
an even more appalling situation. There were no Protestant churches
in the territory! Eveline Alexander visited New Mexico in December
1866 with her husband, Colonel Andrew J. Alexander, who was in-
specting the army posts in New Mexico. Eveline's mother, Mrs. Cornelia Martin, who resided at the family home in Auburn, New York,
later recalled her daughter's letters describing the deplorable situation
in New Mexico. Choosing to ignore the extensive work conducted by

9

the Catholic Church in the area, Eveline commented on her visit, conveying despair at "the great destitution of that country of all religious privileges. . . ."[3]

If one accepted these interpretations, then New Mexico Territory was a very wicked place indeed. As Mrs. Alexander and her mother viewed the situation, the time was ripe for Protestant crusaders to bring their enlightened message to dispel the clouds of spiritual darkness in Santa Fe. There was one ray of hope in this otherwise dismal picture. On December 7, 1866, Eveline Alexander found a cause for rejoicing during her visit to Santa Fe. "This morning I went to church, quite a rare occurrence in this country," she noted in her diary. "Service was held in a room in the building known as the 'palace'—being the residence of the governor. The clergyman was an old Presbyterian who has only been here two or three weeks."[4]

The old Presbyterian mentioned by Mrs. Alexander was David F. McFarland, assigned by the Board of Domestic Missions, Old School, of the Presbyterian Church, to open a mission station in Santa Fe. Recruited from his position as principal of the Mattoon Female Seminary in Mattoon, Illinois, McFarland arrived in Santa Fe in November 1866. He organized the First Presbyterian Church of Santa Fe with twelve members on January 6, 1867. Welcome assistance for his remote outpost soon came from an unexpected source. Eveline Alexander's correspondence with her mother inspired the ladies of Auburn, New York, who belonged to the Auburn Female Bible Society, to reorganize as the Santa Fe Association. The women pledged to send Bibles, tracts, and, perhaps, a teacher to help McFarland in the little school he had started as an important adjunct to his mission.[5]

McFarland, always dogmatic in his views, soon endeavored to inform the widespread audience of the national church about the lamentable state of society in his part of the country. In a series of three articles published in *The Presbyterian Banner* in April 1867, McFarland began his polemical discourse by criticizing the lack of interest displayed by his brethren in New Mexico's problems. "What member of the Church," he queried, "knows as much respecting the moral conditions of these Territories, as he knows about India, or China, or any other far distant heathen country?" Following this condemnation with a revelation of the regrettable hold that Catholicism had upon his neighbors, McFarland discussed at length the plight of the New Mexico Indians, whose religious practices had allegedly been drastically altered by association with Catholic priests. "Much, very much, of that mongrel mixture of heathenish ceremonies and Catholicism," McFarland charged, "holds supreme sway among the great mass of the native inhabitants at this time." The distressed missionary then concluded on an optimistic note, predicting that the vast resources of his church would soon be employed to spread the light among the heathen dwelling in darkness at her very door.[6]

These lamentations did not fall on deaf ears. McFarland's articles came to the attention of John C. Lowrie, secretary of the Board of Foreign Missions, Old School, of the Presbyterian Church. At the same time this distinguished churchman was considering Mc-Farland's impassioned plea, he received a letter from Mrs. Cornelia Martin, who desired to share with the secretary her daughter Eveline's comments about the destitute condition of a particular Indian tribe in New Mexico—the Navajos. Lowrie was finally convinced by the weight of the evidence before him that the time had arrived for the Presbyterian Church to enter the field of Indian mission work in the Southwest. From all indications it appeared that the Navajo tribe would serve admirably as a testing ground for such an enterprise.[7]

The Navajos may also have been singled out to initiate a program of Presbyterian mission work among the Indians in the Southwest because of recent publicity given to the unique status of the tribe. Traditionally these warlike Indians had referred to themselves as *Diné*— the people. To many white settlers in the Southwest this designation conveyed a sense of the arrogance that had been displayed for centuries in the aggressive acts of this proud tribe. Exasperated at continued clashes between the Navajos and their white and Indian neighbors, Brigadier General James H. Carleton, commander of the military district of New Mexico, had ordered a campaign during the winter of 1863–1864 to subjugate the Navajos once and for all. After defeating the Indians on the battlefield, Carleton intended to relocate the conquered people from their ancestral homes in northwestern New Mexico and northeastern Arizona to the Bosque Redondo. This site was named by Spanish explorers for a round grove of trees located in eastern New Mexico along the Pecos River. Here, the Indians could be concentrated and closely supervised by the army from nearby Fort Sumner. The initial phases of Carleton's plan worked to perfection. By March 1864, a punitive expedition led by Colonel Christopher Carson had broken the last pockets of Navajo resistance. The victorious soldiers then forced most of the Indians to make the Long Walk, as they described the journey, to their new homes.[8]

11

Chapter 2

General Carleton's grand plan for the relocated Navajos envisioned a self-sustained community of Indians who would be converted from hunting and gathering by teaching them the appropriate agricultural techniques needed to supply their food requirements. Early accounts from eyewitnesses who viewed the experiment gave qualified predictions for successful results. The Navajos were trying to adapt to an agrarian lifestyle, although they were not very happy with their lot. They particularly resented the concession demanded of them to share the new reservation with several hundred Mescalero Apaches who had also been defeated in Carleton's subjugation program. Senator Doolittle and his colleagues noted this discontent when they visited the Bosque Redondo for three days during their tour of New Mexico in June 1865. One member of the Doolittle entourage, who mentioned that the impressions of the subcommittee members were generally favorable, observed that the dissatisfaction of the Indians could not be ignored when evaluating the success of the project.[9]

General Carleton was not really concerned about any dissatisfaction expressed by the Navajos. As he saw it, they, and all Indians, were doomed to extinction in any event, so why not let them gradually fade away on a reservation shielded from contact with the onrushing tide of white settlement. Carleton revealed this extraordinary viewpoint in his reply to the questionnaire circulated by the Doolittle Committee. One of the questions asked: "Are they [Indians] increasing or decreasing in numbers, and for what causes?" Carleton, noting that the Indians were decreasing very rapidly, mentioned among the causes for the decrease

the causes which the Almighty originates, when in their appointed time He wills that one race of men—as in races of lower animals—shall disappear off the face of the earth and give place to another race, and so on, in the great cycle traced out by Himself, which may be seen, but has reasons too deep to be fathomed by us. The races of the mammoths and mastodons, and the great sloths, came and passed away; the red man of America is passing away![10]

A vehement "Not so" would have been the rebuttal offered in 1867 by Lowrie and McFarland, and by Eveline Alexander and her mother. Since Indians were also God's children, they could be uplifted to the point where they could take responsible positions in white American society. "I think our church ought by all means to enter any door amongst these poor Indians," Lowrie wrote to McFarland, "as soon as practicable." The board secretary then asked McFarland to supply an estimate of expenses for sustaining a missionary in New Mexico for a year, although Lowrie felt sure that the Board of Foreign Missions would not hestitate about entering this interesting field no matter the cost. Many times the board was obliged to act in faith, Lowrie concluded, and in this case he was sure the funds would somehow be provided.[11]

As soon as practicable turned out to be longer than originally contemplated by the Presbyterians in New Mexico and New York. Late in 1867, the status of the Navajo experiment at the Bosque Redondo had to be regarded as questionable, to say the least. The Mescalero Apaches, after fleeing from the reservation in the fall of 1865, had disappeared into the vast and sparsely populated reaches of southeastern New Mexico. Crop failures caused by droughts and insects had dealt crippling blows to the plans for agricultural self-sufficiency. Finally, opposition to the scheme from Carleton's political enemies in New Mexico was another factor contributing to declining support for the project by government officials. But if the plan was abandoned, then what to do with the Navajos? Certainly they were no longer warlike in nature; the cultural shock of their removal had obviously shattered their combative spirit. Among the recommendations in the January 7, 1868, report by the Peace Commission was a call for a formal peace treaty with the Navajos. Armed with authority to proceed toward this goal, members of the commission visited the Bosque Redondo late in the spring of 1868. They agreed that the deplorable conditions warranted returning the Navajos to their old homeland if they so desired. In a treaty signed on June 1, 1868, the negotiators consummated this agreement. The Indians then retraced their steps under military escort to a new reservation in northwestern New Mexico and northeastern Arizona.

In the Navajo treaty of 1868, the signatories agreed that all war between the parties to the agreement would forever cease. Within the reservation boundaries accepted by both sides, the United States agreed to build an agency building, a carpenter shop, a blacksmith shop, a chapel, and a schoolhouse as soon as a sufficient number of children could be induced to attend school. Heads of families could select tracts of land not exceeding 160 acres for the exclusive possession of the person selecting the land as long as it was cultivated. The Indians pledged to compel their children between the ages of six and sixteen years to attend school, while the United States, in turn, agreed

13

to provide for each thirty children a schoolhouse and a teacher who would teach the elementary branches of an English education. The Indians also were to receive seeds, agricultural equipment, and other forms of annuities at the new reservation. Finally, the United States promised an appropriation of $150,000 for the travel expenses of the Indians from the Bosque Redondo, along with the purchase of 15,000 sheep and goats, 500 beef cattle, and a million pounds of corn to help the Indians get a new start as peaceful farmers.[12]

With resettlement of the Navajos assured, John Lowrie moved quickly to implement his plan for a missionary to enter "this interesting field." The New York ladies who belonged to the Santa Fe Association, re-named the New Mexico, Arizona, and Colorado Missionary Associ-ation, agreed to help search for a volunteer to fill the position at the new Navajo reservation. In the summer of 1868, inquiries sent out by the association finally produced a willing candidate in the person of James Madison Roberts, a student at the Western Theological Sem-inary in Allegheny, Pennsylvania. After accepting the invitation, the young man found himself caught up in a veritable whirlwind of ac-tivity. He completed the requirements for graduation from the sem-inary; married Mary E. Koons, to whom he had been engaged for several years; and then received his instructions from the Board of Foreign Missions.[13]

Lowrie told Roberts to proceed as soon as possible to Santa Fe where David McFarland would be waiting with directions to his as-signment with the Navajos. McFarland had reported the absence of adequate housing at the reservation for a missionary family, so Lowrie urged Mrs. Roberts to remain at Santa Fe until her husband could secure acceptable quarters. Lowrie had also requested a special dis-pensation from the War Department for Roberts to purchase supplies at officer's rates for himself and his family at military posts near his mission station. Unfortunately, this request was denied, but with $200 from the mission board to cover travel expenses, and with a final admonition to be economical in their expenses, the young couple started on their great adventure, arriving in Santa Fe on November 26, 1868.[14]

News of Roberts's assignment to aid the Navajos soon appeared in Presbyterian publications. In the December issue of *The Record*, a spokesman for the Board of Foreign Missions announced that the first step had been taken toward sending the gospel to the Navajos. As-suming that not everyone might have heard of this interesting tribe, the writer noted that the correct pronunciation of the tribal name was Navahoe. Although serious uncertainties remained in planning for the mission's future, readers' prayers would surely remove all difficulties and a good work could be done for the tribe. In the next issue of this periodical, another report from the mission board indicated great concern for expected opposition to the new mission from another religious denomination. The writer predicted that agents of the Roman Catholic Church would now work diligently to thwart the efforts of the Presbyterians. The Romanist priests, who had long neglected their own work among the Navajos, would surely try to revive their ancient claims to provide for the spiritual needs of the Southwest Indians. In addition to this interdenominational rivalry, cost was another matter for concern. This factor had to be regarded as significant because, according to the writer, exorbitant shipping charges on supplies sent from the United States to far away New Mexico made the cost of living in the latter area very high. However, even with these impediments, the writer still believed that all would be well if only an open field and God's blessing could be secured.[15]

Ready to face all these challenges, Roberts set out from Santa Fe for his mission station at Fort Defiance, Arizona, site of the Navajo agency, just across the border of Arizona and New Mexico. The fort had been established in 1851 to deter the Navajos from committing depredations in the area. Although the army had abandoned the fort during the Civil War, Kit Carson used it briefly, with the name Fort Canby, as his base of operations against the Navajos in 1863 and 1864. When the Indians returned in 1868, the Department of the Interior appropriated the remaining buildings to serve as agency headquarters for the new Navajo reservation. Military operations for the region were then conducted from Fort Wingate, relocated on a site about forty miles to the southeast.[16]

As he approached Fort Defiance on January 15, 1869, James Roberts's senses would have responded to two impressions—color and cold. The overwhelming red coloration of the barren soil and the high sandstone cliffs looming ahead could not escape notice. At the same time, at an altitude of almost 7,000 feet, the numbing chill in the air might have been disheartening to someone anticipating a mild winter in sunny Arizona. In any event, as he drew nearer to his destination, Roberts would have noted a distinctive cleft in the great barrier before him. The army had constructed the fort at the mouth of this canyon, hoping to take advantage of the sporadic water supply from a small stream. In 1869, the deteriorating wood and adobe structures of the post were grouped around a rectangular parade ground. All in all, the first sight of his new home could hardly have been received with great joy by someone accustomed to the characteristics of a prosperous and civilized society back East.

Whatever his personal feelings at the time, Roberts's immediate concerns were to establish contact with the Indians; secure suitable housing for himself and Mrs. Roberts, who remained behind temporarily in Santa Fe; and conduct a burial service for Theodore H. Dodd, agent to the Navajos, who died the day after Roberts's arrival. In their very brief acquaintance, Roberts felt that he had found a friend in the desperately ill man. Dodd had started to prepare three rooms in one of the agency buildings for use by the Roberts family. All was ready except for installation of doors and windows. After completing the sorrowful task of interring the deceased agent, Roberts realized that construction on his living quarters would probably be disrupted until the arrival of a new agent, who he hoped would not be an enemy to the religious work. In the interim, the missionary secured lodging with members of an Indian family, all of whom, as he recalled, professed an ardent desire to learn to read and write the English language.[17]

Roberts must have been somewhat apprehensive about the kind of reception he would receive from the Navajos because his presence at Fort Defiance was not at their behest. In a few days he secured an audience with several of the chiefs of the tribe, who asked him quite bluntly what he intended to do at Fort Defiance. Knowing that this was not the time to play the role of zealous proselytizer, Roberts replied simply that he had come to teach the Navajos to read and write in the school promised to the Indians in their treaty with the government. The chiefs then indicated their approval, promising to persuade the Navajo children to come to his school. They also declared, according to Roberts, their gratification that the new missionary was not a Catholic.[18]

All things considered, Roberts regarded these first experiences at an Indian agency as satisfactory. He was content with his surroundings and with his reception by the Indians. By the end of January, he had recruited three Navajo children who came to him during the day for their lessons. Also, by the end of January, Dodd's replacement arrived for duty. James C. French, who had served previously at the agency for the Ute Indians at Abiquiu, New Mexico, was a man who had considerable experience in dealing with Indians. Assessing his personal characteristics, Roberts was pleased to note that French was not a drunkard. Employees at the agency soon completed work on the living quarters for the missionary family, and Roberts sent for his wife to join him at Fort Defiance. When Mrs. Roberts arrived on February 13, the young couple moved at once into their new home.[19]

The satisfaction experienced by the Roberts family with their new surroundings was not shared by James French. The Indians were restless. Though the Indians had been promised a large number of sheep and goats to renew their flocks at the new reservation, those pledges had not been fulfilled. French received numerous complaints about Navajos stealing cattle and sheep from nearby ranches and from other Indian tribes in the vicinity. The distraught agent was completely frustrated in his efforts to recover the stolen property. In his reports to his superintendent in Santa Fe, French endeavored to shift some of the blame for these depredations to other shoulders. He insisted that many of the Indian raids were made by Apaches posing as Navajos. On the other hand, if Navajos were clearly involved, then they were outside bands, renegades of a sort, over whom he had no control.[20]

French did find time occasionally in his busy schedule to listen to Roberts's plans for his mission. The relationship between missionary and agent was, at first, quite congenial. French indicated that he was friendly to the cause of education for the Indians. He told Roberts of his plans to erect the schoolhouse and chapel stipulated in the Navajo treaty sometime during the summer. This was welcome news to the missionary, but the first note of discord appeared when Roberts started to worry about the legal status of his mission on the reservation. He wanted French to give him title or permanent lease to at least 100 acres of ground that could then be developed as a mission farm and school. Roberts insisted that he could not, in all fairness, ask his church to spend funds to improve the mission facilities if the mission would, in fact, be controlled by the government and subjected to changes in its condition at the whim of each new agent. Roberts developed this argument further when he revealed to French that he had heard on good authority that the first choice for Dodd's replacement was a Catholic. Presumably this ill-advised act was thwarted only by the territorial governor's timely intervention. If a Catholic had come as agent then, as Roberts saw it, a Protestant missionary would soon have been informed that his services were no longer

needed. French listened and then tactfully dodged the issue by suggesting that he would have to procure more information on the matter
from his superiors before he could respond.[21]

On an eventful day early in the summer, Roberts received support
for his mission farm scheme from an unexpected source when a distinguished visitor arrived at the agency. Vincent Colyer, secretary of
the Board of Indian Commissioners, was on an inspection tour among
the tribes of the Southwest. He wanted, of course, to see how the
Navajos were getting along on their new reservation. Colyer noted
several problems, some serious, others almost humorous in nature.
He regretted that many treaty provisions were still unfulfilled. On
the other hand, the industrious Indians had planted a large grain crop
and a large harvest was anticipated. Characteristics of the typical
Navajo received his attention. "They are more like the Irish than any
people I can compare them with," he observed. "Brave, hardy, industrious, restless, quick-witted, ready for either mischief, play, or
hard work, they are a people that can be guided into becoming the
most useful of citizens, or, if neglected, the most troublesome of
outlaws." The neglect leading to outlawry could be avoided by maintaining a strong police force on the reservation or, in other words,
"treat them precisely as you treat the rougher classes in our large
cities, promptly suppressing all petty misdemeanors, and they will
behave just as well as the whites of equal culture and ability."[22]

Colyer found time during his visit at Fort Defiance to join French
and Roberts on a tour through the countryside around the agency
site. At one point the trio discovered a small valley with a water supply
about nine miles from the agency headquarters. Roberts insisted at
once that the spot would be a perfect location for his mission farm
and school. Colyer agreed and, as Roberts recalled, he urged the hard-
pressed agent to proceed at once with implementation of the missionary's grand plan. Roberts's obsession with his mission farm scheme
permitted his imagination to envisage a truly utopian community for
the Indians. Assuming that irrigation water could somehow be secured, his students could then be put to work raising food for their
own consumption while obtaining, at the same time, a learning experience that would be useful for the rest of their lives. French, ever
the patient listener, sidestepped the issue once again, explaining that
his superiors would still have to make the final decision on the matter.
Meanwhile, Roberts was convinced more than ever that he was on
the right track with his innovative proposal.[23]

Colyer's final observation about conditions at Fort Defiance concerned a matter that some might have regarded as trivial when compared to the other problems encountered at the agency. Colyer could not refrain from commenting rather humorously about a domestic problem in the Roberts's household. "Mr. Roberts, missionary of the Old School Presbyterian board," Colyer recalled, "had a school commenced among them [Navajos] at Ft. Defiance, and reported them uncommonly bright and promising, but the vagabonds of the tribe stole his chickens, milked his cow, threatened his kitchen by burglariously [*sic*] breaking in at night, and kept Mrs. Roberts on the rack of anxiety daily."[24]

This petty thievery by the Indians doubtlessly irritated James Roberts, but other financial problems at the mission gave him greater cause for concern. Since he was not on a fixed salary, he had been instructed to communicate his needs periodically to John Lowrie. Then the mission board would either send funds for his anticipated expenses or reimburse him for money already spent out of his own pocket. This system worked reasonably well, although there were times when letters with funds for Roberts's account were either late or lost in transit. James French tried to ease the cost-of-living burden at the agency by supplying meat for the Roberts's table and corn for their cow and chickens. In addition, Roberts finally received notice that he would be allowed to purchase supplies for his family at a discount from government stores at Fort Wingate. With this assistance, Roberts candidly admitted that food expenses for his family at the Navajo agency were less by about half than they would have been at his former home in Ohio.[25]

For a time it appeared that a way might be found to provide another source of financial assistance to Roberts, with subsequent relief to the treasury of the Board of Foreign Missions. Roberts learned that David McFarland in Santa Fe had recommended to appropriate government officials that Roberts be designated as principal teacher to the Navajos, with authority to enlist a staff of as many as five other teachers for his proposed mission farm and school. Roberts and McFarland knew that the treaty with the Navajos provided for federal funding for one or more salaried positions (for school teachers) at Fort Defiance. McFarland's move was designed to ensure that Roberts would be first in line, in a supervisory position, when the government authorities eventually decided to allocate these funds.[26]

Forces at work far from New Mexico prevented this dream from becoming a reality. In the fall of 1867, the ladies of the New Mexico, Arizona, and Colorado Missionary Association had raised enough money to send a teacher to assist McFarland at his school in Santa Fe. The young lady selected was Charity Ann Gaston of Knoxville, Illinois. Miss Gaston, a former missionary teacher to the Choctaw Indians in the Indian Territory, arrived in Santa Fe in November to begin her work at the school. In New York, the ladies of the missionary association were also aware of the potential for a teacher's position at Fort Defiance. Learning that Charity Ann and David McFarland were experiencing a bit of friction in the conduct of the school of Santa Fe, the ladies exerted pressure among friends in the Department of the Interior to obtain the teacher's job at the Navajo agency, along with the coveted federal salary of $600 per year, for their protégé. When Charity Ann heard that her appointment was approved, she set out at once for Fort Defiance, arriving there on October 12, 1869, to teach at the Indian school.[27]

If Roberts and McFarland were aware of the plans of the missionary association, they must have assumed that Roberts would still be awarded the position of principal teacher, with Charity Ann the first on his staff of assistants. Roberts was surely disappointed when, at long last, he received a letter from the Office of Indian Affairs explaining the government's position. Commissioner Ely Parker informed Roberts that when two or more schools were functioning at Fort Defiance, then it might become necessary to have a person to exercise a general supervisory role over them. Meanwhile, according to the government's interpretation of the Navajo treaty, only one teaching position could be funded, and that one had been awarded to the lady teacher now at the agency.[28]

The lady teacher at the agency was, of course, Charity Ann Gaston. Among her early experiences at Fort Defiance, one in particular made a profound impression. On one occasion, she witnessed a distribution of annuity goods to the Navajos. In a later communication to the women's missionary association in New York, she vividly described this event:

Now I want to set before you the scene I have been witnessing the last few days. There has been a general issue of goods by the agent, and the whole tribe has been here to be counted and receive their tickets for the drawing of their goods. Almost every thing that they use is given out to them, cotton cloth, and prints, handkerchiefs, woolen yarn, tin pails,

needles, thread, hand cards for carding wool, etc. The women with babies
or small children get the tickets for them and draw their goods.

Their condition and appearance are said to be better than last year.
When they were in the "corral," I went with some friends to the top of a
building near by and looked down upon them as they were all together,
thousands of them; and how sad were my thoughts as I remembered that
not one of *all* the vast multitude knew aught of the blessed Jesus or the
love he bore for poor sinners.[29]

For all the Presbyterians at Fort Defiance, redeeming that vast multitude of Navajo sinners depended, in large part, on expanding the
opportunity for the Indians to obtain a proper Christian education.
While Roberts's failure to secure a government teaching position may
have rankled for a time in his mind, his hopes for a teacher's sinecure
from government funds depended, in any event, on implementation
of his grand plan for the mission farm and school. The small school
that he had conducted before the arrival of Charity Ann Gaston was
not a resounding success. Roberts noticed that the few children attending grew weary of reciting every day, as they struggled to learn
English by repetition of examples. On the other hand, Roberts found
it very difficult to make any progress in learning the Navajo language.
He hoped to master it eventually, but he thought it would take at
least three years before he could become reasonably fluent. Aware of
the reluctance of youngsters to come to the day school, he was convinced that his concept of a mission farm and boarding school would
be more attractive to the children. Surely more satisfactory results
could be obtained if the young people could be placed in a situation
where, as Roberts believed, he could introduce them at once into the
costume and habitation of civilized life.[30]

Days passed with still no word from Washington on Roberts's plan
for the farm and school. The wheels of bureaucracy seemed to grind
exceedingly slow, except when government officials were motivated
to act quickly to advance their own interests. Perhaps Roberts had
this impression when he heard of President Grant's intent to place
army officers as Indian agents. Predicting that James French would
soon be replaced at Fort Defiance, he was not surprised when this
anticipated action occurred on September 1, 1869. On that date, Captain Frank T. Bennett, detached from his regular assignment with the
army at Fort Wingate, took charge of the agency. Roberts, who was
worried at first that the new man might not be in sympathy with the

mission farm proposal, was relieved when Bennett assured him that he favored the project. Bennett agreed with French, however, that the issue would still have to be resolved by a high-level decision.[31]

Actually Captain Bennett was concerned with more pressing problems than the nebulous scheme of his resident missionary. He found the old agency buildings in a miserable state of repair. In his opinion, if any agency was allowed funds for improvement of agency buildings it should be Fort Defiance because it was the most forsaken place he had ever seen. Paperwork in his office piled up. There were no carpenter or blacksmith tools at the agency. He anticipated a problem in issuing ration tickets to the Indians. His predecessor had a stamp for making the tickets, but the stamp had been sent to Santa Fe for repair, and had not been returned. There were only two horses and one mule at the agency; there was no saddle to be found, and the only conveyances available were heavy government wagons. In a masterpiece of understatement, Bennett reported to Major William Clinton, Superintendent of Indian Affairs for New Mexico in Santa Fe: "I find this a very dismal place and my surroundings are anything but pleasant. . . ."[32]

Clinton read about Bennett's problems with compassion, but he was more concerned with a letter received in mid-August from Commissioner Parker. The commissioner was very disturbed by a proclamation issued on August 2, 1869, by Robert B. Mitchell, governor of New Mexico Territory. The angry governor had abruptly declared the Navajo and Gila Apache Indians to be outlaws if they were found outside the limits of their reservations without military escort. The outlaw Indians were to be treated as common enemies of the country. Citizens of New Mexico could use whatever force might be necessary for their protection, even if it should result in the killing of the Indians. Parker regarded this proclamation as dangerous in the extreme. He instructed Clinton to do everything in his power to prevent violence.[33]

Of course, this was easier said than done. There were no clearly defined boundary markers around the perimeter of the vast reservation. Neither the Navajos nor their neighbors could know for sure when roving bands of Indians left the confines of the reservation. Early in September, angry Navajo chiefs visited Bennett complaining bitterly about the murder of two Indians by Mexicans [Mexican-Americans] who then brazenly stole the Indians' livestock. Bennett could not obtain any evidence supporting the Indians' charges, but he was sure that many Mexicans in the vicinity were taking advantage of the governor's proclamation to kill and rob peaceable Navajos. On other occasions the Navajos were on the receiving end of similar accusations. In December, when Bennett received reports from Utah of extensive depredations and murders committed by the Navajos, the agent could only note that his orders to the Navajo chiefs to end these raids had little effect because the chiefs insisted that the culprits were irresponsible young men over whom they had no control.[34]

As if these problems were not sufficient to drive any good Indian agent to distraction, Bennett had to cope with still another dilemma soon after his arrival at Fort Defiance. At the end of the summer, shipments of annuity goods, including various items of farm machinery, arrived at the agency. Bennett expressed his candid opinion of the utilitarian value of these shipments to Clinton in a respectful request "that no more money be expended for fancy plows, planters, reapers and mowers or threshing machines or anything of that sort, as there are now several such articles that are not nor have they ever been of any service to the Navajos." Bennett strongly advocated a shift in direction in moneys spent for the Navajos from useless machinery to a much more pressing need, namely, feeding the Indians, who depended on rations distributed at the agency until their crops matured at the end of the summer. Luckily, the crops of wheat and corn did provide a relatively good harvest, although there was some damage from an early frost. Bennett then sorrowfully noted that lack of adequate storage facilities and a tendency of the Indians to waste the precious grain had placed the Navajos in a very precarious position as winter drew near.[35]

On November 18, 1869, Bennett had only about six days' rations of wheat and ten days' rations of beef for the Indians. Although the majority of the Indians would eventually be forced to turn to him for their continuing subsistence, he had no idea when (or how) he could replenish his depleted supply. If the government did stop the ration program then, Bennett warned, the Indians would inevitably turn to stealing and war. There was one bit of cheering news among these gloomy predictions when, on November 25, the 1,000 goats and 14,000 sheep promised in the treaty to replenish the flocks of the Indians finally arrived at the reservation. However, the government had certainly not intended the butchering of these animals by the Navajos during the winter to alleviate their food problems. Bennett somehow managed to scrape by until the end of the year when his pleas were finally answered with an emergency shipment of wheat and corn that arrived at the agency for distribution to the hungry Indians. In spite of all of these trials and tribulations, Bennett was satisfied at the end of 1869 that the Navajos were an industrious people who, if properly encouraged, would in a short time become self-sustaining and well behaved.[36]

In the midst of this turmoil, James Roberts, occupied as always with plans for his mission farm, sought support for his project from friends in New York. He wrote to the ladies of the missionary association, explaining that the government would probably pay for construction of a school house and chapel at the farm, but perhaps the association could send at least a thousand dollars to build a residence for the missionaries. Anticipating that he would take as many as twenty families to the farm, he also asked for boxes of clothing material from Eastern donors for his tenants. Roberts advised that the clothing material would be more appropriate than finished garments because many Indians still had their own peculiar ideas of fashion and beauty which they were unwilling to surrender. Of course, there would be children at the farm, so balls, tops, and marbles would be welcomed for their amusement, thereby keeping them from gambling, one of the great vices of all Navajo men, women, and children.[37]

All of these great expectations turned to shattered dreams in November when Roberts finally received a ruling from the Office of Indian Affairs on his mission farm proposal. The decision was brief and to the point. The current treaty with the Navajos had never contemplated anything like a mission farm and manual labor school for the Indians. Therefore, the government could not approve such a project. Roberts, who must have been bitterly disappointed after this setback, bravely reported the outcome to his mission board, stating his determination to take a few boarding Indians into his own home. At the same time, he would continue to teach as many day students as he and Charity Ann Gaston could conveniently handle.[38]

As the year drew to a close, the Presbyterians on the Navajo reservation could only have regarded the results of their efforts as negligible. Still, they were confident in their ability to do good if circumstances would permit. James Bennett noted favorably that Roberts and Miss Gaston had about thirty pupils enrolled in their classes. Both teachers were much encouraged by indications that the students showed interest in their studies. In Roberts's view, if two more buildings were available for schoolhouses, and if two more teachers could be employed to conduct additional classes, then he could secure almost a hundred students. Bennett concurred with this sanguine prediction. He also observed with satisfaction that the chiefs often visited the school and were very pleased with it.[39]

At the offices of the Board of Foreign Missions, a review of progress at the Navajo mission for 1869 might have brought mixed reactions. There were times when Roberts sorely tried the board's patience. For example, on one occasion when Lowrie questioned a fund request by the missionary, Roberts petulantly replied: "If any expect of us to get along somehow or other without even the little conveniences of life which can be had for a little money they will be mistaken."[40] In the eyes of board members, this was hardly a proper attitude for a missionary whose commitment to the good work should somehow transcend monetary considerations. Actually, the board customarily approved Roberts's expenses for little conveniences. When Roberts found that he could not always obtain the agency team and wagon whenever he wanted it, the board magnanimously approved funds to secure horses and a wagon for his own use. He also received permission to purchase a cow and stove. Roberts's grandiose plans for his mission farm, however, were invariably associated in the minds of his superiors with expenditures never contemplated when Roberts was assigned to the mission at Fort Defiance. Among the more extraordinary of his requests, Roberts expected the board to find money to hire a practical farmer to teach the basics of farming at his mission farm. A physician would also be needed to take care of the Indians' health. One might surmise that the board members were not as dejected as Roberts when they learned of the government's rejection of his mission farm scheme. They could have reminded the missionary that the age-old adage about learning to crawl before you try to walk could well have been applied to the Navajo enterprise.[41]

There was cause for optimism in considering possibilities for expansion of missionary efforts by the Presbyterian Church in the West at the end of 1869. An agreement was finally reached to reunite the Old School and New School branches of the church in the North into one great denomination known as The Presbyterian Church in the United States of America. By this action many church leaders saw the way clear for a much more aggressive missionary policy in the West. In a typically zealous declaration inspired by this event, one writer exhorted:

When two great military divisions [Old School and New School], that have been operating in an enemy's country, at last come together, making one Grand Army, the world looks on expecting in some quarter a decisive demonstration. . . . Would it not be well . . . to advance to the next great mountain chain, and seizing it, to make it a stronghold for the Presbyterian Church, from which it can debouch on the States north and south and to the Western Sea?[42]

James Roberts would certainly have regarded Fort Defiance as a crucial point along the next great mountain chain. Perhaps the pooling of previously divided resources for western missionary work would bring a well-deserved increase in the niggardly allowance allocated in the past to the Navajo mission. But before judgments could be made about Western areas most deserving of expanded support, events in the nation's capital were destined to place an altogether different perspective before Presbyterian decision makers.

3

The Peace Policy Enlarged, 1870

Please send us if not a real active Christian man as
Agent, at least one who has morals enough not to fall
into the wicked vices of this western life the next month
after his arrival here.
—James M. Roberts
June 1870

An alarming note of discord between Congress and the White House on the issue of agency appointments threatened to undermine the harmonious support in Washington for the Grant Peace Policy early in 1870. Many congressmen did not approve President Grant's decision to appoint army officers as Indian agents. The legislators had long regarded selection of appointees for those positions as their prerogative, giving them the opportunity to dispense these patronage plums to deserving constituents. When Grant persisted with the appointment of army officers, congressmen reacted by inserting in the army appropriation bill of July 15, 1870, the stipulation that army officers could not hold civil appointments.[1]

While the president fumed at this maneuver, the secretary of the Board of Indian Commissioners saw in this action an opportunity to advance his own plan for improving conditions in the Indian service. Vincent Colyer expressed his displeasure with the apparent favoritism shown to the army by the president in a letter to Felix Brunot, chairman of the Board of Indian Commissioners. "The 'Army Ring' is about as huge a power as the old 'Indian Ring' and ten times as dangerous . . ." Colyer warned. "I find very few Republicans dare place themselves squarely against it, and yet I am satisfied that if it is not reduced or broken up it will destroy the Republican Party." When it became evident that the Congress would be successful in ousting the army officers at the Indian agencies, Colyer was determined that these positions should not be filled again by congressional patronage appointments. He decided that he would try to convince the president that the limited success of the Quaker experiment could be expanded dramatically if other religious denominations could be persuaded to follow the Quakers' lead. In other words, why not have all agency appointments filled by good Christian men chosen from names submitted by the mission boards of the nation's great churches?[2]

Colyer submitted his proposal to Secretary of the Interior Cox, who forwarded it with his favorable endorsement to President Grant. In mid-June, Colyer received word of the president's approval of his plan. Cox then agreed that Colyer, in his position as secretary of the Board of Indian Commissioners, was the best qualified person to solicit the cooperation of the churches. Colyer had already made overtures to at least one of the churches to participate in his plan. Early in June, he advised John Lowrie that the president would probably soon place the care of the Indians in the hands of Christians willing to assume the responsibility. Colyer assured Lowrie of the kind feelings of Secretary Cox toward the Foreign Mission Board of the Presbyterian Church. He hoped that Lowrie would be able to convince the board members to undertake the supervision of one or more Indian reservations, beginning, perhaps, with the Navajos.[3]

Would the Presbyterians participate in the grand scheme? The spirit of the times permitted nothing less than enthusiastic acceptance of the challenge. Doing good to the Indians was at the top of the list of benevolent outreach commitments devoutly desired by many Presbyterians. At the annual meeting of the General Assembly of the church in May 1870, the delegates adopted a number of resolutions, including:

That the Assembly views with deep concern the unevangelized condition of the aboriginal population of our land, and deprecates the increasing tendency among many of our citizens to treat them as a race to be exterminated, rather than as the proper objects of Christian effort, to be thereby civilized and gathered into the fold of Christ, and the Assembly hereby authorizes the Board of Missions to put forth its utmost efforts to accomplish this humane and benignant purpose.[4]

This directive seemed quite clear. When the Foreign Mission Board met on June 20, the members expressed their gratification for the liberal and benevolent policy of the government toward the Indians. They indicated willingness to recommend someone for appointment as agent to the Navajos as soon as practicable. They also promised to enlarge Presbyterian missionary work among the Indians as far as men and means could be obtained for the purpose. Lowrie notified Colyer at once of the board's favorable action, promising that Colyer would be advised as soon as the right man could be found to go the Navajo reservation.[5]

The die was cast, and the Grant Peace Policy veered in another direction. General approval in Washington for the new innovation was exemplified in the comments of Secretary of the Interior Cox who envisioned the conversion of Indian agencies into mission colonies where agents and missionaries would work together as one harmonious and complete whole. Cox saw implications in the policy for the suppression of drunkenness and immorality on the reservations because righteous married men and their families would be placed in the various positions of employment at the agencies, instead of single immoral men and mere adventurers. With right principles guiding the program, Cox was confident the government would soon discover solutions for all the questions associated with the Indian problem.[6]

The Board of Indian Commissioners approved the new program in principle, although board member Nathan Bishop warned his colleagues of pitfalls ahead. Bishop felt that the program's success would be assured only if President Grant could continue in the presidency for another twenty years. Since this was hardly possible, as soon as Grant's successor came to power the whole concept would probably be abandoned. Office seekers would once again replace Christian agents. All the progress made in civilizing and Christianizing the Indians would soon be ended. This pessimistic appraisal by Bishop failed to dampen the spirits of the board, however, and the members passed a resolution declaring hearty approval of the plan to place the Indian tribes under the care of the various religious denominations.[7]

With the decision made to go full speed ahead with the new program, the next step was to secure commitments from other denominations to join with the Presbyterians in the allotment of agencies. Colyer's letters soliciting support brought many favorable responses from church mission boards. In their eagerness to participate, some of the respondents announced that they had already recruited good men who were ready to receive their appointments as Indian agents. All, of course, were anxious to know which tribes would be assigned to their care. Acting again on the suggestion of Secretary Cox, Colyer tried to allot Indian tribes to churches in congenial pairings. His enthusiasm for his task might have been aptly described as the joyous reaction of a child playing with a new toy. Working with a map and a set of watercolors, he marked out his distribution of agencies using different hues for each denomination. He then enclosed the map with a long letter to Cox announcing his selections. Trying to show a rationale for his choices, Colyer explained that, in most cases, he made allotments of tribes to churches with a record of previous mission work among those tribes.[8]

In the Southwest, the presence of James Roberts at Fort Defiance clearly established a claim for the Presbyterians on the Navajos. But Roberts was the only Presbyterian missionary to the Indians in the vicinity. How, then, to explain the placement of four other agencies in New Mexico and Arizona on the Presbyterian list of agency responsibilities? The Catholic Church certainly expected to receive several of these agencies, since its claim for mission work in the area predated that of the Protestant denominations by centuries. When the initial distribution left the Catholic Church with only eight agencies throughout the entire West, angry church officials, after reluctantly accepting these agencies, refused to associate any further with this part of the Peace Policy. The Church decided, instead, to direct its expanding work among the Indians from a new Bureau of Catholic Indian Missions in Washington, D.C. In any event, by the end of August 1870, the Foreign Mission Board of the Presbyterian Church had responsibilities in the Southwest for appointments at the Navajo and Hopi agencies in Arizona; the Southern Apache and Mescalero Apache agencies in southern New Mexico; and the agency for the Jicarilla Apaches and Moache Utes at Cimarron in northeastern New Mexico.[9]

While John Lowrie set out to locate good men for appointments as Indian agents, James Roberts at Fort Defiance rejoiced in the expectation that Frank Bennett would soon be replaced by someone who understood the basic principles of good moral behavior. The collapse of an effective working relationship between missionary and agent came early in March 1870, when Roberts performed a marriage ceremony at the agency contrary to Bennett's wishes. It all started when a member of a government party surveying the Navajo reservation approached Roberts, requesting the missionary to marry the young surveyor to a Navajo girl. Roberts agreed to perform the service, assuring the young man that this action was the only proper way to justify living together with the girl. The girl's relatives consented to the marriage and the ceremony was duly performed.[10]

Frank Bennett received the news of these events after the fact. When he heard about the marriage, he called Roberts to his quarters where he expressed amazement that Roberts would perform such a ceremony, knowing all along that the girl was a "public woman" diseased with syphilis. According to Bennett, Roberts then "questioned my authority, using very loud language saying that he would have married the young man if his mother had been there on her knees protesting." Bennett submitted his comments to his superintendent William Clinton, who forwarded them to Commissioner of Indian Affairs Ely Parker with the endorsement:

Any act of his [Roberts] calculated to create insubordination amongst a set of illiterate Indians is very wrong. As at a military post there can be but one commanding officer, I would therefore recommend the Reverend Mr. Roberts be made to understand that there can be but one head to an Indian agency, and that all persons residing there are subject to his orders.[11]

Roberts hastened to tell his side of the story to the Commissioner of Indian Affairs. Without trying to disguise his sense of outraged decency, he deplored the immoral conduct exhibited by white employees at Fort Defiance. Most of them kept Navajo women "for the express purpose for which a man would keep a public whore." Surely this was no way to introduce American civilization and Christianity among the Navajos. Roberts defended his performance of the marriage ceremony as clearly within the scope of his authority as a minister of the Gospel. Viewed in this perspective, the whole matter was really none of Bennett's business. When Roberts also advised Vincent Colyer about his unjust treatment, Colyer offered his sympathies to his "Dear Christian Friend." In an attempt to smooth ruffled feathers, Colyer reminded Roberts that the whole Indian system had been revolutionized. If Roberts would just be patient, his views would surely prevail in time, because bad agents would be removed and good Christian men put in their place.[12]

Commissioner Parker sided with Bennett and Clinton in the dispute. He told them in no uncertain terms that persons residing on any reservation must be subordinate to the agent's instructions in any actions affecting the Indians. If, in Bennett's judgment, the welfare of the Indians demanded exclusion of any person from the reservation, then Bennett had express power to carry out this banishment. Here the matter ended, although the relationship between Roberts and Bennett never returned to its previous condition of camaraderie. Roberts found solace in the assurance that Bennett would soon depart. In a plaintive communication to Felix Brunot, the missionary insisted that the worst enemies to the work at Fort Defiance were encountered among the Americans employed there by the government. Assuming that Brunot might be in a position to influence the selection of Bennett's replacement, Roberts called for help. "Please send us if not a real active Christian man as Agent," Roberts pleaded, "at least one who has morals enough not to fall into the wicked vices of this western life the next month after his arrival here."[13]

The great marriage ceremony dispute was not the only problem James Roberts experienced at the Navajo agency early in 1870. He also encountered difficulties in the conduct of his school. The year began on a promising note as Roberts reported that school affairs were moving along smoothly. He felt he was making a little headway in his study of the Navajo language, although the improvement of his communications skills in the classroom was not noticeable to Charity Ann Gaston. Roberts spent two hours each day in the school conducting blackboard exercises and scripture readings in the English language. Charity Ann found it exceedingly unfortunate that the students could not really comprehend these lessons or the message of Jesus and his salvation. "Though we have prayer and reading the scripture every day in school," she noted, "it is not in their language and they do not understand much of what it means." A calamity befell the students and teachers on April 1 when the school was closed. Needing a residence for an agency employee, Frank Bennett abruptly commandeered a building previously provided to house the school. Roberts woefully admitted that he had no idea when other accommodations might become available for the scholars to pursue their studies. Since the students would not attend during the summer months, it might be fall before classes could be resumed.[14]

In another area of concern, Lowrie was surprised and perhaps irritated to learn that Roberts had not abandoned his scheme for locating a mission farm remote from the agency headquarters. Ignoring his previous setbacks on this issue, Roberts calmly announced his intent to resume the search sometime in the spring for a suitable farm site. In May and June, the adventuresome missionary traveled to the northernmost reaches of the reservation near the New Mexico–Colorado border. On this journey he noted the location of several promising places that could conceivably support a farming venture.

Although the area was at least seventy-five miles from Fort Defiance, Roberts blithely ignored the logistical problems associated with support of this remote location as he continued to dream about a Navajo Utopia rising from the wilderness.[15]

Last, but certainly not least, of Roberts's continuing problems was his chronic shortage of funds. Early in 1870 he informed Lowrie that he had received no drafts from the board to cover his expenses since the first of the year. This embarrassing situation had reduced him to the point of borrowing money from friends in Santa Fe to cover the credit extended to him at the commissary at Fort Wingate. The haphazard nature of reimbursement for his expenses was understandably annoying. He insisted, finally, that it was only proper, from a good business standpoint, to arrange for a regular salary as a reward for his services among the Navajos.[16]

While Roberts fretted about his shabby treatment, Frank Bennett's concerns for the welfare of the Navajos undoubtedly led him to believe that the gravity of his problems far outweighed the petty grievances of Roberts. For one thing, Bennett had to deal with a slavery problem. In New Mexico it had been rather commonplace to encounter cases where Indians were subjected to various forms of forced labor. Jean Baptiste Lamy, bishop of the Catholic Church in New Mexico, commented on this deplorable situation in his remarks to members of the Doolittle Committee during their visit to Santa Fe. "There are a good many Navajo captives among the Mexican families; they make the best of servants," Lamy asserted.

Some families abuse them, while others treat them like their own children. Most of the Mexican families have them; there are more than a thousand of them, perhaps two or three thousand. Part of these captives have been taken in war by the Mexicans, and part have been purchased from the Indians, such as the Utes, who are constantly at war with the Navajos. These slaves have been bought and sold in this manner for years. . . .[17]

Recognizing the seriousness of this issue, Bennett directed the Navajos who were agitating for release of their people to call on William Clinton in Santa Fe. On January 18, several of the Navajo chiefs appeared in Clinton's office to present their cases. In company with a deputy United States marshal, Clinton followed the Indians to several homes in the vicinity where they found six Navajo women living with Mexican families. The Navajos insisted that the women had been

33

bought from the Utes. They also assured Clinton of the women's desire to return to their people. The superintendent was unsure of the limits of his authority on the matter, so he bought time by promising the chiefs that he would seek an opinion on the merits of the case from the Commissioner of Indian Affairs.[18]

Clinton sent Commissioner Parker a statement of the pertinent issues and the commissioner responded early in March. Parker pointed out that slavery was clearly illegal, but was this really slavery? There was no way to interfere if the Navajo women had voluntarily signed a contract for hire. Perhaps it would be best for Clinton to ascertain for certain the facts in each case. Clinton surely assumed that subsequent inquiries would reveal, in each case, some form of labor contract, complete with the mark of the Indian. However, he did make one effort in June to pursue the subject. After visiting several families, hoping to arrange some sort of a settlement, he finally gave up when the Mexicans refused to show any indication of willingness to cooperate. At Fort Defiance Bennett then chose to drop the whole matter, reasoning, perhaps, that it would be better to let the whole controversy fade away, if possible, than to face the probability of court actions that could lead to violent repercussions.[19]

At the Navajo agency Bennett struggled through the winter to find the wherewithal to feed the Indians. In January, he realized that his supply of rations was, once again, running dangerously low, that no money was available to replenish his stock, and that there was little hope for a supplemental appropriation from Congress for this purpose. He continued to issue reduced rations periodically, with each Indian allotted one-half pound of shelled corn or wheat and one-half pound of fresh beef per day. By the end of April his supplies were exhausted. Acting on his own responsibility, he arranged with the commander of the military district of New Mexico for an issuance of military subsistence supplies to be used until the Navajos could harvest their crops late in the summer.[20]

Early in the year there were great expectations that 1870 would be when the Navajos would become self-sufficient in their food supply. In February, officials in the Interior Department found $30,000 in the budget that could be used, in part, to buy seeds and implements for the Navajos to put in a crop when weather permitted. Bennett recalled that in the spring, every man, woman and child who could handle a shovel or hoe, went to work in the fields. Regrettably, Mother Nature did not smile upon the Navajo farmers' efforts. Hopes for a bounteous harvest faded when a severe frost at the end of May, followed by a summer drought, ruined the Navajos' crops. Knowing that the government still intended to halt support for the issuance of rations, Bennett presented his case for continuing the program. "The question must be fairly put," he argued, "as to whether it is not better to feed them here, as an industrious, peaceable, quiet, friendly race of people (with the exception of a few thieves and bad men), or to feed a great majority of them (as prisoners of war), at some military post, the balance becoming a miserable, roaming, thieving set of vagabonds." After this announcement, Bennett could only wait with the hope that his distress signal raised in the Southwest would be visible to the eyes of legislators in faraway Washington when the Congress convened in its next session.[21]

Reports of depredations on settlers in the area continued to plague Bennett and Clinton, who were trying their best to restrain the Navajos. When the citizens of New Mexico concluded that these efforts were ineffectual, William A. Pile, who took office as territorial governor in the summer of 1869, called on residents in exposed areas to form posses to pursue and punish any thieving Indians. One reaction to this proclamation created a very tense situation on the Navajo reservation in August 1870. An irate party of fifty armed Mexicans arrived at Fort Wingate on August 25 en route to Fort Defiance to recover several hundred sheep and horses alledgedly stolen from the Mexicans. Officers at Fort Wingate managed to detain most of the posse members at the fort, while a detachment of soldiers and a few leaders of the posse proceeded to Fort Defiance to lay the charges before Frank Bennett. The party managed to retrieve a few sheep and horses but, according to the leader of the troops, Bennett refused to let him arrest any of the accused Indians because apologies had been tendered by the culprits to Bennett and the Navajo chiefs, along with promises that incidents of a similar nature would never occur again.[22]

After the departure of the still-angry posse, the commander at Fort Wingate castigated Bennett for humiliating his men in an action that would only encourage the Indians to continue stealing. When Clinton received word of this interdepartmental bickering, he defended Bennett's action to Commissioner Parker, arguing that the whole matter was precipitated by the evil effects that ensued from armed posses of citizens roaming over the country making war wherever and whenever they pleased. Eventually inflamed tempers cooled, but the inalienable right professed by residents on a remote frontier to seek vigilante justice when other forces of law and order appeared lax in their duty was never more clearly illustrated.[23]

Other news from the Navajo agency early in 1870 dealt with lesser but still troublesome matters. Indian agents received news in May via a circular letter from the Interior Department that they were expected to serve as enumerators for their tribes in the 1870 census. Bennett could not conceal his annoyance at this burden added to his other weighty problems. "As regards the taking of the census," he explained,

I would report that it will be utterly impossible for me to take the census in accordance with instructions and blanks furnished, for the reason that at least nine out of every ten [Navajos] have no names. For instance, at the last issuance of annuity goods, I issued extra goods to over one hundred sub-captains, at least half of whom had no names, and I was obliged to improvise names for them.

On another issue, Clinton brushed aside another report of a Navajo raid on a Mormon settlement in Utah when he sent his findings on the incident to Commissioner Parker. Clinton observed, with a rather wry sense of humor, that the Navajos "did not think that there was any great wrong committed . . . as they had been told that the Mormons were enemies of the United States."[24]

At this point, considering all Frank Bennett's anxiety during his tenure as agent to the Navajos, one might have expected that he would have eagerly looked forward to replacement by a civilian appointee selected by the Board of Foreign Missions of the Presbyterian Church. This was not the case, however, as Bennett indicated in September that he would be glad to resign his army commission to continue as agent at Fort Defiance if he could receive assurance that he would be given the Navajo appointment. There was really no hope for favorable consideration of his proposal with the record of his altercations with James Roberts still fresh in the minds of those who would make the selections. Even as Bennett made his offer, Presbyterian periodicals in September carried notices of the job openings at Indian agencies.[25]

An advertisement in *The Presbyterian* on September 3, 1870, described the criteria that would be used in the selection process:

The Board of Foreign Missions of the Presbyterian Church has been requested to nominate suitable persons for appointment by the

Government as Agents among some of the Indian tribes in Arizona and elsewhere . . . the object being to secure the best guaranty of character and qualifications on the part of persons appointed to these posts, and to obtain as Agents men in full sympathy with the benevolent work of all Christian people among the Indians.

Men are wanted of undoubted integrity, of careful and accurate business talents, of good judgments, of energy, and yet conciliatory in manner, and of such religious or benevolent disposition as would make them willing to take an active part in promoting the welfare of the Indians. The salary of such Agents is $1,500 each, with quarters and transportation. Securities must be furnished by the Agent and his personal friends to the amount of $25,000, conditional on the faithful discharge of his duties.[26]

How many men reading this notice would be attracted by the job description? Was the skill level demanded commensurate with the salary? Would anyone care to leave a comfortable home in the States to move to "Arizona or elsewhere"? For answers to these questions the board members could only wait to see what the mail would bring, hoping that the spirit of the Grant Peace Policy had ignited flames of missionary zeal among "persons in full sympathy with the benevolent work of all Christian people among the Indians."

John Lowrie may have been pleasantly surprised at the response to the board's advertisement. He could hardly have anticipated the large number of inquiries that poured into his New York office. He disqualified some of the applicants at once. Many were primarily interested in finding relief for health problems. For example, one writer from Rochester, New York, admitted candidly that his principal reason for applying was to seek improvement in his health in Arizona. "I cannot any longer stand this climate and the exposure to the cold," he wrote. "I am yesterday and today prostrated by a severe attack upon my lungs, brought on by exposure to the coolness and dampness. . . ." The applicant, who also professed great interest in the challenge to work with the Indians, closed with the assurance that he had voted for both Lincoln and Grant. Lowrie filed this letter with the marginal notation: "Health will not do." He accorded the same treatment to an applicant from Champaign, Illinois, who, after admitting that he suffered from "adhesions of the left lung and congestion of the diaphragm," insisted that his general health was tolerable and a move to a warmer climate would doubtlessly cure all of his ailments.[27]

In Santa Fe David McFarland took a personal interest in efforts to secure the right men for the agencies in New Mexico and Arizona. Knowing that applicants would be screened by Lowrie in New York, McFarland wrote to him early in September with an inspired suggestion. Why not appoint James Roberts as agent to the Navajos at Fort Defiance? Roberts could easily procure assistants for his missionary work, and he would then "have everything his own way." When Lowrie declined this proposition, McFarland offered another startling proposal. He had heard a rumor that the Board of Home Missions was considering withdrawal of support from his struggling mission at Santa Fe. With this in view, McFarland wondered if he might not receive an appointment as an Indian agent or, better still, an appointment as Superintendent of Indian Affairs for New Mexico. In the latter position, he could remain in Santa Fe and continue to help his little mission. Lowrie chose to ignore all of these schemes. By mid-September of 1870, he had transmitted all of his recommendations for agency appointments to the Interior Department.[28]

Unfortunately, Lowrie's failure to recommend his nominees for specific agencies delayed the decision on appointments. Officials of the Interior Department had hoped that Lowrie would make these pairings, but when they mentioned this discrepancy to the mission board, the members simply indicated that they had no preference in the matter. Any assignments made by the government would be acceptable. News of the selections finally reached the mission board from the office of the Secretary of the Interior on October 22, 1870. Samuel D. Williamson of Washington, D.C. received the appointment to the Navajo agency. Williamson had been highly recommended to Lowrie, with an endorsement by the Chaplain of the Senate, heading the list of those who appreciated his exceptional talents. When notified of his consideration for an agency appointment, Williamson assured Lowrie of his ability to work side-by-side with any missionaries at his agency in a manner that would be pleasant, profitable, and supportive of the cause of Christ.[29]

Assuming the Navajo appointment finalized, Lowrie was surprised when he learned that Williamson had notified Commissioner Parker early in November of a change-of-heart about his appointment. Another job offer to serve on the National Lincoln Monument Association was too attractive to turn down, so Williamson felt obliged to accept the more lucrative position. Parker then asked Lowrie to supply an alternate selection, hopefully an attractive young man of good business qualifications, as the Navajo agency was regarded as very important. Numerous recommendations in Lowrie's files indicated that James H. Miller had served honorably as adjutant of a Pennsylvania regiment in the Union Army during the Civil War. He now resided in Neosho, Missouri, where he was a public school teacher, a real estate salesman, and a ruling elder in the Neosho Presbyterian Church. When informed of Lowrie's recommendation, Miller expressed his readiness to accept the challenge, and he was duly appointed to the Navajo agency.[30]

Looking back at this point, John Lowrie could not have been faulted for expressing a certain amount of impatience with all the paper work and other headaches required for participation by the Presbyterians in the Grant Peace Policy. Was it worth all the time and effort? A representative answer to this question appeared in a Presbyterian periodical in October with the title "New Hope for the Indians."

With upright and benevolent men as Indian Agents; with the friendly influence of the Indian Department, fostering education, and favouring missionary labors; with the growing purpose in the country that justice and fair dealing shall be done to the Indians; with the conviction deepening in the minds of all thoughtful and Christian people, that all our duty has not yet been fulfilled towards these poor, depraved, perishing neighbors; with prayers and gifts, and purposes of self-denying labour for their conversion—surely there is new hope for this people! It is their coming under Christian influence, resulting in their civilization, or it is their speedy extinction as a race that is soon to be decided.[31]

While this new hope inspired upright and benevolent men in the East to commitments to bring justice and fair dealing to the Indians, the "poor, depraved, degraded, perishing neighbors" at the Navajo agency at Fort Defiance found their destiny influenced by the intro-duction of several new factors into the never-ending struggle for survival.

Smallpox had long been regarded as one of the major diseases contributing to the "speedy extinction" of the Indian race. To combat this disease among the Navajos, an army medical officer carried out an extensive inoculation program in the fall of 1870, among all the Navajos he contacted on the reservation. There was no provision, however, for regular medical treatment for the Navajos. Hoping to provide this service on a continuing basis, John Lowrie decided to send a missionary with medical training to New Mexico. John Menaul had a previous record of foreign mission work on the island of Corisco off the west coast of Africa, where he served from December 1868, to April 1870. Suffering from deteriorating health in the tropical climate, and despondent over the death of his wife, he returned to the United States seeking another position. Lowrie advised James Roberts in August of Menaul's reassignment to mission work in the Southwest. He described Menaul as "an Irishman by birth, but his education at College and Seminary is American. He has considerable knowledge of medicine, able to practice well in ordinary cases. He has a remarkable power of adapting himself to almost any circumstances. . . . He is truly devoted and earnest as a follower of Christ."[32]

Anticipating that the new recruit would join him at Fort Defiance, Roberts wrote to Menaul describing the items that the latter would need to set up housekeeping at the agency. In this fraternal gesture, Roberts provided an interesting insight into the rigors of life at a frontier mission station. An extra stove was available at the mission, but as there was no pipe on hand to make it functional, Roberts advised Menaul to try to buy pipe in Santa Fe. Tableware, washtubs, and oil lamps could be obtained from supplies at Fort Defiance. There was no bedding or furniture available. Roberts simply noted that he had made all of his furniture except for a bureau that he brought from the East. Above all, Roberts urged Menaul to bring along a washing machine and wringer, as washing was the hardest thing to get done at the agency.[33]

When Menaul reached the Navajo agency on November 16, Roberts was somewhat disappointed when he learned that his new comrade's first choice for a location in the field was the Zuni Pueblo, about forty-five miles southeast of Fort Defiance. While in Santa Fe, Menaul had heard that the Zunis wanted a teacher to come to their community and educate their children. Anxious to learn more about the conditions at Zuni, Menaul persuaded Roberts to accompany him on a visit to the pueblo. The missionaries found the Indians receptive to their plans, promising the use of rooms for a school and living quarters, although, in Menaul's observation, "the town being huddled together with cattlepens all around it, with their manure and other filth accumulating in it of centuries, I cannot think of living in it longer than I can get some kind of shanty thrown up outside of town." With Menaul apparently determined to start a mission at Zuni, the two men returned to Fort Defiance where Menaul began to arrange his affairs for the move to the pueblo.[34]

Roberts, who might have wished to provide greater assistance to his brother missionary at this time, had other pressing problems to consider. After obtaining another building at the agency for his school in mid-August, he was disappointed when he could not find time to take part in the renewed classroom exercises. He found that he had to use his carpentry skills on many occasions to keep the mission facilities in repair. He was also obliged to work many hours in the family garden. Adding to these concerns was the poor health of Mrs. Roberts. His comments on the latter issue provoked a sharp exchange between Roberts and Lowrie. When Roberts wondered if the board could send someone to assist his wife, Lowrie rather brusquely pointed out that army wives on the frontier operated their households efficiently without the kind of aid envisioned by Roberts. This brought an angry rejoinder from the missionary. He reminded Lowrie that army wives had access to the services of laundresses for a pittance at frontier posts. In addition, officers could always detail soldiers to help with housework. Roberts had tried to get Indian girls to help Mrs. Roberts, but none of them had stayed longer than a few days. He told Lowrie bluntly that his wife was entirely discouraged and desiring very much to go home. If help was not forthcoming, then Roberts saw no recourse but to abandon the mission, as he could not believe "that our Blessed Master calls any lady to wear herself out in a year or two for the sake of a few dollars."[35]

Roberts received support for his complaints about financial difficulties at the mission from John Menaul. Menaul agreed with Roberts on the need for a fixed salary for missionaries on duty in the Southwest. A reasonable salary scale should provide teachers, male and female, seven hundred dollars a year; a single missionary, if boarding, eight hundred or, if keeping house, nine hundred; a man and wife twelve hundred and each child one hundred per year. With this evidence of a determined and united front from Roberts and Menaul, it appeared that the Board of Foreign Missions would have to give serious thought in the coming year to either increasing the support or abandoning the effort at the remote outpost on the Navajo reservation.[36]

While Roberts and Menaul fretted about their problems, on November 30 the first shock wave of the congressional action designed to remove army officers from positions in the Indian service reached New Mexico. On that date, Nathaniel Pope of Illinois relieved Major William Clinton as Superintendent of Indian Affairs for New Mexico. Pope was a Union Army veteran whose quest for an appointment as a regional superintendent of Indian affairs could not have been hindered by his relationship as nephew of General John Pope, commander of the military district of Missouri. The desperate nature of the Navajo food problem struck Pope at once when he arrived in Santa Fe. He immediately sent a telegram to Commissioner Parker warning that there would be no rations of any kind available at Fort Defiance after December 15. The reply to this ultimatum only repeated what those in New Mexico had heard too often. There were no funds available for feeding the Indians, but efforts were underway to have those funds provided at an early date. Suspecting that the early date might be a long time coming, Pope courageously authorized purchase of 300 head of beef cattle which, together with 50,000 pounds of corn borrowed from the Quartermaster Department of the Army, would be sufficient to feed the Navajos until the Congress, reconvening early in the new year, could provide additional funding for provisions for the Indians.[37]

Another change in a government position that was directly concerned with the formulation of Indian policy occurred in October 1870. In Washington, D.C., Jacob Cox resigned as Secretary of the Interior after his outspoken opposition to President Grant's adventurous foreign policy in the Caribbean made him *persona non grata* in the administration. To fill this vacancy the president selected Columbus Delano, a former Republican member of the House of Representatives, who had been appointed Commissioner of Internal Revenue by Grant in the previous year. Any concerns that the new secretary might not be in accord with the principles outlined in the Peace Policy were soon dispelled by Delano's statement that he had been corresponding with John Lowrie whose suggestions he intended to follow. Delano also promised that everything possible would be done, within the limits of congressional appropriations, to provide the Indian agencies with suitable buildings and adequate means for the successful prosecution of the system of management adopted by the government to benefit the Indians.[38]

Other government officials shared Delano's optimistic predictions. In his annual report for 1870, Commissioner of Indian Affairs Parker reflected upon the record of past disappointments with Indian policy whereby "the Indians made but little progress toward the healthy Christian civilization in which are embraced the elements of material wealth and intellectual and moral development." By invoking the cooperation of the entire religious element of the country in the new program, however, it could be expected that this action would "bring about and produce the greatest amount of good from the expenditures of the munificent annual appropriation of money by Congress for the civilization and Christianization of the Indian race." And in his report to the Congress on December 5, President Grant reviewed the actions expanding his Peace Policy during the year, finding the results favorable indeed. "I entertain the confident hope," Grant proclaimed,

that the policy now pursued will in a few years bring all the Indians upon reservations, where they will live in houses, and have schoolhouses and churches, and will be pursuing peaceful and self-sustaining avocations, and where they may be visited by the law-abiding white man with the same impunity that he now visits the civilized white settlements.[39]

Eager to do their part to achieve the president's goal, as the year 1870 drew to a close the Presbyterian appointees to Indian agencies in Arizona and New Mexico prepared for the journey to their duty stations. Questions pertaining to expectations in their new jobs must have passed through their minds. Would there be suitable housing at the agencies? How would they be received by their Indians? And what did it really mean to have these tribes under the care of religious denominations; that is, what was the extent of their authority over the administration of affairs at their agencies? While an attitude of wait-and-see was really the only recourse available at the time for answers to these questions, all of the recruits probably would have echoed the cheerful optimism expressed by the new Navajo agent. From his home in Neosho, Missouri, James H. Miller assured John Lowrie of his intent to leave for the Southwest as soon as his official orders arrived. As for the future, Miller hoped "by the help of God and my brethren in the Church to do good among the Indians."[40]

4

Trying to "Do Good" to the Navajos, 1871

I humbly hope and pray that I may be made the
instrument of doing some good for the Indians.
—James Miller
August 5, 1871

While the Presbyterians appointed as Indian agents were en route to their duty stations early in 1871, several distinguished gentlemen associated with the Peace Policy gathered for an important meeting on January 13 in Washington, D.C. Present at this convocation were members of the Board of Indian Commissioners, Secretary of the Interior Columbus Delano, Commissioner of Indian Affairs Ely Parker, and numerous representatives from the churches supporting the Peace Policy. Following a brief audience with President Grant, the delegates assembled at the Interior Department to discuss their recent efforts to solve the Indian problem.[1]

Speaking for the administration, Secretary Delano assured one and all of the government's satisfaction with progress to date toward civilizing the Indians. Hoping to clarify relationships between agents, their mission boards, and the government, Delano explained that a record of a good Christian lifestyle was not, in itself, sufficient to ensure that a man would succeed as an Indian agent. He must also possess good health, energy, and experience in business affairs to achieve efficiency in his official as well as his religious capacity. The government would not interfer in the relationship between an agent and his mission board but it would, of course, reserve the right of instant dismissal should the appointee prove unworthy. Delano concluded by expressing his personal belief that the Peace Policy would surely succeed, "as it was sustained by a Power that was higher than any which could be derived from men only."[2]

The churchmen in his audience doubtlessly appreciated Delano's encouraging words, but they may have still pondered the question—what precisely was expected of an agent entering the Indian service in the 1870s? Actually, instructions to a new agent were spelled out in considerable detail. After posting a performance bond of $25,000 and taking the prescribed oath, the appointee received a letter from the office of the Commissioner of Indian Affairs outlining an agent's responsibilities. First, the appointee should proceed without unnecessary delay to the duty station. On arrival, he would officially relieve his predecessor by examining his records. If all was in order, receipts were given for transfer to his care of all agency property and funds. The appointee was expected to maintain the agency headquarters among the Indians in his charge, devoting his time, always, to their welfare and improvement. As agent, he was to notify the commissioner's office of all important matters transpiring at his agency. From time to time, he could make recommendations which, in his judgment, were wise and expedient for improving the well-being of the Indians. An agent was required to transmit all of his official correspondence, along with monthly reports, through the superintendent's office. Finally, he was to render statements of his official accounts quarterly in quadruplicate on appropriate forms supplied by the department.[3]

None of these instructions applied to the relationship between agent and missionaries at an Indian agency. James Miller, for example, could only speculate upon the reception he would receive from the brethren at Fort Defiance where, unknown to the new agent, the antagonism between James Roberts and his mission board had deepened early in 1871. The board was still reluctant to provide fixed salaries for Roberts and Menaul. Hoping to convince the board members of the difficulties created by their adamant position, Roberts complained incessantly about his monetary hardships, with numerous references to the high cost-of-living on the frontier. When the accumulation of these lamentations became unbearable, Lowrie finally assured Roberts that the mission board had endeavored to send all of the funds required for reasonable requests. Referring to insinuations by Roberts that he might leave the mission if his demands were not met, Lowrie hoped that this was not intended as a threat to the board. He reminded Roberts that he went to the Navajos because Christ had called him. Reflecting on the record of achievements at the Navajo mission, Lowrie was discouraged to note such little progress after two years. In fact, the board could not discern that any Navajo had yet been pointed to

Christ as his savior. Surprised by this stinging rebuke, Roberts quickly
replied with great contrition. He admitted his unworthiness to cope
with the challenges of the western wilderness. But he was sure that
the board's admonitions would be very helpful, and the long-awaited
arrival of James Miller would undoubtedly open the doors to better
things ahead.[4]

Miller, his wife Elizabeth, and their two-year-old son arrived at Fort
Defiance on January 30. The new agent relieved Frank Bennett on
February 3.[5] The Miller family observed at once the same deplorable
condition of the buildings at the agency noted earlier by Bennett. One
adobe building in a sad state of repair was available for the agent's
residence. None of the four rooms had any floors, the rooms were
badly lighted from four small windows, and a new roof was sorely
needed. A room was attached to this building to serve as an office,
but it too had no floor and only one window. The chapel and schoolhouse promised in the treaty of 1868 still had not been built. The
missionaries conducted their school in a small room in another of the
agency's ramshackle buildings. Although Miller estimated the cost
for new facilities at no less than thirty or thirty-five thousand dollars,
he felt sure it would be cheaper in the long run to erect new buildings,
rather than try to repair the old.[6]

The first meeting between Miller and James Roberts resulted in an
uplifting of the missionary's flagging spirits. After appraising Miller's
attributes, Roberts enthusiastically concluded that he was just the
right man in the right place, full of energy, thoroughly Christian, and
blessed with a large amount of missionary spirit. Apparently the time
had arrived at Fort Defiance for one of the seeds planted by the Grant
Peace Policy to bear fruit. Missionaries and agent were presumably
of kindred spirits in their regard for the basic issues related to the
Indian problem. Surely all would now work together in fraternal
harmony in pursuit of a common goal. Regrettably, this concept of a
cordial working relationship at the Navajo agency was soon strained
to the breaking point on the issue of the immoral lifestyle adopted
by several agency employees.[7]

Like anyone moving into a supervisory position in a new job, James
Miller was reluctant to initiate major policy changes with undue haste.
In Roberts's view, this cautious attitude was hardly in keeping with
the pressing need to cleanse the temple of evildoers at Fort Defiance.
Roberts wanted all the irreligious employees at the agency fired at
once. The zealous missionary was particularly upset about the open

cohabitation of some of these men with Indian women without the benefit of appropriate marriage rites. While Miller may have agreed in principle with Roberts's position, the new agent thought he must move slowly in this purge until replacements could be found who were both moral and well-qualified for the jobs.[8]

When news of their bickering reached the mission board, John Lowrie was understandably distressed by this display of animosity among the Presbyterians at Fort Defiance. He finally asked Miller to speak frankly with the errant men, assuring them that their "licentious intercourse" could not be allowed. They would have to reform their lifestyles, or they could not expect to continue as employees at the agency. Miller bowed to these wishes and promised to discharge those whom he regarded as beyond reform. He also admitted his compassionate concern for the future of men with families of several children. It would be an act of cruelty, in Miller's opinion, to abruptly terminate their employment, so he determined to persuade these men to legitimatize their marriages with an appropriate Christian ceremony, which would then make them acceptable employees at the Navajo agency.[9]

While Roberts worried about the irreligious conduct of agency employees, his fellow missionary John Menaul found it difficult to decide on a final location for his ministry in order to help the Indians. A station at the Zuni Pueblo was still foremost in his thoughts early in 1871. In ensuing months, however, several factors revised his thinking. First among these was a joyous event occurring at Fort Defiance on February 2, 1871. On that date, John Menaul and Charity Ann Gaston were married. In a gesture of friendship, Menaul invited outgoing agent Frank Bennett to attend the ceremony. James Roberts and his wife, still regarding Bennett as an opponent, were not at all pleased with this arrangement. Roberts felt obliged to perform the wedding, but Mrs. Roberts refused to attend and, as Menaul later recalled, her deliberate snub was intended as a clear disapproval of Menaul's invitation to Bennett.[10]

Other cracks began to appear in the friendship between Menaul and Roberts. It might have been better for all concerned if the Menauls had moved to Zuni right after the marriage, thus eliminating any cause for rivalry between the two mission families at Fort Defiance. But Charity Ann was still employed to teach the Navajo children. She could not in good faith abruptly terminate her commitment to this post for a move to Zuni. Adding to Menaul's reluctance to leave Fort Defiance was a broad hint from Lowrie that Roberts's days as missionary to the Navajos were numbered. If Roberts did return to the United States, then Menaul might be the logical person to continue the important work among the Navajos.[11]

James Miller may have unintentionally contributed to the growing schism between the missionaries by conferring a small but noticeable accolade upon John Menaul. Frank Bennett had been asked at the end of 1870 to give his opinion about the desirability of introducing looms and spinning among the Indians on a large scale. Bennett thought it was an excellent idea. Although an attempt to initiate the scheme while the Navajos resided at the Bosque Redondo had not succeeded, Bennett felt that the Navajos in their old familiar homeland would be much more receptive to the proposal. James Miller also saw merit in this proposition. He made a formal application to the Office of Indian Affairs to fund this position at Fort Defiance, with the understanding that Menual, who had been trained early in life as a weaver, would receive the post if it were approved. The pragmatic Menaul saw several advantages in this scheme. "In so doing," he explained to Lowrie, "I could do even more for the Indians spiritually, besides the greater influence I would have in civilizing them. Then again it would be a saving to the Board by the amount of wages I would receive."[12]

If Roberts was miffed by Miller's apparent display of favoritism, he kept his ruffled feelings to himself. Nevertheless, the warm relationship between the missionaries at the Navajo agency noticeably cooled from this time forward. Certainly James Miller did not appreciate the problems emanating from the missionary establishment at his agency. He encountered an ample amount of other difficulties in the day-to-day conduct of agency affairs to keep him fully occupied. He was greatly concerned with the chronic problem of rations, or the lack thereof, for his estimated 9,000 Navajo charges. On one occasion, only a few days after his arrival, the desperate Indians had broken into the agency corral, stealing and later slaughtering the work oxen for food. Frank Bennett and Superintendent Pope had muddled through at the end of 1870 by borrowing food supplies from nearby army garrisons. They also made minimal purchases of other supplies with promises to pay when appropriations for the Navajos were approved in the coming year. Miller and Pope continued their makeshift procedure until March 8 when the Commissioner of Indian Affairs notified Pope of an appropriation for $50,000 to sustain the Navajos until their 1871 crops could be harvested. However, all outstanding debts had to be paid from this fund. After making these deductions, Pope realized that he would need additional funds in late summer until the Indians could reap the fruits of the harvest.[13]

When hungry Navajos were not fed, some of them would steal livestock from ranches in the vicinity to ward off starvation. Miller received the usual complaints from irate citizens about these depredations, and conscientiously tried to retrieve stolen property. When the Navajo chiefs were unenthusiastic about cooperating with this policy, Miller called for two companies of cavalry from Fort Wingate to apprehend the thieving Navajos. The two Indians finally arrested by the soldiers in this campaign promptly escaped from confinement in Santa Fe where they were awaiting trial. Totally disgusted at this turn of events, Miller could only note that the arrests still had a good effect on the balance of the tribe, as reports of thefts were noticeably absent in his office for some time afterwards. Local citizens appreciated Miller's diligence in this matter. "Unlike many former Indian agents," observed a writer in a Santa Fe newspaper, "Mr. Miller does not look upon his copper colored wards as saints and incapable of doing wrong. . . ."[14]

The difficulties created by his "copper colored wards" obviously occupied much of Miller's time, but he did find an opportunity to devise a plan for settling his missionary problem. Beginning in the spring and continuing through the summer, he promoted a scheme to relocate Roberts and Menaul elsewhere on the reservation. The agent argued that all of the idlers and worst Indians of the tribe congregated at Fort Defiance. Obviously the morals of the children attending the mission school could only be endangered by this bad influence. Miller, Roberts, and Menaul explored the countryside around the agency in August until they found a small valley about forty miles from Fort Defiance where a mission compound could conceivably be established. The agent presented a strong case for the adoption of this new plan. He felt that the valley was well suited for a mission farm, with adequate tillable land and a nice stream of water for irrigation purposes. In Miller's opinion, "both Mr. Roberts and Mr. Menaul are much pleased with the place and are very desirous of getting into their new field."[15]

James Miller may or may not have been aware of the previous rejection of plans for an elaborate mission farm for the Navajos. Perhaps he was determined to test the waters once again for this scheme in an attempt to have the mission station, and its attendant problems, removed from the immediate vicinity of his agency. If the missionaries were very desirous, at first, to make the move suggested by Miller, their ardor for the proposition soon cooled. Early in November, Roberts confessed that the relocating enterprise was not proceeding smoothly. As Roberts described the situation, the chiefs did not want Americans located so far in the interior of their reservation, although one can also sense that the missionaries were having second thoughts about moving to an even more isolated location. Not really sure of the best course of action to pursue at the time, Roberts and Menaul decided to stay, for the time being, at the agency, where news about changes contemplated in the program for educating the Navajo children claimed their attention.[16]

The school at Fort Defiance was now a success, according to Charity Ann Menaul. She reported forty pupils, male and female, on the rolls at the close of the spring term in June 1871, with a daily average attendance of twenty-four. The curriculum included lessons in the English alphabet, orthography, reading, writing, printing on the slate and blackboard, and arithmetic. She also taught knitting and sewing to the girls. During the year they had made twenty-four dresses and thirty-three shirts. The only negative note in this otherwise glowing report was recognition of the many absences of the students caused by the transient nature of their parents' residence at the agency.[17]

In the spring of 1871, a rumor had circulated at the agency concerning the funding of teachers for the next school year. According to the information received, the government would probably employ two teachers at salaries of $1,000 each, a substantial increase over Charity Ann's initial salary of $600. All agreed that Charity Ann Menual would be one of the teachers. James Miller was very impressed with her work, attributing much of her success to her increasing fluency in the Navajo language. As for the remaining teaching position, Roberts hoped, at first, that this appointment would go to Mrs. Roberts. If this came to pass, then he intended to bring a lady from the States to help in the Roberts's household. He would then teach occasionally, while concentrating on learning the Navajo language.[18]

Roberts's decision not to promote his own candidacy for the second teaching position may have puzzled the members of his mission board. After all, he had been a prominent candidate for this post when it was originally established. John Menaul thought he knew the reason for this change-of-heart. According to Menaul, Roberts feared he would lose his financial support from the mission board if he went on a government payroll. Therefore, he intended to continue drawing money from the board in his capacity as missionary to the Navajos, while his wife brought in badly needed additional funds with her government salary. Reporting to Lowrie about a conversation with Roberts, Menaul quoted his fellow missionary as saying: "If the Board wishes to please us, as it now does, then it will give us a salary, and if we do government work here and draw wages it is nobodies [sic] business."[19]

The matter dragged on through the summer while Miller waited patiently for an official announcement of the $2,000 appropriation. In the interim, he revealed his plans for distribution of the money if it were granted. James Roberts and Charity Ann Menaul would receive his recommendation for appointment as teachers. With this revelation, Roberts quickly made a formal request through government channels for the second teaching position. Miller endorsed the request with one condition. The creation of a salaried position for Roberts would be predicated upon a proven need for a second school at the agency. When all of this news reached the mission board, Lowrie gave his candid opinion about the prospects for his missionaries at Fort Defiance. He expressed hope, of course, that Roberts would receive the appointment as teacher. Certainly teaching was always regarded as part of proper missionary work at an Indian reservation, as long as no restrictions were placed on giving religious instruction. But the board secretary also gave a very candid appraisal of the situation among the Navajos. "If Mr. Roberts cannot be appointed as teacher," Lowrie wrote to both missionaries, "then we hope he will find other openings for useful labor. I must confess we are much discouraged at the results of his mission thus far. . . ."[20]

In October 1871, Miller received the long-awaited directive on the school issue from the office of the Commissioner of Indian Affairs. If Miller regarded the first school, conducted by Charity Ann Menaul, as filled to the capacity of thirty students mentioned in the treaty of 1868, then he could open another school. Two teaching positions would be funded in appropriations for the current year. The commissioner told Miller that he could use his own discretion about appointing James Roberts to the second position. Salary terms could be set by Miller, but if the agent decided to appoint Roberts, the missionary should receive the same salary that would be paid to any good teacher, male or female. Acting with these guidelines, Miller told Roberts to start his school. Since the missionary saw little to be gained from another day school at the agency, he decided to conduct the new school as a boarding school in his home. He began to recruit students for the new educational endeavor, admitting six Navajo boys whom he described as the happiest, most contented, and obedient boys that he had ever encountered. This was a small beginning but, with apparent disregard for the space limitations in his home, the ever-confident missionary was sure that he could soon secure the thirty students anticipated in the Navajo treaty.[21]

James Miller most assuredly welcomed any kind of resolution to his difficulties with the missionaries at Fort Defiance. Other problems at his agency gave him greater cause for alarm. Once again the Navajos' crops had failed. In the spring, the Indians had worked hard preparing the ground and planting in all parts of the reservation. By August, however, the prospects for a good harvest appeared very bleak because of drought conditions throughout the area. On October 1, Miller dejectedly admitted that an early frost had badly damaged the remaining crops. Nothing could be expected for the Navajos in the months ahead from this source of food. The anxious chiefs were already asking if they could count on government subsistence during the coming winter.[22]

Miller and Pope finally concluded that the answer to this perennial dilemma was to provide the Navajos with the means to develop a source of food already proven adaptable to the arid environment of the Southwest—namely, sheep. The sheep provided to the Indians under the terms of the 1868 treaty had not only survived but multiplied. It was very evident that the Navajos prized these animals above anything the government furnished them. Perhaps one-third or even one-half of the annuity goods promised to the Indians for the year could be issued in the form of sheep, thereby supplying the Indians with a source of food and wool for blankets.[23]

While officials in Washington considered these recommendations, at Fort Defiance the Navajo food problem could not be avoided as winter drew near. Adopting the same emergency procedures used in the previous year, i.e., obtaining rations from various sources on promises to pay, Pope delivered enough corn and beef to the agency in the fall to last until the end of the year, but what then? In desperation, Pope called for an emergency appropriation to meet the needs of the Indians in the months ahead. He received assurance from the Commissioner of Indian Affairs that he would lay the matter before the Congress in the form of a request for $60,000 for subsistence to June 30, 1872, and $125,000 for the following fiscal year ending June 30, 1873. With this hopeful but indecisive information at hand, Miller could only tell the worried Indians to be patient, that surely the federal government in Washington will not permit the Indians to starve on the Navajo reservation.[24]

Implicit in the instructions defining the responsibilities of Indian agents was the assumption that they would maintain a condition of peaceful co-existence between the Indians in their jurisdiction and other Indians and white men residing in the vicinity. On two occasions during the year James Miller's skills as a peacemaker were put to the test. In the spring, Miller helped to defuse a potentially dangerous confrontation between the Navajos and the Indians of the Hopi and Zuni pueblos by helping to negotiate an agreement whereby all parties would restore stolen properties to their rightful owners. In November, Nathaniel Pope warned Miller of Mormon intrigue in the vicinity of Fort Defiance. According to rumors, the Mormons were trying to induce the Navajos of Arizona and New Mexico to make war on their white Gentile neighbors. Pope hoped that all intercourse in the future between the Navajos and Mormons would be prevented if possible. Miller assured the worried superintendent that he had taken preventive measures. He simply told the Indians to have nothing to do with "that people" as long as the difficulties between Mormons and the government continued.[25]

At the end of 1871, another problem at Fort Defiance offered less hope for a peaceful solution. James Roberts had reached an impasse in his crusade to rid the agency of irreligious employees. Although Miller had terminated the employment of several of these men, two of Roberts's primary targets remained on the payroll. The agent refused to fire his chief clerk, Thomas V. Keams, and the agency butcher, Anson C. Damon. Keams was Miller's right-hand man. Frank Bennett had hired Keams on February 1, 1869, as Spanish interpreter at the agency, and had also permitted him to conduct much of the routine agency business. Miller found it expedient to continue and expand this practice. At the end of 1871, Miller rewarded his industrious assistant with an appointment as clerk at an annual salary of $1,200. Anson C. Damon had secured employment in May 1866 as butcher for the Navajos at the Bosque Redondo. When the Navajos moved to Fort Defiance, Damon moved with them, continuing his employment as butcher at the new agency. To Miller, the expertise of these two men was simply indispensable. However, since they continued to live with Navajo women without the benefit of proper Christian marriages, it could not be expected that Roberts would rest easy in the days ahead in his continuing campaign to reform the morals of the agency staff.[26]

If James Roberts saw a defeat in the continuance of Keams and Damon as employees at Fort Defiance, he certainly approved Miller's selections to fill two new positions at the agency in 1871. In the spring, Miller had requested permission to employ a physician and a farmer at the Navajo agency. In July, the Commissioner of Indian Affairs approved these positions, with annual salaries of $1,200 for the physician and $1,000 for the farmer. Miller thought he had just the right men for these jobs. He selected Benjamin M. Thomas as farmer. Thomas, an ardent Presbyterian, came to New Mexico from Valparaiso, Indiana, at the end of 1870 to improve his poor health. Learning of the vacancy for a farmer at the Navajo agency, he applied for and received appointment to the position. For physician, Miller, acting on John Menaul's recommendation, expected to secure the services of Dr. James Aiken of Reeseville, Pennsylvania. Menaul regarded the young man, who was an elder of the Reeseville Presbyterian Church, as a very promising doctor who would be well suited for work among the Indians. Unfortunately, Aiken decided to reject the Navajo assignment. This position remained unfilled at the end of 1871, but Miller was on the right track, in Roberts's estimation, in his understanding of the requirements for good Christian men in these important positions.[27]

While the roster of white employees at Fort Defiance experienced significant changes in 1871, a transformation also occurred in the ranks of leaders of the Navajo tribe. Barboncito and Armijo, two of the old chiefs, died during the year. Ganado Mucho, another old chief, then assumed a position of authority in the tribe. Ganado Mucho, like the departed chiefs, advocated a peaceful approach when negotiating with representatives of the United States. However, in further restructuring of the tribal hierarchy, Manuelito, a younger and more militant subchief, ascended to a prominent position. Only time would tell how his role in tribal affairs would be defined, but the white residents at the Navajo agency certainly hoped he would also understand and appreciate the peaceful intent of the Grant Peace Policy. Choosing to consider these events as good omens, Miller and Pope looked ahead to peaceful co-existence between the Navajos and their neighbors in 1872, always keeping in mind that continuance of a food supply for the Indians was crucial for this optimistic projection.[28]

At the end of 1871, James Roberts and John Menual evaluated their status among the Navajos and both men's hopes for the future. James Miller had finally obtained confirmation of Roberts's appointment as a second teacher at the agency. Roberts now had an assured income, but another problem loomed ahead. The government expected him to maintain an enrollment of at least thirty students in his school. He recognized, as part of that challenge, the need to master the Navajo language. On Sundays, he prepared one church service for the white residents at Fort Defiance and another service for the few Indians who came to hear him preach. He decided to pay one of the interpreters at the agency ten dollars a month to translate the sermons into the Navajo language. He then memorized the words before making his presentation to the Indians. This arrangement, however, lasted only until the end of the summer, when the interpreter left the agency. At the end of the year, Roberts continued to struggle with this troublesome issue.[29]

John Menaul's recollections of the events of 1871 should have been pleasant ones. Occasionally, he found opportunities to exercise his skills as a doctor and, in May, Miller placed the missionary on the agency payroll at a salary of forty-five dollars per month to supervise the issuance of grain to the Navajos. This stipend, along with his wife's earnings as a teacher, gave the Menaul family a combined income adequate for their needs. Perhaps the weaving project for the Navajos would also be approved, thereby providing an opportunity to further develop a useful position among the Indians. Yet John Menaul was troubled, feeling unsure that his role at the Navajo agency was what God had intended for him. He had the unpleasant feeling that James Roberts still opposed his staying on at the agency. In revealing comments at the end of the year, Menaul disclosed his innermost feelings to John Lowrie. He wanted to be in the right place, wherever God wanted him to be, but was he wasting his time and efforts at Fort Defiance? In a candid confession, he acknowledged an impulse to move on, perhaps returning to Africa, or to a new challenge in India or China. He fervently hoped that the new year would bring with it a revelation, perhaps of divine origin, that would dispel these doubts in his mind.[30]

While men at Fort Defiance labored in 1871 to make the Peace Policy a success among the Navajos, in the nation's capital the efforts of a prominent public servant to implement the new Indian policy on a national scale brought condemnation rather than commendation. Early in the year, a congressional committee investigated allegations that Commissioner of Indian Affairs Parker had defrauded the government in the purchase of supplies for the Indians. Parker was cleared of the charges, but angered by this humiliation, and feeling that his job had been relegated to a position subordinate to the Board of Indian Commissioners, Parker resigned effective August 1, 1871. In November, President Grant filled the vacant position by selecting Francis A. Walker for that important post. Although the new member of the Peace Policy team had little knowledge of Indian affairs, he had a reputation as an effective administrator derived from his brilliant work as superintendent of the Ninth Census. He had also served gallantly with the Union Army during the Civil War, with a record of wounds received in battle and a period of confinement in a Confederate prison. The announcement of Walker's appointment may have raised the hopes of many of the new appointees to positions at Indian agencies who saw an opportunity in his selection to find solutions in the coming year for many of their problems that were related, as they viewed the situation, to bureaucratic obstacles often encountered at the home office.[31]

Many government spokesmen agreed on one basic premise at the end of the year—the results of the Peace Policy had exceeded all expectations. During the search for a successor to Ely Parker, Henry R. Clum, chief clerk in the Office of Indian Affairs, served as acting commissioner. In his annual report, Clum found much to be thankful for in the operations of the Indian service in 1871. Peace generally prevailed in the relationship of the Indians to the government. Tribes previously hostile were changing their ways. Abandoning their roving ways, they appeared content to establish themselves on reservations where they could be properly cared for and civilized. Entrusting the offices of superintendents and agents to men of good standing and moral character in the spirit of the Peace Policy gave hope for early achievement of the benevolent intentions of the government toward the Indians. "By a judicious management of their [Indian] affairs," Clum exulted, "with a sufficient supply of means requisite for the purpose, it may be confidently expected that their future advancement in civilization will be measureably rapid and gratifying."[32]

Secretary of the Interior Columbus Delano shared these sentiments. While agreeing in his annual report that the humane policy inaugurated by the government had produced gratifying results, he also ventured to suggest courses of action for the future. Some sort of incentive program could be adopted to encourage the Indians in directions which would induce them "to cultivate habits of industry, and foster a desire for mental and moral culture." Of course it was unreasonable to expect that "unlettered barbarians" could evolve into intelligent, law-abiding citizens in a short time, but the rewards for their industry could be made so attractive as to "obliterate their long standing prejudice against labor. . . ." In addition, a compulsory education system could be based on a policy of withholding annuities from those who refused to use the available educational facilities. Perhaps all of these goals could be expeditiously achieved by gathering all Indians under an efficient territorial government in the Indian Territory where there was plenty of land available to accommodate every scattered tribe. When this goal was reached, then all Indians would be "surrounded by such influence as to be more easily managed, thus enabling the Government to work out its humane policy toward them to its legitimate results."[33]

The members of the Board of Indian Commissioners had a busy year, to say the least, in 1871. In March the Congress asked the executive committee to begin auditing accounts in the Office of Indian Affairs. Another committee of the board continued to oversee the purchase and inspection of annuity goods for the Indians. The demand of this paperwork burden on the time of board members was overwhelming, but some of the members still found opportunities to visit several Indian tribes. In June chairman Felix Brunot held a council at Fort Laramie, Wyoming Territory, with Red Cloud and other chiefs of the Sioux Indians. Brunot noted with satisfaction the manifestation among the Sioux to maintain peaceful relations with their white neighbors. In a visit to tribes of the Pacific Northwest, Brunot found many of them laboring industriously on reservations, adopting the costume and habits of white men. Commenting on all of these activities, Brunot expressed his approval of all of the commissioner's achievements in 1871. He viewed the system of appointing Indian agents nominated by missionary societies as a distinct improvement at the agencies where the system was fully operative. He was convinced that the increased experience gained by the board could only lead to still greater success in the reformation of Indian policy, thereby confirming "the wisdom of the policy of peace so uniformly advocated by the

President, and supported by the liberality of Congress and the humane sympathies of the people. . . ."[34]

President Grant joined in these expressions of satisfaction with the results of his Indian policy. At the end of the year, he found that the exertions of various Christian societies and of the Board of Indian Commissioners had induced many Indians to settle on reservations, to cultivate the soil, to perform productive labor of various kinds, and to partially accept civilization. With continued care for these concerns, Grant hoped that other Indians still pursuing old habits of life would be led to embrace the only opportunities left to them to avoid extermination. Concluding his remarks, the president called for liberal appropriations from Congress to continue the policy of peace, "not only because it is humane, Christianlike, and economical, but because it is right."[35]

Looking forward to the new year, James Miller might have considered the anticipated debate in Congress over appropriations for the Indian service as most critical for his predicament at the Navajo agency. At the end of the year, the supply of rations for the Indians at Fort Defiance was again almost exhausted. Nevertheless, recommendations to correct this situation had been submitted to Eastern decision makers, who would surely give serious consideration to finding a lasting solution for this problem. It was also evident that the missionaries at the agency were still groping for a way to carry out their tasks harmoniously and productively. However, with a year's experience behind him in these delicate matters, Miller could hope for better days ahead because, if nothing else, he had a better understanding of the issues and personalities associated with this part of his responsibility. What one word might have best expressed the feelings of James Miller as a new year came to the Navajo reservation? Frustration? Anger? Hope? One would like to believe that the latter sentiment prevailed. With no way to anticipate the personal tragedy that lay ahead for him, Miller must still have believed, as he had written to John Lowrie, that he could truly become "the instrument of doing some good for the Indians."[36]

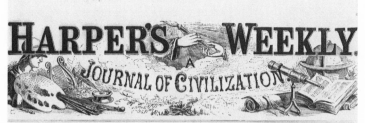

HARPER'S WEEKLY

JOURNAL OF CIVILIZATION

VOL. XIV.—No. 703.]   NEW YORK, SATURDAY, JUNE 18, 1870.   [SINGLE COPIES, TEN CENTS.
[$4.00 PER YEAR IN ADVANCE.

Entered according to Act of Congress, in the Year 1870, by Harper & Brothers, in the Clerk's Office of the District Court of the United States, for the Southern District of New York.

ON THE WAR-PATH.

ON the first of the present month a motley delegation of Indians waited on Commissioner PARKER, at Washington, for the purpose of conferring with him in regard to Indian affairs in the Territories of the Northwest. The English names of the principal men are RED CLOUD, SPOTTED TAIL, and SWIFT BEAR. RED CLOUD, who for more than twenty years has been the head chief of the Sioux Nation, is a man of herculean stature, six and a half feet in height, and large in proportion. Indeed there is not a small man in the delegation; but in every other respect the sight of them instantly dispels every illusion in regard to the "noble savage" which one may have received from Indian romances. Large, coarse features, prominent cheek-bones, faces painted in every imaginable style of ugliness, are the characteristics of the party. The women are particularly ugly, with pug or flat noses, wide mouths, and big feet. They are all magnificently dressed in Indian style. All wear splendid buffalo-robes, ornamented with embroidery and jewels.

The object of this visit to Washington is to obtain protection and redress. In a conversation with Commissioners PARKER, SPOTTED TAIL, stated his grievances in round terms. The government, he said, does not fulfil its treaty obligations; and that supplies promised and money owed are not forthcoming at stated times; and that white men, wherever they can find many buffaloes or gold, come to the Indians' land or take the Indians' ponies and other possessions. The Commissioner promised that these grievances should be redressed, and gave the delegation some excellent advice in regard to fighting and stealing.

While the members of the delegation are enjoying the hospitalities of the government at Washington, their brethren in the West have suddenly appeared on the war-path. Colonel MORROW, who commands the military forces

Sketch purporting to show President Ulysses S. Grant and "a motley delegation of Indians" in Washington, D.C., June 1870. Presumably the clasped hands and the tomahawk set aside on the ground signify acceptance by all parties of the peaceful intent of the Grant Peace Policy. (*Harper's Weekly*, June 18, 1870, Vol. XIV, No. 703. Courtesy Library of Congress)

61

Agent W. F. M. Arny and the delegation that journeyed to Washington, D.C., in 1874. Arny is fourth from the left in the back row with the famous blanket showing the centennial dates 1776–1876 draped over his shoulder. Chief Manuelito of the Navajos is seated fourth from the left in the front row between his wife and son. Standing at Arny's left is "Rocky Mountain Bill." At the extreme left in the back row is "Wild Hank." At the far right in the back row is the interpreter Jesus Alviso. (Courtesy Smithsonian Institution, Washington, D.C.)

Commissioner of Indian Affairs Ely Parker. A Seneca Indian and brigadier general in the Union Army at the end of the Civil War, he had the responsibility for overseeing the implementation of the Grant Peace Policy. (Courtesy National Archives, #111-B-4121)

President Ulysses S. Grant was sure that his Peace Policy would lead to the civilizing and Christianizing of the Indians. (Courtesy Library of Congress)

Brigadier James H. Carleton, commander of the military district of New Mexico from 1862 to 1867, believed that the Almighty had destined the Indians to disappear from the face of the earth. (Courtesy Museum of New Mexico)

Sheldon Jackson, superintendent of the Presbyterian home mission work in the Rocky Mountain West in the 1870s. (Courtesy Presbyterian Historical Society, Philadelphia, Pa.)

John Lowrie, secretary of the Board of Foreign Missions of the Presbyterian Church, coordinated the efforts of his church to respond to the goals established in the Peace Policy. (Courtesy Presbyterian Historical Society, Philadelphia, Pa.)

David F. McFarland, first pastor of the Presbyterian Church in Santa Fe, New Mexico. (Courtesy First Presbyterian Church, Santa Fe, New Mexico)

San Francisco Street in Santa Fe (circa 1865) looking east toward the
Catholic church. (Courtesy Museum of New Mexico, U.S. Army Signal
Corps Collection, Negative No. 11330)

Next page, top. Fort Defiance, Arizona shortly after its construction in 1851.
Used as the agency for the Navajos after the Civil War. (Courtesy Western
History Department, Denver Public Library)

Next page, bottom. James M. Roberts, first missionary assigned to the
Navajo Agency at Fort Defiance, Arizona, in 1868. (Courtesy First
Presbyterian Church, Santa Fe, New Mexico)

General Oliver O. Howard, the "Christian General," authorized creation of the Navajo tribal police force. (Courtesy Library of Congress)

John Menaul, Presbyterian
missionary at the Navajo agency
from 1870 to 1875. (Courtesy
Menaul Historical Library,
Albuquerque, New Mexico)

Charity Ann Menaul (née Gaston),
teacher at the Navajo agency, was
saddened when she first arrived at
Fort Defiance by the realization that
none of the Navajos "knew aught
of the blessed Jesus or the love He
bore for poor sinners." (Courtesy
Menual Historical Library,
Albuquerque, New Mexico)

Grave of A. H. Donaldson in the old Fort Defiance cemetery. Died April 30, 1880. (Author's photograph)

The Navajo Reservation and Vicinity in the 1870s

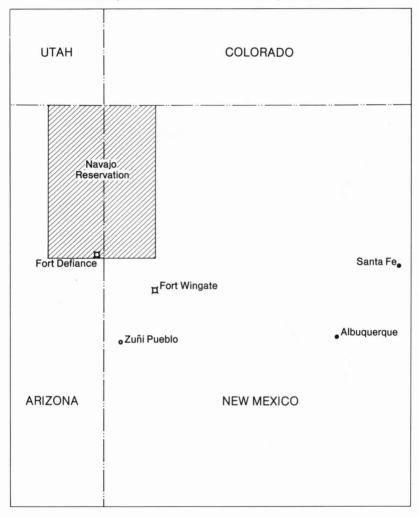

Navajo Agency at Fort Defiance, Arizona in 1869

A. Carpenter's Shop
B. Blacksmith's Shop
C. Storerooms
D. Headquarters
E. Interpreter's Quarters
F. Missionary's Quarters
G. School House
H. Council House

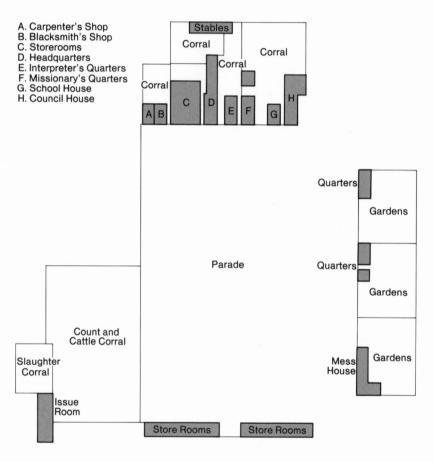

Source: Compiled from enclosure in Bennet to Clinton, December 23, 1869, OIA, M234, Roll 557

5

A Martyr for the Cause, 1872

Yet it seems hard to serve a country in whose ears the
daily cry of murders ring, and it gives no protection even
to its own agents in the carrying out of its work.
—John Menual
June 13, 1872

If 1871 was a good year for the Peace Policy, 1872 opened on an even more promising note. Recalling the success of the meeting of Peace Policy advocates in January 1871, members of the Board of Indian Commissioners decided to convene a similar assembly early in 1872. Gathering with the commissioners in the nation's capital on January 11 were Secretary of the Interior Columbus Delano, the new Commissioner of Indian Affairs Francis A. Walker, and churchmen who supported the new Indian policy. Felix Brunot, chairman of the Board of Indian Commissioners, opened the great meeting by explaining his purpose in calling together the delegates from various interest groups. Quite simply, by sharing their experiences all parties could contribute to a more unified program that would do justice, "as becomes a great Christian nation, to the people for whose care God has placed upon us the entire responsibility." With this commendable goal in mind, Brunot called for the views of the churchmen regarding the progress to date of the Peace Policy.[1]

Speaking for his church, John Lowrie explained how the Presbyterian endeavors had resulted in noticeable progress in the civilization of the Indians assigned to his care. Nothing had occurred in the past year to weaken the faith of his mission board in the humane policy of the government to the Indians. The influence of the men appointed to the agencies assigned to the Presbyterians would go far to correct the great evils of the past by judicious application of the best principles of religion and education. Agreeing with Secretary of the Interior Columbus Delano's recommendation to place all Indians in the Indian

73

Territory, Lowrie reasoned that this would facilitate "the spreading of the Gospel by the different missionaries among the tribes, and they would advance rapidly toward civilization, soon being able to stand side by side with the whites. The object of the missionaries is to give them the Gospel, and civilization will follow as the result."[2]

At Fort Defiance James Miller might have had difficulty in accepting John Lowrie's implication that the benefits of the white man's civilization would necessarily have followed the introduction of the gospel message by missionaries on an Indian reservation. There were other more practical considerations requiring his attention as he sought to find ways and means to civilize the Navajos. The new year did not begin favorably for James Miller. On January 1, after issuing the last of the corn, he feared his supply of beef would only last until the middle of the month. Near the end of January, Miller saw the rations situation as desperate, with the Indians, in many cases, eating seed grain to relieve their hunger. Early in February, a writer in the *Santa Fe New Mexican* insisted that this sad state of affairs was not exaggerated. The reporter described Miller as a capable and efficient agent, with an unbounded influence over the Indians, "but unless he is provided with the means to supply the absolute, necessary wants of the Navajos, who look to him for the means of maintenance, he can do nothing to prevent them from leaving the reservation and committing depredations."[3]

Miller's short-term solution, as usual, was to borrow food supplies whenever and wherever possible, promising to repay these debts from future appropriations. On February 21, he obtained 20,000 pounds of corn from Fort Wingate, and he hoped to secure another 50,000 pounds from that source in the near future. Miller's superiors offered little encouragement. The Commissioner of Indian Affairs, reminded of his comments about a special appropriation at the end of 1871, admitted that there were still no funds on hand for the Navajos' subsistence. On March 19, Miller was out of rations again. In complete despair, he told Nathaniel Pope he could no longer be held responsible for the Indians' actions. Early in April, he asked Pope for authority to sell the agency's six oxen, or issue them to the Indians for food, as there was no hay or grain available to feed the animals. In the *Santa Fe New Mexican*, Miller warned citizens of the territory to refrain from grazing their sheep near the reservation, as it would be a great inducement for the Indians to steal rather than starve.[4]

The residents of the territory believed they had solid reasons to fear the growing threat of Indian raids. For many of these apprehensive citizens, the blame for Indian discontent could be placed squarely upon the doorstep of the government, with its misguided approach to solving the Indian problem. Since the genesis of the prevailing Indian policy was derived from the schemes of Vincent Colyer, few tears were shed on the western frontier when he resigned his post as secretary of the Board of Indian Commissioners in January 1872. Typical of comments in the Southwest on receipt of the news of Colyer's departure was a cynical statement by a disgruntled citizen who reported new outrages perpetrated by the "peaceful Apaches." Perhaps the great Colyer might now find an opportunity to experience some of the hazards created by his mollycoddling of the Indians. "As Colyer [sic] has resigned the Secretaryship of the Board of Indian Commissioners," quipped the writer, "we hope the sanctimonious old humbug will take a situation as mail driver on the Tucson road for a few weeks."[5]

Meanwhile, on the Navajo reservation it was time for spring planting. Somehow Nathaniel Pope found funds to purchase more seed grain for the Navajos. The determined Indians planted their crops, hoping that their industry would finally be rewarded with a bountiful harvest in 1872. In May, James Miller's cupboard was bare again. John Menaul recognized the severity of the situation when he noted that the desperate Indians had killed everything eatable about the post, including his cow. At the end of the month, as he prepared for an exploratory tour to the farthest corners of the reservation, Miller borrowed a little corn and beef for the Indians, but the sense of impending disaster was not dispelled by this stopgap measure. Early in June, a traveler returning from Fort Defiance gave a frightening account of the situation. Blaming the mismanagement of "the Indian ring in Washington" for the crisis, the writer insisted:

Some one hundred children have died within the last few weeks, for want of proper sustenance, and the despondent appearance of all would touch the heart of the most obdurate. Nor is this all. The employees of the agency have not been paid for many months and justly feel aggrieved thereat, whilst they live in constant apprehension of an Indian outbreak.[6]

James Miller surely would have reported the death of one hundred Navajo children from starvation, so this statistic must be regarded as highly suspect, but the visitor to Fort Defiance touched upon another disquieting factor in his comments. The laments of employees who had not been paid for many months added another dimension to the mounting problems at the Navajo agency. Many of the employees, unpaid for the past eight months, had been forced to borrow money to feed their families. When the complaints reached the Office of Indian Affairs, Commissioner Walker insisted that no payroll estimate had been received from Nathaniel Pope for the employees at Fort Defiance. When the angry commissioner instructed his superintendent to remedy this situation without undue delay, Pope, anxious to correct his administrative oversight, presumably forwarded the required forms posthaste.[7]

A notable change in the distribution of job responsibilities at Fort Defiance occurred early in 1872. John Menaul's medical skills had still not been fully utilized at the Navajo agency. Anxious for an opportunity to remedy this situation, Menaul formally requested appointment at the end of February to the unfilled position of physician at the agency. Among his qualifications, the missionary noted his study of medicine in the last year of his seminary program. While residing in Philadelphia, he had also attended clinics and lectures at famous medical colleges in that city. Impressed by these credentials, James Miller strongly endorsed Menaul's request. On March 8, the pleased missionary received confirmation of his appointment as physician to the Navajos. Miller clearly indicated his appreciation of the favorable development of Menaul's career when he told Lowrie: "Mr. Menaul is becoming a general favorite with both employees and Indians and bids fair to be a useful man."[8]

For the Menauls, early 1872 was a happy and productive period in their lives. John Menaul, recovered from his feeling of uncertainty about his calling at the end of the previous year, was delighted with his new responsibilities. The many Navajos he treated as agency physician seemed pleased with the remedies he prescribed. In a few months, with a medical practice averaging eleven patients daily, he had to request a new shipment of medicines to replenish his depleted supply. James Miller also called upon the busy missionary to implement the weaving program discussed earlier at Fort Defiance. The government showed its favorable reaction to the recommendations of Miller and Pope for increasing wool production on the reservation by giving Pope authority in the spring of 1872 to purchase 10,000 sheep for the Navajos. Anticipating this favorable action, Pope had sent a loom to Fort Defiance at the end of January with a directive to begin teaching its use to the Indians immediately. When Menaul added weaving demonstrations to his medical responsibilities, he did not understate his position when he observed that his time was "pretty well occupied" with his several duties.[9]

In the school conducted by Mrs. Menaul, evaluation of the results of her teaching was rather difficult. According to Miller, Charity Ann was performing admirably, with about forty pupils enrolled in her classes. Not all of these children were regular in attendance, but she still maintained a respectable number of students. When interviewed by a reporter for the *New Mexican* during a visit to Santa Fe, Miller described Mrs. Menaul's school as doing well, with the children learning to read in English as fast as could be expected. Nathaniel Pope had a more critical opinion of the school. As he viewed it, the school was not really a success because only a small proportion of those enrolled appeared on a regular basis. Nevertheless, the school was still a going concern, presumably satisfying in principle the treaty requirements for thirty pupils. Pope did believe that the time might come when the school could become a success "by the exercise of proper care and attention."[10]

The record of achievement exhibited by the Menauls was not shared by James Roberts. In January, Miller finally wrote finis to all plans for relocation of Roberts and Menaul in an area away from the agency headquarters. The Navajos had announced their firm objection to erection of any buildings in the area previously contemplated because it was too cold there in the winter, and it was the best place on the reservation for grazing their livestock. Meanwhile, the Roberts's boarding school at the agency was not doing very well. Regarding the situation as hopeless, James Miller began to build a case for the missionary's removal. Miller insisted he could not sustain Roberts in his position unless he could increase his school enrollment to thirty students. This goal appeared unattainable. Roberts never had more than six students in his school, there was little hope for any increase in the future, and, in Miller's opinion, the Indians had become very prejudiced against Roberts because of the missionary's puritanical demeanor. If there was no indication of improvement in this unhappy situation, Miller felt he would have to appoint someone else in the teaching position Roberts held.[11]

At first Roberts appeared oblivious to the precarious status of his position. He thought the little boarding school in his home was doing just fine, although he admitted candidly that a major reason for his boys staying in the school was to get something to eat. Apparently feeling secure in his future at Fort Defiance, Roberts seemed unconcerned when the enrollment at his school dropped to three in February. The missionary finally revealed an explanation for his reluctance to substantially increase the number of students in his boarding school. It was rather common knowledge, he insisted, that many Indian children had the "loathsome disease" so common among the employees of the agency and the majority of the Indians. Roberts was sure that the unspeakable disease was easily contracted from close contact with those afflicted. With this concern, he did not feel he should bring too many Indian children into direct contact with his family.[12]

At the end of February, Roberts's illusions were abruptly transformed into reality when Miller and Menaul called upon him and strongly urged him to resign his position at Fort Defiance. An unanticipated action taken by the Navajos precipitated this confrontation. Word had spread throughout the agency of a plan devised by the Indians, who were thoroughly dissatisfied with Roberts, to go to Santa Fe and demand an order from Nathaniel Pope for the missionary's removal. Understandably dismayed, Roberts insisted that the Indians would never have thought of this course of action if his enemies among the agency employees had not put them up to it. Assuming that John Lowrie would make the final decision on Roberts's status, all of the interested parties hastened to clear themselves of blame for the sad state of affairs. Miller told Lowrie that he had done everything in his power to suppress the Navajos' opposition to Roberts, but the Indians had been determined to go to Santa Fe to voice their complaints. If this had actually happened, it could only have dealt a serious blow to all of their positions at the agency. Perhaps it was all for the best. Of Roberts's pupils, all but one had now departed. As a matter of course, Miller would have been required to discontinue the school.[13]

Roberts represented his case to Lowrie as the injured party in a scheme by Miller and Menaul to dislodge him from his post. After careful consideration, Roberts concluded he had a better right to remain at the Navajo agency than other parties who ventured to take so much interest in his welfare. Continuing with his defense, Roberts decided a visit by the Indians to Santa Fe would not be detrimental to his record. On the contrary, their complaints would reflect just as much and more upon James Miller. As Roberts saw the situation, the Navajos did not really want him to leave them. Miller's antagonism to his position probably resulted from jealous statements by John Menaul, whom Roberts finally recognized as "the cause of the whole matter. . . ."[14]

Defending himself against these allegations, Menaul, seeing himself as blameless, gave his views on the delicate situation. Just because he had friendly relations with employees at the agency, Roberts had assumed this rapport was gained at the sacrifice of Menaul's Christian principles. Menaul denied this insinuation. Surely the sincerity of a man's devotion to Christianity need not be measured by the number of his enemies, a position firmly maintained by Roberts, who felt he was always in the right on these matters. Menaul did acknowledge the existence of a group of discharged employees who were agitating for Roberts's dismissal. Taking a very cynical attitude, these men vowed that they were following the precepts of Roberts's brand of Christianity by doing unto him as he had done to them. Finally, in Menaul's opinion, Roberts's misguided decision to defy his opponents came from a dogged determination not to provide the discharged men with "evidence of weakness on the part of the Church which he represents. . . ."[15]

John Lowrie had heard enough. On March 23, 1872, the mission board sent a notice of dismissal to Roberts. "We are of one mind," Lowrie wrote, "that, in the circumstances of the case, it is best for you to leave the Navajo work, and to return to the States. . . ." Sadly reconciled to this peremptory directive, a few days later the Roberts family left Fort Defiance on the long journey back to their home in Ohio. According to James Miller, the contrite Roberts admitted as he departed that his work at the agency might have been more productive if he had not pursued a wrong course from the beginning.[16]

Relieved by Roberts's departure, James Miller also prepared for a journey. Nathaniel Pope had asked Miller and Benjamin Thomas, the agency farmer, to try to locate other areas on the Navajo reservation where the Indians might find conditions more suitable for farming. Miller had heard good reports about the fertility of the land watered by the San Juan River in the remote northern reaches of the reservation. On June 4, Miller and Thomas, with two other agency employees, left Fort Defiance on their quest. Miller surely welcomed the opportunity to take a bit of a holiday from the trials and tribulations of his agency position. He found, instead, a martyr's death. On June 11, while Miller and his companions were asleep in their camp, two Indians intent on plunder fired upon them. Miller died instantly when

79

a bullet struck him in the head. After quickly burying the deceased agent, his unharmed comrades brought the sad news of Miller's death to Fort Defiance, identifying the fleeing assassins, from the style of their dress, as Ute Indians.[17]

The news of Miller's death shocked the territory. After reporting details of the tragedy, a writer in the *Santa Fe New Mexican* expressed confidence that the military and Indian authorities would use every means to bring the cowardly murderers to speedy justice.[18] John Menaul accepted the renegade Ute theory, but he found enough guilt in the matter to have a large amount left over for the government. He forcefully expressed his angry appraisal of the situation in a bitter denunciation of the whole concept of peaceful coexistence with the Indians:

This is but one of the scores of murders committed in this country by Indians, and all by reason of an imbecile Government with its farces of Treaties and Missioners [*sic*] crying peace, peace when there is no peace, but war to the death. These warrior Indians are not fools. When a peace is called for, a number of them come in, they get a good ration, clothing, and, on peace pretensions, guns and ammunition. These stay around the Agency to receive these supplies and just hand them over to those on the war path. . . . What the end of these things will be I do not, or even wish to know. I know that it is all in the hands of a good and gracious God. . . . Yet it seems hard to serve a country in whose ears the daily cry of murders ring, and it give no protection even to its own agents in the carrying out of its work.[19]

While the search continued for the Indians responsible for Miller's death, life went on at the Navajo agency. Charity Ann Menaul accompanied the agent's bereaved widow and child on the return journey to the home of Mrs. Miller's family in Schellsburg, Pennsylvania. Benjamin Thomas relinquished his position as farmer at the end of 1872 to become agent for the Southern Apaches at Tularosa, New Mexico. In an action that would have infuriated James Roberts, Pope appointed Thomas Keams, Roberts's former adversary among the disgruntled men employed at the agency, as acting agent for the Navajos until John Lowrie could find a successor for Miller. Problems at the agency did not diminish under new leadership. When a severe frost on June 18 badly damaged the Navajos' early crops, reports of depredations committed by starving Indians increased. In July, Pope exceeded his authority once again by purchasing supplies of beef and corn on credit, hoping to placate the Indians until their fall crops could be harvested.[20]

In August a very distinguished visitor arrived at the Navajo reservation. Following a mission as an emissary for peace to the Apache tribes of Arizona, General Oliver O. Howard, recently relieved from his position as head of the Freedmen's Bureau, visited the area to evaluate the Navajo situation. Howard had full authority to make whatever changes he deemed necessary to alleviate the Navajos' distress. On August 4, Howard, Nathaniel Pope, and Thomas Keams had a lengthy meeting with Ganado Mucho, Manuelito, about a hundred other Navajos, and several Apache chiefs. After declarations of peaceful intent by all factions, Howard approved two new programs viewed as beneficial to the future of the Navajos. With the concurrence of the Navajo chiefs, Howard appointed Thomas Keams as a special agent to plan for the creation of a large subagency along the San Juan River. Howard then authorized Keams to take steps at once to organize a Navajo police force.[21]

Although often credited with first proposing the Navajo police plan, Howard should rightfully have shared that distinction with John Lowrie. In March 1872, Lowrie had conveyed his thoughts on this subject to Secretary of the Interior Delano. Lowrie wondered why Indian policemen could not be used instead of white soldiers for all Indian peacekeeping functions since the white soldiers were, in most cases, intemperate and immoral men, exerting the worst influence on the Indians. A plan using the Indians could be modeled on England's use of Sepoys in India. The Sepoys, who made excellent soldiers, did not cost a tenth part of the expenses of European troops. Besides, as Lowrie viewed the situation, the semimilitary drill adopted in training the Indians would be a valuable civilizing element for their advancement. Secretary Delano agreed with the feasibility of Lowrie's plan, promising to act upon his suggestions whenever and wherever a practical application of his theories could be applied.[22]

That practical opportunity occurred at the Navajo reservation in August 1872. Acting on General Howard's directive, Thomas Keams started recruiting Indians for his police force. With a shrewd eye for politics, he selected Manuelito, perhaps the most militant among the leaders of the Navajos, to head the peacekeeping force. Keams charged the police specifically with guaranteeing the boundaries of the reservation, arresting thieves, recovering stolen property, and offering general aid. The new scheme was an instant success. On August 28 the *Santa Fe New Mexican* reported receipt of a letter from Keams stating that Manuelito and his patrol had recaptured twenty-nine horses, mules, and burros from Indian thieves, and turned them over to the agent. A request for 100 carbines for the police from the arsenal at Fort Union, New Mexico, was not approved, but the Office of Indian Affairs assured Pope that steps would be taken to secure all the carbines and ammunition needed from other sources. Keams's gratification with early results of the great experiment was evident early in September, when he described the police force as the best method ever adopted for finding and recovering stolen stock brought on the reservation.[23]

Thomas Keams welcomed the various decisions enlarging his authority at Fort Defiance, but he did not appreciate one of General Howard's directives. The so-called Christian general was disturbed by reports of immoral conduct by many of the employees at the Navajo agency. He had heard that these men openly indulged in gambling and profanity, and some of them lived with Navajo concubines. He thought these iniquitous individuals should be discharged as soon as possible. Keams, perhaps wondering if James Roberts had been in touch with Howard, refuted these accusations to Nathaniel Pope. He insisted that none of the employees were addicted to gambling and profanity. Admittedly some of the employees lived with Navajo women, but they were married according to the customs of the Navajos, which in no way conflicted with their morals. "I judge this false information has been given by some party," Keams insisted, "who from mercenary and office seeking motives, under the cloak of Christianity, seeks to injure these men."[24]

While Thomas Keams worked to perfect his police force, John Lowrie responded to the government's call for selection of a new agent at Fort Defiance. The appointment went to William F. Hall, a resident of Washington, D.C., who was employed at the time in the office of the Auditor of the Treasury. Like James Miller, Hall had applied for the Navajo position in 1870. Learning of Miller's death, Hall hastened to remind Lowrie of his continuing availability. The usual character references attested to his moral and physical fitness for the job. The candidate pointedly told Lowrie of General Howard's urgent desire for Hall to receive the appointment. Hall also stated that he was blessed with a wife who was determined to be a missionary. He insisted that their adoption of this noble and holy cause would surely bring results advantageous to both the Indians and the government.[25]

After agreeing that his wife could join him at a later date, William Hall arrived at his post at Fort Defiance on September 7, 1872. Two days later he gave his initial impression of the situation at the agency to Nathaniel Pope. Surprisingly, he found the Navajos in a happy, contented, and prosperous condition. His foremost concern was for the physical plant at the agency. There was an urgent need for new buildings. The roofs were falling in, the sides were giving way, the timbers were rotten, the doors and windows were unmanageable, and the general state of the buildings was entirely inadequate for their intended use. Thomas Keams reinforced these views. After a heavy rain early in September, which caused some of the walls and roofs to cave in, Keams made temporary repairs, but he agreed it would be a great saving to the government to erect entirely new buildings.[26]

Perhaps optimistic estimates of the Navajo food supplies in late summer of 1872 provided the basis for Hall's extraordinary statement about contented Indians. Nathaniel Pope received some government funds in September, which permitted him to contract at once for delivery of new supplies of beef and corn to the agency. This food supply, supplemented by the fruits of a better than usual harvest of Navajo crops, appeared adequate to sustain the Indians until the end of the year. In September, Hall supervised the issuance of 7,414 sheep to the Navajos, bringing the number of sheep and goats on the reservation, in the estimation of Thomas Keams, to about 125,000. Prospects also appeared bright for creation of the subagency on the San Juan River, when the Commissioner of Indian Affairs approved the project in late September. Thomas Keams visited the area in the fall, noting on his journey a brief stop by the grave of James Miller. He regarded the area as a perfect agency site. Enough corn could be raised there to support the whole Navajo nation. Enthused by this report, Pope asked for commitment of a small number of soldiers to the proposed site to protect the Navajo farms and deter the neighboring Utes from trespassing in the area.[27]

While government officials labored to solve the Navajo food problem, John Lowrie considered a proposal to fill the vacancy created by the departure of James Roberts from the Navajo agency. Williamson Crothers, Presbyterian agent for the Hopi Indians in Arizona, recommended William Truax of Chicago, Illinois, for this position. Truax, who was employed as general agent for the Theological Seminary of the Northwest in Chicago, was looking for an assignment in the Southwest with hopes of improving his health. From Santa Fe, David

83

McFarland added his endorsement to the Truax candidacy. McFarland felt that no better or more suitable man could be found for work in New Mexico. If Lowrie did not wish to move at once to fill the vacancy at Fort Defiance, then Truax could find employment teaching at one of the Indian pueblos near Santa Fe. Lowrie decided to follow the advice of his men in the field. On June 18, 1872, he notified Truax of a commitment by the mission board to provide five hundred dollars toward his support as a missionary for one year. Truax was to proceed to New Mexico and make his own decision on the best field for his services where, hopefully, he could then "bring many precious souls to Christ."[28]

On October 19, 1872, a notice appeared in the *Santa Fe New Mexican* announcing the arrival of two gentlemen to labor as teachers among the Indians of New Mexico under commissions from the United States government and the Presbyterian board of missions. The two travelers were William B. Truax of Chicago and James M. Roberts. Roberts's appearance must have caused raised eyebrows among the Presbyterian brethren in New Mexico. After the dismal record of Roberts's work at Fort Defiance, he probably managed to secure another assignment in New Mexico only because John Lowrie was absent from his post as board secretary when the members consented to Roberts's proposition. Confined to his bed late in the summer by a serious illness, Lowrie had received one previous inkling of a scheme by Roberts to return to mission work in the Southwest. Roberts had wanted to make another attempt to conduct a boarding school for the Navajos at Fort Defiance. Aware of the cause of many of his previous difficulties, he promised to operate the new venture strictly according to the views of the agent and John Menaul. As for financial support for his school, Roberts felt sure he could raise a fund of $50,000 for this purpose by lecturing throughout the East during the summer months.[29]

Certainly John Lowrie would have spoken out against adoption of this plan, or any other presented by Roberts, if he had been present during the board's deliberations on a new assignment for the missionary. In any event, Roberts got his appointment, and when Lowrie returned to his office at the end of September, he found a letter from Roberts waiting for him. The missionary and his family, who were ready to start for their new post among the "heathen," requested a check from the board at once for five hundred dollars to cover their travel expenses. This time there would be another member in the

Roberts's party. Recalling one of his urgent needs during his previous tour of duty at the Navajo agency, Roberts announced his recruitment of an assistant who would join them in Chicago. This lady would keep house and assist Mrs. Roberts, who hoped to teach school occasionally at the agency.[30]

In Lowrie's less than enthusiastic reply to Roberts's comments, he revealed an aspect of the new arrangement that might have been instrumental in convincing the board to give Roberts another chance. Contrary to his original expectations, Roberts would not return to Fort Defiance. There would be no possibility of duplicating old mistakes in hostile surroundings. The agent for the Pueblo Indians in New Mexico had provided a teaching position for Roberts. According to the terms of this agreement, the government would pay an annual salary of six hundred dollars. The mission board would pay traveling expenses for the Roberts family, but not for the assistant. The possibility for supplementing Roberts's salary from mission funds would remain open for subsequent negotiation pending a report on his needs.[31]

Perhaps deciding that half a loaf was better than none, the Roberts family set out for New Mexico. They were joined in Chicago by Jennie Flatt, the assistant for Mrs. Roberts, and by William Truax. When the party reached Santa Fe, the missionaries discussed their assignments with John Cole, agent of the Christian Church for the Pueblo agency. Cole thought Roberts would find a receptive audience for his services at the San Felipe Pueblo, located about thirty miles southwest of Santa Fe. Public announcement of this decision included expressions of renewed hope for uplifting the Indians. "The appointment is a good one," a reporter in the *Santa Fe New Mexican* noted, "and no doubt will be followed by the very best results in the education and enlightenment of the Indians."[32]

As fate would have it, the Indians at San Felipe were not destined to be educated and enlightened by James Roberts. William Truax, who had, in effect, a roving commission from the mission board, finally decided he would like to try his hand at the San Felipe Pueblo. When asked if he would accept another site for his efforts, the usually combative Roberts, perhaps eager to show his new spirit of cheerful cooperation, agreed to locate at the Santo Domingo Pueblo only a few miles from San Felipe. Reporting to Lowrie on these selections, Roberts and Truax announced their intent to use the "old deserted convents" in the two villages for dwellings and school purposes.[33]

To his dismay, Roberts, intent on occupying the "old deserted convent" at Santo Domingo, encountered unanticipated difficulties. The Catholic mission buildings stood vacant, but certainly not deserted. The doors were securely locked and, according to the Indians, the keys were in the hands of a nonresident priest who had no intention of making the facility available to the Presbyterian interloper. Disheartened by this new situation, Roberts then decided to shift his field of operations to the Taos Pueblo, about fifty miles north of Santa Fe. Unfortunately, opposition from his adversaries in what he called "the Romish church" continued to plague the frustrated missionary at his new location. At the end of the year, Roberts reluctantly admitted to Lowrie the necessity for abandonment, at least temporarily, of the venture at Taos Pueblo because the priestly opposition was overwhelming. However, he hoped to go forward with his labors at the non-Indian community of Taos, about three miles from the pueblo, where he felt he could do good work for the Mexicans.[34]

The decisions by Roberts and Truax regarding their locations deprived the Navajos, momentarily at least, of a replacement for the teaching position vacated by Roberts earlier in the year at Fort Defiance. The future of the other teaching position at the agency also appeared uncertain. In November, William Hall reported both positions vacant. Charity Ann Menaul, who had accompanied the family of the deceased James Miller to their home in Pennsylvania in June, had still not returned from her prolonged visit to the East. The prospects for conducting any kind of a school at the agency appeared very bleak indeed as the year drew to a close. Hall lamented the absence of any building on the reservation that could be regarded as actually suitable for school purposes. In Santa Fe, Nathaniel Pope noted the inability of previous teachers to persuade the children to attend regularly. Pope hoped that a school conducted at the proposed subagency site on the San Juan River would have a better chance of success, but until a decision could be made on that proposal, attempts to educate the Navajo children would probably be suspended.[35]

Regrettably, Nathaniel Pope missed the outcome of the San Juan River proposition. On November 19, 1872, an announcement of Pope's abrupt and unexplained dismissal appeared in a Santa Fe newspaper. Proclaiming astonishment at this unexpected turn of events, the writer thought the new appointee, L. Edwin Dudley, from New York, might be a good man, but it would be difficult for him to perform the duties of his office more faithfully and competently than Nathaniel Pope. Rumors circulating in Santa Fe about Dudley's background brought differing reactions. Another commentator writing in the newspaper thought Dudley would probably be a valuable acquisition to New Mexico. However, at the Presbyterian church, David McFarland viewed Dudley's arrival in a less favorable light. Preferring to reserve judgment until Dudley could be observed in his new office, McFarland still felt that previous efforts to advance the cause of the Indians under the Peace Policy might be jeopardized because it was said on good authority that the new superintendent was a Catholic.[36]

A few days after his arrival in Santa Fe on December 13, Dudley became convinced that the San Juan River relocation scheme would not be approved, if at all, before spring of the following year. Anticipating the delays implicit in bureaucratic policy making, Dudley preferred not to dwell on false hopes for speedy action on this proposal. Another aspect of innovative experimentation at Fort Defiance appeared more promising. Agent Hall assured his new superintendent that the Indian police force, headed by Chief Manuelito, had definitely proved its worth. In fact, the most notable improvement in the conduct of the Navajos at the end of the year was the dramatic decrease in stealing which, in Hall's opinion, was attributable in large measure to organization of the special mounted police.[37]

At the end of 1872, William Hall's initial enthusiasm for his job at Fort Defiance had waned considerably. He thought the Indians seemed impervious to all civilizing influences. They had no conception of Christianity in any of its forms. Whether or not they could ever be taught to shape their conduct on a moral basis or a sense of right was a most perplexing question. A glaring example of their ignorance and superstition was their devotion to tribal medicine men who only pretended to cure the sick by incantations, while charging outrageous prices for their spurious services. A trip to Santa Fe at the end of November did nothing to raise the spirits of the crestfallen agent. Along in his hotel room on a Sunday evening, he could not sleep. In rooms below the click of billiard balls, the clink of whiskey glasses, and the oaths and obscenities of reckless men profaned the Sabbath. Indeed, he thought the whole territory was peopled by a community of gamblers, thieves, robbers, murderers, and adulterers. This display of uncivilized conduct had shattered his hopes of bringing his wife and two children to join him. Conveying this tale of woe to John Lowrie, Hall concluded with a prediction that he would soon be obliged to resign, as he could no longer tolerate the fearfully depraved condition of the people, especially the "Mexicans."[38]

There was one glimmer of hope in this otherwise gloomy portrayal. While in Santa Fe, Hall was delighted to receive a visit from William Truax, who was not content with his assignment at San Felipe Pueblo. Would Hall accept his services at Fort Defiance to establish and conduct a school? Hall quickly accepted this offer, considering himself fortunate in obtaining the companionship of such a Christian friend and brother. The addition of one good man to the roster of employees at Fort Defiance was offset by the departure of another at the end of 1872. At Tularosa in southern New Mexico, the position of agent to the Southern Apaches became vacant when the Commissioner of Indian Affairs discharged the Presbyterian appointee, Orlando F. Piper. Benjamin Thomas relinquished his job as farmer at the Navajo agency to accept this position, departing in December to assume his new responsibilities. Among the remaining employees at Fort Defiance, Thomas Keams apparently did not enjoy the support of William Hall. On the contrary, the new agent seemed determined on a course of action that would result in termination of Keams's employment. The designation of Keams as a special agent by General Howard had been based upon two premises, a need for supervision of the subagency on the San Juan River and the requirement for creation of a Navajo police force. At the end of 1872, the subagency plan lay dormant, and the police force, in Hall's opinion, could be effectively reduced to about thirty men. This reduction in Keams's responsibilities would leave him with only his routine clerical duties, which Hall insisted he could handle very well himself.[39]

While the situation at the Navajo agency might best be described as in a state of flux at the end of 1872, in the nation's capital the president and his associates praised the results of the continuing evolution of the Peace Policy. Commissioner of Indian Affairs Francis Walker believed that the present policy was now proven to be sound and beneficent. Reducing to a minimum the loss of life and property on the frontier, it had allowed the freest possible development of settlements and railways. The irresistible tide of western migration, which could not be denied or delayed, would soon reduce the last hostile tribes to the condition of supplicants for charity. Indeed, this was the only hope of salvation for the "aborigines of the continent." However, they must also realize that the Great Father's charitable attitude was not intended to perpetuate the Indian's natural reluctance to perform manual labor. On the contrary, if they would eat they must work, and the government was prepared to provide instruction in the civilized arts. Acknowledging that it was always a tiring proposition to elevate people from degradation to self respect, Walker urged perseverance in the continuation of present policies, so that later generations of Indians would be saved from becoming "a pest and a scourge to themselves and to the larger community. . . ."[40]

Reporting on the activities of the Board of Indian Commissioners in 1872, Felix Brunot noted that he and his colleagues had observed a marked change for the better in the confidence exhibited by the Indians in their government. Many of the tribes now had a more positive intent to comply with their obligations and to accept the advice of their agents and superintendents. Convinced that there was much evidence disproving the assertion that adult Indians would not work, Brunot attributed much of this change in attitude to the efforts of the missionary boards whose reports showed success far beyond expectations. Seeking to put an end to rumors that the president's Indian policy might still fail, the board chairman insisted that these misrepresentations came from "bad men with whose schemes it has interfered. . . ." Certainly the policy had saved the nation millions in money and kept thousands of Indians pacified. Finally, Brunot predicted that, before the end of the president's second term, "the success of these measures will have become so patent to all that not even the inveterate Indian haters of the border will venture to find fault with them."[41]

Certainly the members of the Board of Foreign Missions of the Presbyterian Church had little reason to find fault with the results of the Peace Policy near the end of 1872. Admitting that perhaps not all agents appointed by the board had been well-adapted to their work, a board spokesman still insisted that the new policy was generally working well. Fortunately, protecting the Indians from the evils inflicted upon them by lawless white men was recognized as a primary goal of the program. However, the civilizing of the Indians would not come from military or civilian measures. Civilization was the offspring of the Christian religion. "It matters not that many or most of the Indians are deeply debased," the writer concluded, "so were our own ancestors; but no condition of humanity is hopeless. The power of Divine grace can reach, and enlighten, and lift up to our own level the most degraded of our race."[42]

Secretary of the Interior Columbus Delano would not have diminished the role of the civilian arm of the government in the process of civilizing the Indians. Of course religion had its place with other measures in achieving this goal but, for Delano, industry was the great civilizer. Pursuing this thought in his annual report, Delano believed that little could be done to really elevate the Indians until they were led into habits of industry and recognized the advantages of labor. Regrettably, adult Indians, fixed in their ways, would not benefit very much from this process. They could only be held in restraint, but there was hope for improvement in the younger generation, and the energies of his department would be directed to that task. In summation, Delano concluded that the Indian Office was working in a most satisfactory manner. Measured by any true standard, the Indian policy of the government had proved a success because the president was "endeavoring in good faith . . . to fulfill the nation's duty toward a helpless and benighted race."[43]

In his annual state of the union address in December, the president agreed that 1872 had been a good year for the Peace Policy. President Grant was pleased to report that the program had been as successful as could be anticipated within so short a trial period. It had reduced the expenses of the management of Indian affairs, decreased the number of depredations upon white settlements, provided an opportunity for the extension of railways through the public domain, and enabled the establishment of settlements in remote districts of the country. At the same time these achievements were recorded, there was clear evidence that the general condition of the Indian tribes had been noticeably improved. With all these achievements, the policy would definitely be maintained without any changes excepting those which might render it even more efficient.[44]

Although all of these confident statements seemed to reflect an optimistic outlook for continuing success for the Peace Policy in the coming year, in New Mexico many citizens who were sympathetic to the spirit of the reform program were still disappointed that one issue relating to Indian-white relations close to home remained unresolved. The Ute Indians charged with the murder of James Miller were still at large. Detachments of cavalry pursuing the culprits had only succeeded in obtaining conflicting testimony from Ute leaders about the killer's identities. Chief Ouray, well known and respected as a friend of the white men, had finally suggested an arrangement permitting removal of the troops from Ute lands. The chiefs of all the Ute tribes would then press the search by their own people for the renegades.

In this manner, the capture could soon be effected, and the murderers would be promptly turned over to the military. Here the matter rested at the end of 1872. While the search continued, Miller's friends could only hope that retribution for their comrade's death would surely be forthcoming early in the new year.[45]

6

A Renewed Crusade to Cleanse the Temple, 1873

If I can be the instrument to educate and lead to a
Christian life one poor Indian, it would be *more honor &
profit* than all the positions that politicians can give me.
—W. F. M. Arny
August 29, 1873

Far removed from the problems of Navajos and their neighbors in
the Southwest, members of the Board of Indian Commissioners and
their guests gathered at the Arlington Hotel in Washington, D.C. on
January 15, 1873, for their annual meeting to review events relating
to Indian policy in 1872, and discuss plans for the new year. Felix
Brunot, speaking for the commissioners, congratulated the assembled
delegates on the advances made in a relatively short period of time.
Alluding to President Grant's election for another term in the previous
year, he confidently predicted that in four more years the plan would
be perfected to a point where its success would be assured.[1]

When called upon to express his views on the role of the Presbyterian Church in the Peace Policy, John Lowrie admitted that he had,
at first, faced the task presented to his mission board with a sinking
heart because he thought the tribes assigned to the Presbyterians
included the worst Indians that could be encountered anywhere on
the continent. Even with these misgivings, however, he had adopted
a position, which still prevailed, of providing unlimited support to
the present policy of the government. Following the reports from the
various mission boards, General William Hazen, speaking for the
army and its role in the Peace Policy, gave assurance that all army
officers supported the government's policy because they realized it
was the only policy which had produced results favorable to peace
on the frontier and the civilization of the Indians. Concluding their
deliberations, the delegates, after passing a resolution endorsing the

position taken by President Grant, instructed a committee of five, including John Lowrie, to convey the resolution to the White House.[2]

While this annual ritual of congratulatory declamations took place in the nation's capital, at Fort Defiance, Arizona, William Hall was working on a plan to solve the many problems associated with the quest to civilize the Navajos. In an extraordinary recommendation prepared for the Secretary of the Interior in February, Hall forcefully argued for relocation of the Navajos to the Indian Territory. As Hall viewed the situation, there was simply no hope for the Navajos to become self-sustaining on their vast and barren domain. Although they were an intelligent people and not averse to labor, only a very small amount of the land on their reservation was suitable for agricultural pursuits or stock raising. On the other hand, each Navajo family residing in the Indian Territory could receive 160 acres of land for their needs. Recalling also the utter insufficiency of the agency buildings at Fort Defiance, Hall then concluded his argument by insisting that the mineral wealth of the Navajo reservation must soon attract white intruders. If the Indians were removed before this inevitable confrontation, then over 3,000,000 acres of the public domain could be freed for exploitation.[3]

After recording this expression of his dismal expectations for the future at Fort Defiance, Hall then turned his attention to the always present problems at his agency. Acting on the advice of William Truax, Hall ordered an assortment of school supplies at the end of January, thus enabling Truax to reopen the school at Fort Defiance. The new teacher was encouraged, at first, by the response of the Navajo children to his efforts. Although average daily attendance was only six students, there were numerous occasions when as many as thirty pupils attended. Like his predecessors, Truax found that his greatest difficulty was getting the children to attend regularly. At the end of March, however, when Charity Ann Menaul finally returned to Defiance, Truax gallantly consented to relinquish his position at the school in favor of the former teacher.[4]

Unfortunately, what should have been a relatively simple changing of the guard among the teachers at the Fort Defiance school turned into an incident that seriously strained the relationship between the Menauls and their mission board. John Lowrie was convinced that Charity Ann occupied a position that could be better utilized by a male teacher. In a tactless display of male chauvinism, Lowrie precipitated a crisis with observations to William Hall on the role of Mrs.

Menaul at the school. In Lowrie's opinion, with John Menual already on the agency payroll, it really was not appropriate for Charity Ann to hold a salaried post as a teacher. Any moneys available for this purpose could be used more advantageously to secure Christian men as teachers. When Hall innocently mentioned Lowrie's views to the Menauls, the offended missionary and his wife presented angry rebuttals to the outrageous treatment. John Menaul vehemently insisted that Lowrie had no right to try to tell the government who it should or should not employ. Indeed, as there was no church money involved, the position taken by the mission board was "Popish, Unjust, and Unscriptural." Charity Ann confessed that she was not a little grieved and perplexed at Lowrie's attitude. Since William Truax had now left Fort Defiance, she was the only person available to conduct the school. Certainly it would be unfair to expect her to provide this service without reward.[5]

John Lowrie may have responded with soothing words to these angry protestations, although there is no evidence of a reply in the records of the mission board. In any event, Charity Ann taught at the school as a salaried teacher until the summer vacation. At the same time, John Menaul continued on the government payroll as physician at the agency. The multi-talented missionary was satisfied that his medical ministry to the Navajos was well received. However, he continually lamented about the shortage or, at times, complete absence of badly needed medicines for his patients, most of whom suffered from the prevailing diseases on the reservation, i.e., syphilis in all its stages, rheumatism, and sore eyes. Reflecting his hopes for the future, Menaul was sure that adequate supplies in his medicine cabinet would be a compelling force to lead the Indians to salvation, perhaps to the point of achieving the ultimate goal—elimination of the tribal medicine men.[6]

With Mr. and Mrs. Menaul performing yeoman work at the Navajo agency, William Truax had decided to look for other targets of opportunity for his missionary talents. Arriving in Santa Fe in April, he was encouraged when several parties contacted him with a proposition to take a position as supervisor of schools for all of the Indians in the New Mexico Territory. When subsequent inquiries revealed that this attractive employment opportunity was still very much in the planning stages, Truax altered his plans. In May, a writer in a Santa Fe newspaper reported that Truax, whom he described as a gentleman of most agreeable manners, had left New Mexico for good, leaving behind many friends throughout the area. At the end of May, from his new location in Denver, Colorado, Truax provided several perceptive comments on his impressions of New Mexico. He felt sure, for example, that his wife could never have joined him in that God-forsaken region, as the destitute environment of that territory would have been utterly foreign to her tastes. As for the situation at the Navajo agency, Truax felt that Hall was still vacillating and appeared to have no fixed Christian principles, perhaps because he had reportedly joined the church only a short time before receiving his appointment.[7]

At Fort Defiance, William Hall would surely have resented the insinuations in Traux's charges. While his attitude may have appeared vacillating, he was faced with many diverse trials and tribulations which required day-to-day improvisations to counter each unforeseen crisis. As always, this unhappy predicament was well-illustrated in his problems associated with feeding the Navajos. Food supplies accumulated for the Indians in the fall of 1872 had been constantly depleted. At the end of January 1873, Hall had issued the last of his beef rations and early in March he reported his supply of corn nearly exhausted. When news of this desperate situation reached Edwin Dudley in Santa Fe, the courageous superintendent saw no recourse but to act quickly on his own initiative. He contracted locally to furnish 800 head of beef cattle to the Navajos, hoping that this action would receive after-the-fact approval from his superiors.[8]

Dudley's expectations for official concurrence with his unauthorized act may have been enhanced by his knowledge that a new appointee had recently assumed the position of Commissioner of Indian Affairs. On March 20, President Grant finally announced his selection of the Reverend Edward P. Smith to fill the vacancy created by the resignation of Francis Walker at the end of 1872. Smith, a minister of the Congregational Church, had entered the Indian service in 1871 with an appointment as agent at the Chippewa reservation in northern Minnesota. With what was considered a real Christian man now in a position to give benevolent direction to the Peace Policy, field workers at Indian agencies must have anticipated a greater degree of compassionate understanding in the future for the often deplorable plight of their wards.[9]

Whatever the feelings of Edwin Dudley on these matters, his hopes for support in his action on the beef contract for the Navajos were dashed when he received his first communication from the new commissioner. Smith told Dudley, in no uncertain terms, that Dudley had no authority to make such a contract, and there were no funds available at the time for the Indians' subsistence at Fort Defiance. Dudley should, therefore, immediately void the contract, keeping in mind for the future that all contracts of this nature must not be initiated without prior approval of the commissioner's office. The dejected superintendent could only comply with this order. For the remainder of the spring and early summer, the only rations issued to the Navajos consisted of small supplies of corn borrowed from army supplies at Fort Wingate, New Mexico. Dudley did receive authorization, however, to obtain seed corn and wheat for spring planting on the Navajo reservation, with the hope shared by all that Mother Nature would finally provide a favorable growing season for the Indians' crops.[10]

William Hall also had to devote more than a little of his time to maintain a defense of his position against the swelling tide of opposition to his performance as agent for the Navajos. From a discouraged man who was ready to abandon his assignment at the end of 1872, the beleaguered Hall soon became determined to hold on to his post at all costs. In February John Lowrie told the agent that various sources had mentioned Hall's inability to get on well at the agency. As the case was understood at the mission board, the sooner Hall sent in his resignation the better. Hall's impassioned response to these allegations included his insistence that the charges represented "the embodiement of the most senseless, unfounded, foul, unfeeling, and heartless slander. . . ." Insisting that the condition of the Indians was much better than they had ever experienced before, he was sure that much of the slandering of his good name came from his enemies at the agency who despised the successes attributed to his good work.[11]

At this critical period in the relationship between the churchmen and the employees at Fort Defiance, Hall's attitude seemed to border, at times, on paranoia. On one occasion, his persecution complex led him to expound on his views on the murder of James Miller:

My predecessor's death is still surrounded by a cloud of mystery. I believe he was killed by Ute Indians, but [Benjamin] Thomas and a number of others think he was killed by Navajos. Of one thing I am morally certain. I can almost say I know that I would be killed by my own Indians within a month, if certain parties could secure a successor of their own stamp, and that the unfriendliness of a number of these Indians to Mr. Miller was

97

caused by the most inhuman falsehoods of those who ought to have regarded him with unadulterated gratitude. I firmly believe that if he had not been killed when he was he would have met his death at the hands of these Indians from prejudices created falsely by Whites about them.[12]

In spite of Hall's interpretation of these events, in the spring of 1873 the official culmination of the investigation of Miller's murder dispelled the "cloud of mystery" surrounding the Miller case. Ute chiefs who had promised to search for the culprits announced that one of the murderers had been captured and executed according to tribal custom, while the other had apparently escaped to one of the Hopi pueblos where it would be impossible to apprehend him. Accepting this statement at face value, the government closed its case on the murder of James Miller.[13]

When William Hall had accused his enemies at the agency of slandering his good name, he had one person, in particular, in mind. As he saw it, the slanderer could only have been that wicked man Thomas Keams. Hall declared that Keams was opposed to everything of a religious nature in the conduct of Indian affairs. The crafty special agent, Hall insisted, was using his position to subvert Hall's authority by giving some of the Indians special favors, thus convincing them that Hall was a bad man who ought to be killed and replaced by a good man, namely Keams. Hall was determined to remove this threat to his life. An earlier effort on his part to obtain Keams's discharge had been rebuffed when the Office of Indian Affairs refused to take any action until spring, reasoning that Keams might be useful then if the subagency project on the San Juan River should be revived. But Hall soon received additional support for his removal campaign. In February, Williamson Crothers, Presbyterian appointee as agent to the Hopi Indians, told John Lowrie that their church had no greater enemy in New Mexico than Keams. If the government did not remove his ungodly presence from the agency at once, then the Presbyterian Church should abandon its responsibilities among the Navajos, as the influence of Keams over all the men at Fort Defiance would not permit the advancement of Christian work.[14]

The preponderance of these testimonies made a believer out of John Lowrie. Realizing that it was not within the bounds of his authority to discharge Keams since the special agent's appointment had originated from General Howard's recommendation directly to the Interior Department, Lowrie nevertheless wrote to Secretary of the

Interior Delano reviewing the charges against Keams and requesting his removal. Aware of this mounting opposition to his position at Fort Defiance, Keams sought to find temporary relief from the attacks of his accusers by applying for a leave of absence. However, Edwin Dudley forwarded this request to Commissioner Smith with a recommendation of disapproval, demanding instead that Keams should be discharged. All this pressure against Keams finally brought the results desired by his opponents. In May, Delano instructed Smith to inform Keams that his services as special agent to the Navajos would be terminated immediately. Accepting his dismissal as a fait accompli, Keams left the Navajo agency, ostensibly to take advantage of his new unemployed status to visit family and friends in England.[15]

Any satifaction derived by William Hall from this victory over his old nemesis was soon dissipated when Hall realized that his own position was still in jeopardy. Before leaving Fort Defiance, William Truax had advised Lowrie that Hall did not have the moral courage to surround himself with good Christian employees. On the contrary, at least six of the men were living, according to Truax, with Navajo "concubines." Although Hall was a well-meaning man, he was "floundering in the meshes of those who have no sympathy with the present Indian policy. . . ." Moving quickly behind the scenes, Lowrie began to prepare the way for Hall's dismissal. In April he wrote to W. F. M. Arny, territorial secretary for New Mexico and a professed Presbyterian, suggesting that the post of agent to the Navajos might soon become vacant, in which case Arny would receive Lowrie's recommendation for that important position. Early in June, Lowrie told Secretary Delano that Hall was simply not the right man for the job at Fort Defiance. As soon as he could be conveniently discharged, he should be replaced by Arny, who was already known to the Interior Department, highly recommended to the mission board, and capable of doing much for the welfare of the Navajos.[16]

At Fort Defiance, Hall learned of these maneuvers. He made one final effort to vindicate his actions while, at the same time, he called attention to the dubious character of his intended successor. He insisted that the mission board members had misinterpreted many of the derogatory statements made about his conduct, particularly those related to his association with William Truax. Hall insisted that, despite insinuations to the contrary, Truax had not departed from Fort Defiance because he received no support from Hall. The truth of the matter was that Hall had given him every facility in his power for the successful prosecution of his work. The sole reason for Truax's departure was his own conviction that little could be accomplished in the limited definition of his position. As for W. F. M. Arny, Hall was sure the board would be disappointed in his selection, as many of those who knew his previous record in New Mexico regarded him as a man with limited ability and questionable integrity.[17]

Certainly if the great Peace Policy was intended in some manner to remove the stigma of patronage appointments in the assignments to Indian agencies, then W. F. M. Arny's appointment was the complete antithesis to this principle. Many of his influential friends in the Republican Party in New Mexico and in the nation's capital wrote letters of recommendation to Lowrie supporting the selection of Arny for the Navajo agency. Typical of this pressure was a letter from a former judge in New Mexico who mentioned a conversation with the Secretary of the Interior where Arny's commendable traits were discussed. The writer described Arny as a public officer who devoted himself to a conscientious discharge of his trust, always mingling philanthropy and humanity with the performance of his public duties. Arny's acquaintances among the Presbyterian missionaries in the Southwest also spoke favorably about the applicant's ability. John Menaul believed that Arny was honest and enterprising, although, admittedly, there were those who sometimes distrusted his veracity. David McFarland, writing from the Santa Fe church, noted that Arny had been a zealous member of that church since its organization in 1867. William Truax described Arny as a firm friend of the Indians who had always advocated the cause of education and Christian influence among them. And a letter from Secretary of the Interior Delano, reflecting upon the favorable impression made by Arny during his previous assignments at Indian agencies, served, no doubt, to convince Lowrie that the observations of William Hall probably came from spite rather than true knowledge of the situation.[18]

It probably came as no surprise to all of the interested parties when, on July 19, a directive from the office of the Commissioner of Indian Affairs ordered the removal of William Hall from his position as agent to the Navajos in favor of W. F. M. Arny. When Arny received word of his appointment, he hastened to assure Lowrie that he intended to depart at once from his home in Santa Fe to assume his duties at Fort Defiance where he would direct his efforts to the establishment of a system of moral and religious instruction among the Navajos at a minimal expense to the government and the mission board. Wondering, perhaps, about the reception he would receive from William Hall, Arny was surprised when he arrived at the Navajo agency on August 12 to find Hall adamantly opposed to the relinquishment of his position. Hall insisted that since he had not received official notice of his removal, he did not propose to vacate his post until he obtained proper notification from his superiors. When the exasperated Arny reported this awkward situation to the Office of Indian Affairs, Commissioner Smith angrily reminded Hall that a dismissal notice had been sent to him in July. Therefore, he should comply immediately with the wishes of the government.[19]

With his last defenses breached by Smith's directive, William Hall reluctantly surrendered his post. On September 1, 1873, W. F. M. Arny took charge of the Navajo agency. Meeting with several tribal leaders, the new agent received expressions of willingness to cooperate with him in the development of policies that would, hopefully, benefit all who resided on the Navajo reservation. Notifying John Lowrie of his assumption of the agency responsibilities, Arny included in his remarks a typically zealous statement of his objectives. "If I can be the instrument," he wrote, "to educate and lead to a Christian life one poor Indian, it would be *more honor & profit* than all the positions that politicians can give me."[20]

Soon after Arny's relief of Hall, a government official visited Fort Defiance to inspect the agency operations. Inspector William Vandever, appointed under the terms of an act of Congress on February 14, 1873, realized that Arny could hardly have extensive knowledge about his many problems in his very brief tenure in office. Nevertheless, the inspector's report of September 24, 1873, did focus on issues that could be identified as prime targets for Arny's corrective efforts in the future. Vandever found that the buildings at the agency were sadly in need of repair; there were still immoral employees at the agency who were cohabiting with Indian women; there was no school operating for the Navajos at the time; the Indians were anxious to enlarge the boundaries of their reservation to provide more pasture for their livestock; and it appeared that the Indians would probably be dependent again on government rations when winter arrived. After recording these negative impressions, Vandever still believed that the Navajos excelled in "sprightliness and intelligence" and no tribe could be regarded as "more susceptible . . . of advancement in the arts and customs of civilized life."[21]

Arny agreed that the condition of the agency facilities could only be regarded as deplorable. He immediately submitted a request to Dudley for $500 to employ Navajo laborers for the badly needed rehabilitation of the agency buildings. Like his predecessors, Arny was also convinced that his objective to lead the Indians to a Christian life could not be attained if the Indians were continually subjected to the influence of the immoral men at the agency. In Arny's estimation, the unacceptable employees could easily be identified. Typical of those selected for dismissal were the interpreter Jesus Alviso and the butcher Anson Damon. Alviso was clearly a negative influence. He lived at the agency with *two* Navajo women who were sisters and by whom he had fathered children. According to Arny, he was also addicted to gambling and, insisting that he was only employed to interpret, he refused to help in any other way around the agency. Damon, like Alviso, had lived with several Indian "squaws" and had several children by them. Arny's views on this outrageous lifestyle were neatly summarized in the simple statement, "his moral influence is bad."[22]

Were there no good Christian men left at Fort Defiance to serve as foundation stones for Arny's rebuilding program? Of course the Menauls were the right kind of people in Arny's eyes. Another good man was Seward Chapin, former agent to the Jicarrila Apaches and two bands of Ute Indians at Cimarron, New Mexico. Arny hoped to find employment for Chapin, who had recently arrived at the agency, as the person "in charge of grain and asst. on issue." Arny also thought that an old friend, Henry W. Easton of Abiquiu, New Mexico, would be a good choice for Anson Damon's job as butcher because Easton was a married man with a family who would provide a much better influence than Damon. And providentially, Arny's son William was at loose ends at the time. Supported by his wife and family, he would be an ideal replacement for the man whom Arny intended to discharge from the position of chief herder.[23]

In Santa Fe, Edwin Dudley was not at all pleased with these initial steps taken by his agent at Fort Defiance. Foremost among Dudley's complaints was a suspicion that Arny, who had written directly to Commissioner Smith about his plans, had the mistaken impression that he was in some way empowered to act at the Indian agency independently from Dudley's supervision. With little effort to conceal his displeasure, Dudley urged Smith to remedy this deplorable situation by admonishing Arny to channel any and all of his proposals through Dudley's office. The offended superintendent then began to dismantle Arny's complicated structure of personnel changes by refusing to approve several of his selections as replacements. This jurisdictional dispute continued for the balance of the year. Arny boldly continued to initiate changes and then solicit after-the-fact approval for his actions, but a description of the employment situation at the agency as "unsettled" would be an understatement.[24]

Arny's effort to maintain some semblance of a school at Fort Defiance suffered a similar rebuff. Charity Ann Menaul, referring to the heavy burden of her household duties, had elected to terminate her employment as teacher on June 30, 1873. With an opportunity to begin anew in this field of endeavor, Arny disclosed an audacious plan for developing a realistic and productive educational program for the Navajos. Rejecting the day school concept as completely worthless considering the transient lifestyle of most Navajo families, Arny insisted that regularity of attendance could only be assured in an industrial boarding school environment. Therefore, the government would be wise to allot $7,000 immediately to construct and furnish the necessary buildings for 200 students. At the same time, authorization should be provided for the employment of two teachers, a superintendent of labor, and a patron and matron for the boarding house. The superintendent of labor would spend several hours each day directing the work of the boys on a model farm near the agency, while the matron would teach housework to the girls. If all of these suggestions were implemented, Arny was sure that in four years he could produce 200 native teachers who could then teach other children throughout the reservation.[25]

John Lowrie reacted cautiously at first to Arny's proposals. He did congratulate the agent for his zealous approach to initiating a program of good works for the Navajos. Certainly it was lamentable to learn that so little had been done for them. The board secretary then addressed Arny's educational recommendations with the rather vague assurance that the board members simply concurred with his announced objectives. However, in Santa Fe Edwin Dudley absolutely refused to endorse the great boarding school proposition. Basing his rejection on Arny's intent to employ a staff of teachers and officers that would be appropriate for a first-class school in a heavily populated community, Dudley made it very clear that the system of day schools utilized in the past for Navajo children would continue until the students showed some advancement in their studies.[26]

Arny carefully weighed these two reactions to his proposals. Speaking for the government, Dudley's response was clearly a rejection.

But the language used by the mission board seemed to leave the door open for subsequent consideration if only the ways and means could be found to implement Arny's plans. The clever agent saw a possibility to move ahead in this matter by reviving a proposal that he had initiated soon after he became an agent. He believed that a Presbyterian church established at Fort Defiance would exert a great moral and religious influence over the Navajos. Noting that he and John Menaul were preaching on alternate Sabbaths, he gave the impression that the demand for this service was very evident. With this opening gambit, it was easy for Arny to suggest to the board that a minister and his wife located at the agency could also carry out responsibilities as patron and matron of a boarding school.[27]

While he waited for the mission board's views on this suggestion, Arny was pleased when he received inquiries from two unmarried ladies in the United States who could fill the two teaching positions still funded on the government payroll at the agency. Since Miss Amanda C. Painter and her friend Miss Callie Delph appeared well qualified for these assignments, Arny urged John Lowrie to support him in these selections. Lowrie's first response was favorable, but before he could finalize the arrangements Edwin Dudley intervened in the proceedings. When Dudley heard of the negotiations with the two teachers, he registered a strong protest. "You have already wasted enough money in this field," the angry superintendent wrote to Lowrie, "and ought to make future expenditures where you will realize something for your money and trouble. Fort Defiance is not the place for lady missionaries. . . ." Influenced, no doubt, by this impassioned plea, early in December Lowrie tactfully advised Arny that he had recommended against the appointment of the two ladies at the present time as the perils of a winter journey to Fort Defiance would be too hazardous for them.[28]

With these problems demanding much of his time, Arny surely hoped that the food shortage predicted by Inspector Vandever would not occur. However, from all indications the Navajo harvest had fallen short of expectations. Arny believed that the few crops raised by the Indians would nearly all be consumed before the first of November. From that time on, the government would have to feed them once again. Perhaps anticipating this situation, Edwin Dudley had contracted in mid-summer for 500,000 pounds of corn for delivery at periodic intervals to the Navajo agency. Arny carefully hoarded shipments of this corn in September and October, although he was obliged to send 70,000 pounds of his precious supply to settle the debts of this commodity accumulated by his predecessors at Fort Wingate. Near the end of October, Arny began to issue the corn to the Navajos. He then had to report, with noticeable irritation, that the Indians complained about the absence of beef to supplement this ration. When Dudley corrected this deficiency in November by negotiating contracts for beef to be delivered at Fort Defiance, Arny was able to provide weekly issues of both corn and beef throughout December.[29]

If Arny felt any satisfaction at the apparent resolution, for the time being, of the Navajo food problems, he experienced unexpected frustration from Navajo complaints about another matter. The annual shipment of Navajo annuity goods, scheduled for distribution on September 1, had been delayed. Although these materials started on their way to the agency in mid-July, only a partial shipment had reached Fort Defiance by mid-October. The rest of the supplies were stalled in a warehouse in Pueblo, Colorado. As Arny viewed the situation, he could not issue any of the goods until all had been received. When the impatient agent inquired into the matter, he discovered, to his dismay, that an army officer in Pueblo had refused to permit the forwarding of the remaining supplies because he had no contract to release the material to freighters who were ready and waiting to complete the delivery. On November 1, Arny reported growing anger among the tribal leaders, as they needed the supplies, particularly the clothing, before the arrival of cold weather. Since this crisis received no further mention by Arny for the rest of the year, one would like to think that this matter was finally resolved to the satisfaction of all parties concerned, but the exasperating delay of almost four months surely gave the Navajos reason to question, once again, the credibility of government promises.[30]

One other problem inherited from his predecessor required Arny's attention near the end of 1873. Earlier in the year, William Hall had concluded that the Navajo police force could be substantially reduced as an economy measure. The Office of Indian Affairs, always responsive to money-saving suggestions, had concurred with his recommendation. Shortly before his departure, Hall suggested that the police be dismissed altogether, as he had only occasional need of their services. Hall's superiors agreed again with this suggestion, and when Arny arrived at Fort Defiance, he found instructions to terminate the police force at once. Arny was opposed to this action, fearing that Indian depredations would surely increase, but he tactfully announced his compliance with the order. For the time being then the enlightened policy of General Howard, John Lowrie, and others was set aside but not forgotten by the new Navajo agent.[31]

Although Arny had decided not to make a big issue of the disbanding of the police force, he did take a firm stand when dealing with people who appeared to be questioning his authority at Fort Defiance. James L. Gould had replaced Thomas Keams as special agent after the latter's dismissal by William Hall. Gould came to his job highly recommended by David McFarland in Santa Fe as a young man with impeccable personal characteristics. Arny challenged Gould's selection at once. The petulant agent resented Gould's inclination to work independently of Arny's authority with a feasibility study on the San Juan subagency project. When Arny let it be known that, in his opinion, the position of special agent for the Navajos was only an unnecessary expense to the government, Gould countered by charging Arny with a number of improprieties in his conduct of agency affairs. Among his allegations, Gould charged Arny with diverting to his own use some of the supplies intended for the Navajos. He also insisted that Arny had utilized an Indian as his personal servant while carrying him on the agency payroll as the person responsible for maintenance of the irrigation ditches. Arny defended himself vigorously against these charges. He denied, first, any unlawful diversion of Indian supplies to his own use. Then, although admitting employment of an Indian for miscellaneous duties, he insisted that he paid the small salary of this servant out of his own pocket. In this tug-of-war between agent and special agent, Arny outlasted his adversary. Unwilling to continue his efforts in a hostile environment, Gould resigned in mid-October. With this thorn removed from his side, Arny could turn his attention to the problem of evicting a trespasser from his agency.[32]

William Defrees, the new agent for the Hopi Indians who resided in northern Arizona, made his headquarters at Fort Defiance because he regarded the primitive dwellings in the Hopi villages as unsuitable for the establishment of a civilized domicile. Although Defrees had been recommended for his post as "a consistent Christian man" with a wife who was "a most estimable Christian lady," these commendable attributes could not be translated into an atmosphere of harmonious relations at Fort Defiance. As Arny saw it, the Defrees family occupied rooms that would soon be needed to house the teachers contemplated in his plans for the Navajo school. In Defrees's view, Arny's motive in making this an issue was simply to raise ill feelings toward him among the Navajos. In an attempt to defuse this potentially explosive situation, Edwin Dudley mandated continued joint occupancy of the facilities at Fort Defiance, but only until adequate housing became available for the Defrees entourage among the Hopis. The warring factions were temporarily subdued by the superintendent's edict, and an uneasy truce between the two agents continued for the balance of the year. Irritated, no doubt, by all the acrimonious bickering at the Navajo agency, Dudley could not refrain from expressing his annoyance. "If these gentlemen," he wrote, "were each to exhibit the brotherly feeling which ought to actuate them as members of the same church and officers of the same government, I can see no reason why any trouble should exist."[33]

News of the lack of "brotherly feeling" at Fort Defiance began to reach John Lowrie near the end of the year. John Menaul, who had originally recommended Arny as an honest and enterprising man, had now decided that the agent was a congenital liar and "he is not a Presbyterian or anything that would approximate that faith." Menaul insisted there was not one of the Navajos who liked Arny, as with him it was always "mucha [much] say and nada [nothing] do." One of Arny's former acquaintances in Santa Fe concluded from information received from Fort Defiance that the agent's attitude had labeled him, in the eyes of all who associated with him, as unreliable, treacherous, and "a consummate mischief maker." William Defrees was even more vociferous in his continuing criticism. He insisted that Arny had boasted that he was not a real Presbyterian, even though he held a membership in the Santa Fe Presbyterian church. According to Defrees, Arny was a hindrance and a blot on the otherwise fair pages of Presbyterian history in the territory. He was in his dotage, unstable, vacillating, irritable, and childish. In fact, on his first Sunday at the agency, he went hunting for ducks at a pond not three hundred yards from the place of worship service where he and his cronies fired their guns during the whole time of worship.[34]

Lowrie was worried, of course, that he and his board had made a wrong move with the Arny appointment. He reminded Arny's detractors, however, that the selection was made on the recommendations of Presbyterians in New Mexico who knew him personally and of gentlemen in high places in the East. These comments might have served to chastise the Presbyterians at Fort Defiance for their unchristian attitudes, but Lowrie could not dismiss lightly the criticisms voiced by Edwin Dudley. The angry superintendent charged that Arny had actually brought more unproductive men to the agency, including his own son, who was a wastrel to say the least. Dudley insisted that this young man had lived for several years with a Mexican woman and fathered children by her long before their marriage. Dudley also noted that this degraded youth "drinks anything and everything in the liquor line he can get and swears like a very pirate." With all of these accusations at hand at the end of 1873, Lowrie admitted to Secretary of the Interior Delano that Arny's position at the Navajo agency would have to be carefully scrutinized in the coming year.[35]

In Washington at the end of 1873, government officials seized upon another opportunity to reflect upon results of the Peace Policy in previous months. Edward Smith, who had replaced Francis Walker as commissioner of Indian affairs, concluded that the arrangement whereby Indian agents were appointed on the nomination of religious bodies was working with increasing satisfaction. The churches were generally entering heartily into full support for the program. Hopefully, the government would continue to make sufficient appropriations to teach the Indians how to live in a civilized way. If this support was forthcoming, then persons would surely continue to come forward to work among the Indians "in the spirit of kindness and Christian love, with a faith in God and a faith in man strong enough to sustain them amid the degradation and perversities of barbarism, and cheer them on in the full conviction that no being made in God's image is incapable of improvement."[36]

Reporting for the Board of Indian Commissioners, the board secretary Thomas Cree noted a very great change for the better in the Indian service. Where it had previously been characterized simply as a stupendous fraud, now, with the involvement of the mission boards of the churches, a vastly better class of men had entered the service. Singling out the Presbyterian Church for special notice, Cree found that the amount spent on Indian missions by that great denomination totaled $22,550.55 for the year, and reports from its schools and general mission work were very favorable. Felix Brunot, chairman of the board, agreed with these observations. He particularly appreciated the success achieved in the past year in punishing Indian murderers, selecting for special attention the fine work done by all parties concerned in the case of the murder of agent James Miller by the Ute Indians.[37]

Secretary of the Interior Columbus Delano prepared a lengthy explanation of the intent of the benevolent program. Foremost among the goals was a commitment to place all Indians upon reservations as soon as possible. When this was achieved, the intellectual, moral, and religious culture of the Indians could be advanced with the aid of the Christian organizations who were acting in perfect harmony with the government. Following the introduction of schools and churches by the Christian organizations, the Indians, who would have a better way of life than they had ever known before, would be made to appreciate all of the blessings awaiting them in a Christian civilization.[38]

In his annual message to Congress, President Grant made a statement on the Indian problem that was noteworthy for its brevity. Pleased with the beneficial results of the Peace Policy, he intended to continue it with only those modifications that would be dictated by past experience. There had been some disturbances between Indians and whites during the past year, but these incidents had to be expected until each race came to appreciate the rights of the other. Since the Indian Territory had sufficient land and other resources to support all the Indians east of the Rocky Mountains, it would be advisable to collect those Indians in this location, giving them a territorial form of government as soon as possible to secure their treaty rights.[39]

With constant assurance from knowledgeable men during these early years of the Peace Policy that the program was both successful and permanent, John Lowrie and the members of his mission board were prepared to continue their obligations to nominate Christian men for agency appointments in the Southwest and provide the services of Presbyterian missionaries at these agencies whenever possible. At Fort Defiance, Arizona, as 1873 drew to a close, W. F. M. Arny appeared impervious to any rumors that he may have heard concerning his less than satisfactory conduct of agency affairs. Choosing to ignore the negative and emphasize the positive, he boasted that he had succeeded in "organizing" the Indians. The Navajo chiefs had agreed to report to him weekly and have a general meeting monthly of all interested parties to transact appropriate agency business. At these meetings, Arny proposed to fully discuss the treaty of 1868 with the chiefs, a process which, according to Arny, had never been attempted before. Relying on the success of these efforts to instill orderly procedures into a previously ad hoc relationship with the Indians, Arny was sure that his attempts to Christianize the Navajos would surely be rewarded by significant achievements in the new year.[40]

7

A Visit to the Great Father, 1874

The Navajoes [*sic*] are engaged exclusively in peaceful
pursuits. They are honest, industrious, and—best of all—
decent in their habits, in which, it is needless to say, they
are not comparable with redskins generally.
—*Washington Evening Star*
December 1, 1874

"The peace policy is condemned. The western men say that persons
from the East, with broad-brimmed-hat ideas, and no real knowledge
of the Indian nature, go out among the dissatisfied red men, and only
succeed in running up large bills against the government without
doing any good." This strident attack on the Peace Policy appeared
early in January 1874 in the Washington Gossip section of the *New
York Times*. Although these negative impressions undoubtedly represented the true feelings of many westerners, President Grant found
the criticisms unwarranted and probably motivated by the selfish
interests of a particular group of greedy western men. When questioned about his reaction to the views expressed by opponents of the
Peace Policy, the angry president insisted that misrepresentation and
perversion of the results of his Indian policy had been incited by
residents of the frontier, traders and others, who saw their profit-
making potential substantially reduced by the new reforms. The program was not a failure. On the contrary, the religious agent plan had
worked well in practice. Many of the agents, serving with a genuine
missionary spirit, were teaching the Indians how to support and
protect themselves. In addition, greater progress had been made in
the Indian schools in the past few years than in all previous time.[1]

This optimistic position taken by the president was shared by members of the Board of Indian Commissioners and their guests who
gathered once again in Washington, D.C. on January 14 to share their
thoughts about the past, present, and future direction of their efforts
to help the Indians. Honored as the first speaker called upon to report,

John Lowrie elected to direct his initial observations to the support provided by his church for Indian educational programs. He thought that the Presbyterian schools operated on Indian reservations were generally exhibiting satisfactory results. The greatest problem encountered by the teachers was universally acknowledged to be the difficulty in attaining fluency in the native languages. Lowrie then candidly admitted the embarrassment experienced by his mission board in its efforts among the Indians in New Mexico. Agents in that area complained of the high cost-of-living in the Southwest and the impossibility of securing employees except those of no particular intelligence and poor morals. Elaborating on the cost-of-living issue, the mission board secretary hoped that the government would seriously consider a flexible salary scale for Indian agents, providing an increment above the standard $1,500 annual salary for hardship cases in particularly isolated areas. However, in no case should the salary be so high as to make it a temptation in itself, overshadowing the real motivating force in the selection process—that is, a desire to do good. Reiterating his faith in the spirit of selfless commitment attributed to the Peace Policy, Lowrie insisted that "there are in this land ten thousand men ready to make any sacrifice necessary to carry the blessings of Christianity to all those poor Indians."[2]

While the experts on Indian policy in the nation's capital extolled the virtues of the Peace Policy, far away in the Southwest one of the ten thousand dedicated men envisioned by John Lowrie struggled to develop a program that would, once and for all, succeed in uplifting the Navajos. W. F. M. Arny recognized two pressing challenges early in 1874 that required immediate attention. First, an educational program of some sort for the Navajos simply had to be reinstated in the wake of Charity Ann Menaul's relinquishment of this responsibility in the previous year. Then, with a school underway, renewed efforts would be required to find the wherewithal to feed the Indians. At the end of February, Arny was pleased when two men arrived at Fort Defiance to assist in the quest to achieve these goals. Professor Valentine Friese agreed to accept an appointment as teacher at the agency, and William Truax returned to try to aid the Navajos, this time as agency farmer.[3]

Friese, described by his friend Truax as a Christian gentleman from Pennsylvania, who was studying for the ministry in the Baptist Church, went to work immediately. He found little to build upon from the previous efforts of Charity Ann Menaul and James Roberts. When he could locate only ten small slates and eighteen spelling books in the old school building, he urged Arny to order a long list of school supplies including chalk, alphabet blocks, pencils, slates, readers, pens, pen holders, and ink stands. Although handicapped in his teaching efforts by the shortage of materials, Friese still found his Navajo students eager to learn. For the month of March, the new teacher reported an average daily attendance of between nine and ten students, although twenty-five were actually carried on the rolls at the end of the month. Friese attributed the rather small daily attendance to a period of inclement winter weather, but the students in attendance, who ranged in age from five to twenty years, showed commendable progress in reading, writing and arithmetic.[4]

In April Arny added two more employees to the staff of the Navajo school. On April 14, Mr. Joseph Gow arrived at Fort Defiance. He told the surprised Arny that he had come from his home in Santa Fe at the request of his friend Edwin Dudley, who knew that there was still federal funding for two teachers at the Navajo agency. Presumably Gow would share the responsibility for teaching the Navajo children with Valentine Friese. On the day after Gow's arrival, Mrs. Catherine Stowe, recruited by Arny from the Presbyterian church of Frankfort, Indiana, appeared to serve as matron in a new boarding school contemplated by Arny. Persistent in his dream to open this type of school at Fort Defiance, Arny finally secured after-the-fact approval of Mrs. Stowe's appointment from the Office of Indian Affairs when he argued that the primary responsibility of his new matron would be to perform the duties of a mother to the several hundred orphan children of the Navajos who were scattered over the reservation learning idle and vicious habits.[5]

Joseph Gow's tenure as teacher at Fort Defiance was short lived. With no need for more than one teacher to accommodate the needs of only a handful of students, Arny chose to permit Gow who, after all, was Dudley's appointee, to handle only routine clerical duties at the agency. It probably came as no surprise when, early in June, Gow, seeing no hope for the operation of two schools at Fort Defiance, submitted his resignation. In the small school conducted by Valentine Friese, the professor continued to notice signs of progress among his students. In his annual report prepared in September, Friese noted between thirty and forty pupils on the rolls each month, with an average daily attendance of about twelve and a half. The most advanced pupils were reading in McGuffey's Second Reader, almost all of the students could read reasonably well, and the best students in arithmetic were working in multiplication. Offsetting these positive indications were the deplorable facilities for teaching at the agency. The small room designated for a schoolroom was totally unsuited for this purpose. This problem, in Friese's estimation, could only be solved with construction of the great boarding school envisioned by Arny. The selection by the agent of Catherine Stowe as matron for the proposed school was clearly a step in the right direction. In Friese's opinion, with this evidence of commitment the government should now supply the aid necessary to complete the noble enterprise.[6]

Indeed, the operation of a boarding facility in connection with the school seemed to show early promise for success. In a small building provided by Arny, Mrs. Stowe began to take in Navajo children. These Indian youths, both boys and girls, were neatly clothed by the industrious matron who managed to prepare more than a hundred garments from material furnished by Arny. The fastidious Mrs. Stowe also required the children to wash their faces and comb their hair before going to school. By September, twenty-eight children, at one time or another, had taken advantage of the services offered at the boarding home. With considerable regret, however, Mrs. Stowe found it necessary in September to submit her resignation because of the ill health of her small son. Undaunted by this unexpected turn of events, Arny was determined to continue with the boarding concept. He was sure that the good results recorded from its brief existence demonstrated that this approach offered the only viable plan for achieving success—that of eventually educating all of the nearly three thousand Navajo children. Until a suitable replacement could be found for Mrs. Stowe, Arny announced that his wife and daughter-in-law would continue the operation of the home on a voluntary basis.[7]

With a school functioning once again, Arny could turn his attention to the challenge of leading the Navajos to that much-sought-after goal, achieving self-sufficiency in their food supplies. This burden was now carried by William Truax. After leaving Fort Defiance in the previous year to take up residence in Denver, Colorado, Truax sought opportunities in that city to utilize his missionary training by working among the small Chinese population. However, finding that he could accomplish little without an interpreter, and concerned about his deteriorating health, Truax quickly accepted Arny's invitation to return to Fort Defiance. Although he would have to accept a position as a farmer, Truax believed that he should seize any chance "to bring that large and interesting tribe [Navajos] to a knowledge of the truth as it is in Christ Jesus."[8]

Determined to ignore the previous pattern of crop failures, Truax stepped into a situation that was typically desperate in regard to the Navajo food supply. Near the end of March, Arny dejectedly predicted that at the end of the month all of the beef and corn furnished for the Indians at the agency would be issued. Compounding the problem, Navajo efforts to secure food by hunting had not been productive because the worst winter recorded in many years had kept the reservation completely covered with deep snow. When warmer weather finally returned, Truax exhorted the Indians to prepare more land than ever before for the planting of a large variety of crops. The Navajos diligently followed his directions but, to his dismay, he then discovered that the seeds ordered in October of the previous year had not arrived. An inquiry into the status of this order resulted, finally, in the appearance of the seeds at Fort Defiance on May 30. Truax distributed the seeds as soon as possible to the Indians who streamed into the agency from the farthest corners of the reservation, but the distraught farmer was afraid that an already brief growing season would be further reduced by the unfortunate delay.[9]

While the Indians planted, in Santa Fe Edwin Dudley courageously decided to exceed his authority once again and take drastic measures to provide food for the Indians. He instructed Arny to purchase limited amounts of beef and corn on credit, offering assurance to the merchants that the vouchers would be approved and paid in due time. With this badly needed support, Arny resumed issuance of rations to the Navajos in June. Unfortunately, throughout the summer insects damaged the crops planted by the Indians much more severely than in previous years. Many of the vegetables were ruined and cutworms injured much of the corn. When an early frost on September 3 wreaked havoc among the remaining crops, Truax and Arny knew that their expectations for finding ways and means for the Navajos to feed themselves would have to be postponed for still another year.[10]

Of course, educating and feeding the Indians were important concerns for Arny in 1874, but he also had to be aware of other issues related to his position and the welfare of the Navajos. Although William Truax and Valentine Friese seemed to agree with his plans for uplifting the Indians, Arny could still sense a continuing undercurrent of antagonism from others residing at the agency. Some of the ill feeling generated by personality clashes was eased by the departure of one of Arny's critics. His dispute with William Defrees over the latter's occupancy of living quarters at Fort Defiance was settled when Defrees received funds from the government to erect an agency building near his Hopi Indians. When Defrees and his family left during the summer to occupy their new home, Arny allotted the vacated buildings at once to Truax and Friese. Then, in a forgiving mood, Arny magnanimously welcomed the return of a contrite sinner to the agency. When Jesus Alviso, the interpreter discharged earlier by Arny for his immoral lifestyle, returned to Fort Defiance looking for employment, Arny rehired Alviso because he had professed repentance for his evil ways and promised to do his best in the future to set a good example for the Indians.[11]

Arny may have received with mixed feelings the news of the departure of another employee of the Office of Indian Affairs in New Mexico. On July 1, 1874, Edwin Dudley had to relinquish his position as Superintendent of Indian Affairs for New Mexico, not because he wished to leave that office, but because the government decided to terminate all of the superintendents' positions in the Indian service. This economy measure was not welcomed by some leading residents of New Mexico who saw in the move a regression from an effective structure that had been built up over the years to administer Indian affairs. The disturbed citizens pointed to the many services provided by the superintendents to their agents in the field. They argued that, as a general rule, the Indians, who had little regard for their agents, looked with respect to the superintendent who had both authority and power over them. These protests fell on deaf ears, however, and when Dudley departed, Arny may have been relieved to know that he no longer had to deal with a superior who disliked him personally. On the other hand, he may have realized with regret that Dudley's consistent support in bending the rules when necessary to obtain food supplies for the Navajos would be sorely missed in future crisis situations.[12]

In one other association with an employee at Fort Defiance—John Menaul—Arny tried to maintain at least a surface appearance of cordial relations. The busy missionary labored diligently in his capacity as agency physician, noting in his annual report of August 31, 1874, treatment of 2,204 Indians. However, he avoided contact with Arny as much as possible, believing that the less he knew about the conduct of agency affairs, the better, if he wished to live in peace and keep his position. Early in the year, with a premonition of disaster, he urged John Lowrie to replace Arny if possible, "for the sake of Christ's Kingdom here, for the sake of the Indians here. . . ." When there was no indication that the mission board would act favorably on his recommendation, Menaul let it be known that he was interested in employment elsewhere, perhaps to an assignment in Santa Fe or Albuquerque. Once again it appeared that the troubled missionary was still not certain that he really understood God's intention for his missionary work in the Southwest.[13]

Education, food, and employee relations. While Arny might have regarded these issues as paramount in his quest to do good to the Navajos in 1874, he also confronted other problems that could not be dismissed as insignificant. For example, a war between the Navajos and Mormon settlers west of the reservation threatened early in the year. Arny received reports at the end of January indicating that Mormons had killed three Navajos in a dispute over cattle allegedly stolen by the Indians. Arny's investigation revealed that the Navajos had indeed visited the Mormon settlements without a pass authorizing their absence from the reservation. The angry Navajo chiefs, however, thought that the cold-blooded slaying of the three men without a fair trial was just another intolerable incident of unwarranted vigilante action carried out by ruthless white men against their peaceful Indian neighbors. The Mormon settlers, represented by Jacob Hamblin, described by Arny as the Indian agent for Brigham Young, had no wish to precipitate a full-scale Indian war over this incident. Since the killers were not members of the Mormon Church, Hamblin insisted that his people could not accept any responsibility for the attack. When the army denied Arny's request for a military escort to accompany him to a meeting with the Mormons, the frustrated agent abandoned his efforts to act as mediator in the crisis and the Navajos reluctantly ended, for the time being, their attempts to secure compensation.[14]

Arny had greater success with peacekeeping efforts on the reservation. Although he had reluctantly complied with a directive to dispense with the services of the Navajo police force late in 1873, Arny had never agreed with this abandonment of what he regarded as a very effective program. Aware that cost was one of the determining factors leading to disbanding the police, Arny boldly reactivated the force in May of 1874 with an enrollment of 200 Indians whom he intended to pay from what he described as a surplus of annuity goods. However, when Indian lawbreakers were apprehended and arrested by the police, Arny found that it was impossible to hold the culprits in confinement pending trial. As required by his instructions on these matters, he sent the wrongdoers to Fort Wingate for incarceration only to learn, in every case, that the Indians escaped in less than a week. Although this apparent lackadaisical attitude on the part of his supposed allies in the military obviously angered Arny, he did believe that his policies directed to the maintenance of law and order on the reservation had resulted in the return of much stolen property and a noticeable reduction in thefts from surrounding settlements.[15]

Inspector J. W. Daniels acknowledged Arny's generally successful efforts to keep the peace on the reservation after his visit to the agency late in August. Following the pattern established in the previous year of annual visits by special inspectors, Daniels prepared a comprehensive report on many aspects of agency affairs. Among his positive observations, he agreed that Arny was doing all he could, under the circumstances, to keep the Indians quiet. The inspector also noted that Arny's accounts appeared correct and agency funds had been properly expended for the best interests of the service. Since Arny's records of rations issued to the Indians showed a reduced number of Navajos receiving this support, Daniels concluded that there was a noticeable improvement in the ability of these Indians to provide for themselves.[16]

Addressing the negative aspects of conditions at Fort Defiance, the inspector noted that the agency buildings were absolutely unfit for human habitation. Arny attributed this deplorable situation to damages caused by high water from the melting of abnormal winter snows and very heavy spring rains. Arny had endeavored to obtain the services of Indian laborers to make sorely needed repairs, but his recruiting efforts were in vain as the Navajos refused to work for him when he had to admit that he had no cash available to pay them. For the time being, at least, residents at the agency had to be reconciled to a dismal situation where the already inadequate agency facilities became even more dilapidated in appearance.[17]

Interviews by Daniels with employees at Fort Defiance revealed other problem areas in the conduct of agency affairs. Valentine Friese indicated that his teaching efforts had resulted in some improvement in the reading and writing skills of his scholars, but the children were prone to ignore his pleas for regularity in attendance. John Menaul discussed his work in treating diseases of the Navajos. He admitted that requirements on his time limited his role to the dispensing of medicines from his office rather than visiting outlying areas of the reservation to attend the sick. Daniels's interview with William Truax was particularly edifying. The agency farmer acknowledged that he had been born and raised on a farm, but he had not been actively involved in farming during the past twenty years. Daniels was surprised when he learned that Truax had made no attempt to travel across the reservation to observe Navajo farming practices or to ascertain just how much land they had under cultivation. The inspector concluded from these admissions that Truax was "practically incompetent and physically unfit to perform the duties of his position. . . ."[18]

Daniels's interviews with several of the Navajo chiefs were also informative. When called on to speak, Manuelito was particularly responsive to the inspector's inquiries. The leader of the Navajo police force expressed his concern that the lands of his people might be taken from them. Perceiving that there was plenty of grazing land for all, Manuelito gave assurance that the Navajos would keep the stock on their side of all boundary lines, but he expected their non-Indian neighbors to do the same. Referring to a dispute with a rancher whose employees had killed a Navajo during negotiations over the sale of some sheep, Manuelito insisted that the dead Indian was his cousin and he should be compensated by the rancher for the loss of his relative with 300 sheep, 30 cows, 40 yards of cloth, a box of indigo, and 12 sides of fine leather. If the rancher complied with this demand, then the Indians would be content and no reprisals would be contemplated.[19]

Inspector Daniels had no ready solutions to any of the problems identified in his final report. As an observer without authority to prescribe remedies, he could only assure one and all that his comments on these issues would be carefully studied in the Office of Indian Affairs. Although Daniels's report was confidential in nature, the agent to the Navajos was not oblivious to these threatening issues. With all of the difficulties encountered in the day-to-day operation of his agency, one might have expected that Arny would have concentrated all his efforts at problem solving on purely local matters. However, underlying all of his activities at this time was a determination to secure national recognition for the Navajos and their agent by taking a delegation of Indians to visit Washington, D.C. Arny had started his agitation to obtain approval for this project early in 1874. He carefully pointed out that the Navajos were the only Indians in New Mexico who had not received this privilege to date. To justify the expenditures required for this journey, he insisted that the Navajo chiefs were eager to negotiate a change in the boundaries of their reservation, exchanging a strip of their land to the north for the addition of an equal strip from the public domain in the south. Presumably this exchange would provide the Indians with badly needed pasture land while, at the same time, the unused acreage inside the northern border of the reservation could be opened to white settlers and miners eager to investigate the mineral potential of the area. Of course, as argued by Arny, the delicate negotiations required to achieve an equitable settlement could best be reached by direct conversations in the nation's capital.[20]

At first the response of Arny's superiors was less than encouraging. Superintendent Dudley had acknowledged the apparent desire of the chiefs to make the trip, but he thought that the expenditures anticipated for the journey could be better spent on more sheep for the Indians. Then, in an exhibition of rather petty jealousy, he told the Commissioner of Indian Affairs that he could not spare Arny from the agency for any extended period of time. Besides, if the journey were approved, the Indians could be escorted by others without requiring the agent to make the journey. Commissioner Smith agreed, generally, with Dudley's position. He told Arny that he could not expect to bring the Indians east simply because they desired to come. Regarding the proposed boundary changes, this would be very difficult considering the firm commitments written into the existing Navajo treaty. Still, even though there was no apparent need for the Navajos to make the long trip, perhaps something could be arranged if the Indians would agree to travel at their own expense.[21]

Adept, as always, at trimming his sails to accommodate the prevailing winds, Arny assured Smith that he had, in fact, always tried to discourage the Navajos in their plans for the trip to Washington, but the chiefs had persisted in their demands. Finally, unable to resist their supplications, he had obtained from them, as a sign of good faith, a signed draft of an agreement making the land cession that he had suggested. Then, trying a new tack, Arny pointed out that the Navajos had never really understood their treaty. They were very eager to see the Great Father to hear his explanations of the terms of the great document because they wanted to make all of the arrangements necessary to carry out the provisions in the treaty. Perhaps overwhelmed by Arny's persistence, Smith took steps to present the draft agreement received from Arny for boundary revisions to an appropriate congressional committee, and, in August, he told Arny that $2,500, taken from the clothing fund of the Navajos, had been placed to his credit in Santa Fe for the trip's expenses.[22]

When Arny received this gratifying news, he set to work at once to plan for his journey. He invited eleven Navajos, including Ganado Mucho and Manuelito and his wife. He also requested Jesus Alviso and two other men, identified as Henry W. Easton and William F. Taylor, to accompany him as interpreters. Early in November, Arny had completed all the arrangements for the journey. Leaving his son in charge of the agency, he and his entourage set out on November 5 on the great adventure. Arriving in Santa Fe on November 15, Arny and his party spent several days in the territorial capital exhibiting various examples of Navajo handiwork. The highlight of this display was a unique blanket made specially for the great celebration scheduled for Philadelphia in 1876 commemorating the centennial of the Declaration of Independence. Reporting on this extraordinary example of Navajo weaving skills, an observer noted that the work of the "untutored aborigines" had been directly supervised by Arny, the efficient agent of the tribe. Displaying his characteristic energy whenever anything good could be achieved for New Mexico, Arny intended to give the Indians "a better idea of civilization and if possible to inspire them with a higher ambition."[23]

Moving on to Denver, Colorado, the group reached that city on November 23. They stayed at the American House where, according to a reporter, the Indians were assigned, at their request, to a big room in the basement where "they slept side by side in brotherly and sisterly love." Continuing with his report, the writer was pleased to find that the Navajos were neatly dressed in material of their own manufacture and "their appearance is such as might be carried by some white folks." The Indians, described as honest, industrious, and decent in their habits, were known for their dedication to peaceable pursuits. Crowds of curiosity seekers came to the hotel to see the displays of Navajo crafts, and the ladies of Denver society could view a special display of Navajo styles in the bridal chamber. Reflecting on the purpose of the Navajos' journey, the reporter concluded, rather cynically, that the Indians wanted to go to Washington and "have a friendly chat with the big chief who has made himself so obnoxious to his tribe by apppointing broken down chiefs to lord it over his people in the territories."[24]

If Arny read the report in the Denver newspaper and wondered if he had been included in the category of "broken down chiefs," his wounded vanity would have been restored by the tributes applied to him and his companions in Kansas City, Missouri, next stop along the way in their journey. One witness to the arrival of the party on November 26 found Arny to be a man who had grown gray in the service of his country on the frontier. Evidencing the courteous and accommodating spirit characteristic of a genuine frontiersman, Arny described the plans, which had first been suggested by the Indian chiefs, for achieving in Washington an equal exchange of land along the northern and southern boundaries of the Navajo reservation. The Navajos preferred to obtain fertile land in an area in the south that was warmer and sunnier in exchange for land in the north that was too cold to suit them and subject to heavy winter snows. As for the Indians, the observer noted that these "aboriginal brothers" had brought with them excellent specimens of their handiwork, which would eventually become the property of the Smithsonian Institute.[25]

After a brief layover in Kansas City, the touring Navajos and their agent traveled on to St. Louis, Missouri, where their arrival on November 27 created quite a stir among the inhabitants of that bustling metropolis. In describing the party in the local press, one reporter observed that the Indians, who were all very neatly dressed, exhibited "a more intellectual look than Indians do in general." Regarding their lifestyle, another writer was pleased to learn that the Navajos already had good farms and schools, and they were making notable progress in the mechanized arts. Manuelito, referred to as the war chief of the tribe, appeared as "a stalwart, muscular looking man of swarthy complexion. He is dressed better than the others and wears a plug hat." Agent Arny received very favorable comments. Described as a "fine looking, Quaker-like, old gentleman who has devoted forty years of his life to the improvement of the American Indian," he was also known to be personally acquainted with the chiefs of all the tribes in the West who regarded him as their very good friend. The interpreters Henry Easton and William Taylor fascinated the gentlemen of the press as much as, or more than, the Indians. Cited now as "Wild Hank" and "Rocky Mountain Bill," the two frontiersmen regaled their listeners with stories about their valiant exploits in the West, including desperate fights with Mormons, wild Indians, and Confederate invaders of New Mexico during the Civil War. At the conclusion of these descriptions by the members of the colorful delegation, the reporters invited all interested parties to the Planter's House on the following day to view a display of "Indian curiosities" manufactured by the Navajos.[26]

The display of "Indian curiosities" attracted large numbers of St. Louisans to the open house the next day. Included in the items on display, besides the great centennial blanket, were baskets, beads, moccasins, leggings, bracelets, belts, lassos, spurs, and neckties. When the reception concluded at 11:00 A.M., Arny and the Indians proceeded to General William T. Sherman's headquarters, where they participated in an animated discussion with the war chief of the Great Father. Manuelito opened the council with assurances to Sherman that the Navajos were very happy to see him because they understood that the General had promised to protect them in all their rights. Among those rights that had allegedly been violated, Manuelito emphasized the many instances when Mexicans and Americans had violated the Navajo treaty by trespassing on the reservation. Exhibiting a skill at avoiding troublesome issues that any statesman would have envied, the General simply told his visitors to make their complaints in person to the Great Father when they met him in Washington, since it was the duty of the civil and not the military power to punish lawbreakers. With a final bit of advice from Sherman to the Indians encouraging them to be peaceable and devote their energies to tilling the soil, the meeting closed, according to one account, "to the entire satisfaction of all present."[27]

Leaving St. Louis for Chicago on November 28, the Arny party stopped briefly in Bloomington, Illinois, where Arny took pleasure in presenting the Navajos to old friends in that community which had been his home from 1850 to 1857. On the morning of November 30, the group arrived in Chicago where, as usual, the Indians received extensive coverage in the local press. Descriptions of the Navajos varied from tall and well built with skin "as brown as a Malay . . ." to "of the pure aboriginal type" with high cheek bones, straight black hair, and deep, copper-colored skin. One writer regarded Manuelito as a sociable and affectionate individual who enjoyed hugging all visitors. There was a general consensus among observers that the Navajos were highly civilized and very well educated. Commenting on Arny and his career, another reporter, who dwelt at length on this subject, agreed that the agent appeared healthier and more vigorous than men half his age. He was reportedly dedicated at the time to the education of his wards, who all loved him dearly. During the brief stop to change trains in Chicago, the delegation received visits from the mayor and other prominent citizens, but late in the afternoon they resumed their journey, anxious to reach their destination in the nation's capital.[28]

The Arny party reached Washington on December 2. Newspaper accounts of their arrival attested to the unusually fine appearance of the Navajos. The men, regarded as physically superior to other Indians who had visited the East, were attired in their native dress consisting of pants made of elegantly tanned buckskin and calico shirts of bright colors. Complementing each costume was a fine blanket of their own making. Although the Indians could speak only a few words of English, there was hope for increasing their capacity to communicate with their white neighbors by establishing manual labor and boarding schools on the reservation, thereby separating the children from their parents and increasing the facility with which they could be taught the national language. Regarded as faithful and industrious workers, the Navajos, according to one analyst, were "engaged exclusively in peaceful pursuits. They are honest, industrious, and—best of all—decent in their habits, in which, it is needless to say, they are not comparable with redskins generally."[29]

On December 10 the Arny party, accompanied by Secretary of the Interior Columbus Delano and Commissioner of Indian Affairs Edward Smith, called on President Grant in the White House. The Indians told the president about the revisions desired in the boundaries of their reservation, the incursion of trespassers onto their lands, the unhappy plight of Navajos held in captivity by their enemies in New Mexico, and about the depredations committed against them by Mormons and miners prospecting for gold. After listening patiently to his petitioners, the president skillfully diverted the complaints of the Indians by assuring them that the Secretary of the Interior and the Commissioner of Indian Affairs would take the necessary steps to right these wrongs. Concluding his remarks, the president advised the Indians to remain on their reservation, till the soil, and prepare themselves and future generations of their tribe to become citizens of the United States.[30]

On Saturday, December 19, Arny received a pleasant surprise from some of his friends in Washington. That evening about fifty people gathered at the Tremont House to honor Arny with music, refreshments, and expressions of friendly feelings. When the speakers commended Arny for his labors in the cause of humanity, the pleased visitor responded by extolling the Grant Peace Policy. He compared the president to Jesus Christ, suggesting that both men advocated policies that would bring peace and good will to all. Continuing with a reference to the Bible, he recalled the words of the apostle Paul who told his followers that God made of one blood all men to dwell upon the face of the earth. Referring to the Navajos, he commented on the injustices done to them and agreed that a humane policy toward all Indians would recognize that it was cheaper to feed them than fight them. Just before midnight, the guests enjoyed an impromptu supper and then adjourned after joining in the singing of "Home, Sweet Home."[31]

Arny undoubtedly enjoyed his gala party, but upon at least one occasion he tried to mix business with pleasure during his visit to Washington. He decided to write to Commissioner of Indian Affairs Smith about a delicate yet very serious problem that posed a threat to the well-being of the Navajos at Fort Defiance. He insisted that some of the Navajo women had become diseased from sexual relationships with soldiers at nearby Fort Wingate. In Arny's opinion, the extermination of the entire Navajo nation could be expected if this kind of association with the soldiers continued. To correct this unfortunate situation, Arny urged the commissioner to instruct the commanding officer at Fort Wingate to forbid the Navajos to enter that military reservation. Arny's letter eventually reached General John Pope, commander of the Department of the Missouri, which included the military posts in New Mexico. Referring to Arny's charges as absurd, Pope dismissed the allegations by declining to comment on the chastity of Navajo women, although he did wonder how Arny could have discovered which of the parties in the sexual intercourse had transmitted the disease.[32]

Perhaps satisfied that he had at least tried to right one of the wrongs endured by the Indians, Arny decided to extend the journey of his delegation by visiting other cities in the Northeast. The party stopped only briefly in New York City, but Arny explained to those interested in the Indians that they would spend more time in that city after their return from Boston and Providence. In Boston the local press identified Arny as an intimate friend of the martyred John Brown. Arny supported this contention by exhibiting a revolver that he claimed was a mate to the one that the hero of Harper's Ferry carried in all his campaigns. Attracted again by the colorful appearance of Wild

Hank and Rocky Mountain Bill, one writer noted that the two men were gazed upon "with much astonishment by hunters after novelties." When asked to explain the purpose of their visit, Arny reportedly replied that he brought the party to Boston to show the Indians "that there are more people in Boston than they thought there was."[33]

Moving on from Boston to Providence, Rhode Island, the Arny group reached that city on December 28. During the morning of the next day they visited some of the local manufacturing enterprises including a textile mill and the renowned Corliss Steam Engine Company. They also stopped at a school where Arny delighted the children by rendering an authentic Indian war whoop. In the evening Arny, accompanied by several of the Navajos, lectured to a large crowd at the armory of the Horse Guards. Strongly endorsing the government's Peace Policy, he argued at length that all Indians, for the present, must be humanely cared for as wards of the government. Manuelito then delivered a few remarks which were translated as "Manuelito thanks you for your attention tonight, and is glad to see so many gentlemen and ladies present, especially so many pretty ladies." Following this final indication of concern by New Englanders for the issues related to the Indian problem, Arny and his party set out on the following day for New York City where still another speaking engagement beckoned.[34]

In New York, Arny and the Navajos appeared on New Year's Eve at the Cooper Institute, a prominent facility used extensively for public lectures and debates. One reporter, intending to place the colorfully dressed Indians in some sort of ethnohistorical perspective, described them as mountain Navajos, a branch of the Aztecs. The highlight of the evening came, apparently, when Arny sought to illustrate the Indian problem by reciting a story of a German farmer and his hogs. With careful attention to retaining the dialect used by the speaker, the reporter quoted Arny, speaking as the German farmer:

You come mit me. You see dem hogs? Deys shleepin. You see dat little nigger boy, and you see dat corn? Vell, ven dem hogs wakes up, de little nigger boy, he trow em some corn, and dey eats, and den day lies down again and shleeps again; and ven dey wakes again he he gives em some more and my hogs doesn't run around, and dey makes no trouble.

Comparing this crude allegory to the current difficulties with the Indians, Arny concluded by endorsing a simple solution to all problems. If the government would just feed and clothe the Indians, they would then be content and peaceable.[35]

For Arny, 1874 presumably closed on a note of satisfaction with a job well done. Tired, no doubt, by the rigors of his travels, he could still feel that his efforts had been rewarded by the cordial reception given to his delegation at each stop along the way. For others concerned with the Indian problem at the end of the year, evaluations of achievements under the Peace Policy varied according to location. At Fort Defiance, William Truax and John Menaul could address local issues. In his capacity as farmer, Truax still believed that the Indians could, with proper instruction, raise enough food to feed themselves, even though Arny had found it necessary to resume issuing rations in the fall after the crop failure at the end of the summer. Although disappointed with these unfortunate results, Truax was still gratified by the industriousness exhibited by the Navajos in their farming endeavors. As for his opinion of Arny's record as Navajo agent, Truax's favorable impression of his employer had not changed during the year. He felt that Arny was doing everything in his power to bring the Navajos under the influence of religious training as soon as possible. Truax also believed that the parents of Navajo children were delighted to see their boys and girls learning the great truths of the Bible under the inspired leadership of their agent. All in all, in Truax's estimation, the Navajo agency came closer to fulfilling the hopes of the Presbyterian Church and friends of the Peace Policy than any other in New Mexico and Arizona.[36]

John Menaul did not see the situation at the Navajo agency through the same rose-colored glasses used by William Truax. Near the end of the year Menaul experienced another of his periodic bouts of depression. "To the present time," he lamented to Lowrie, "my earnest desire is to get away from Defiance, and all *Indian Agencies* to somewhere that I may be useful, as at an (at least this one) I. Agency a man's life must be a zero."[37] John Menaul need not have been apprehensive about the mission board's lack of appreciation of his usefulness at Fort Defiance. The board members had the highest regard for his achievements, although their appraisal of the overall condition of the Navajo mission was divided. It was pleasing to note that Menaul and Arny had taken turns conducting religious services each Sabbath, but there was little evidence of significant results derived from these preaching efforts. Still, doors had been opened for the introduction of these worthy endeavors among the Indians that had never been opened before. Reflecting upon the board's commitment to the Navajo mission, one writer for a Presbyterian periodical acknowledged that the vast majority of Presbyterians could not involve themselves directly in the work among the Navajos. However, prayers could be offered for those Indians without ceasing, with the assurance that "under the blessed agency of Christian education and training, they will become fellow citizens with our best people . . . and heirs of the heavenly inheritance."[38]

In the nation's capital, the Commissioner of Indian Affairs also expressed in his annual report for 1874 his hopes for the Navajos becoming, eventually, good citizens. Placing them in the category of "Indian novitiates in civilization," Edward Smith decided that their exposure to the influences of religious teaching had resulted in their abandonment, in large part, of "heathenish practices." Then, examining the status of the Indian program in general, the commissioner described the relationship of his office with the religious societies as harmonious and mutually helpful. Persons secured by the societies to serve as Indian agents were, as a class, performing conscientiously and faithfully. Finally, with an effusive gesture of oversimplification, Smith declared that any man of nerve and common sense, who goes to an agency with the intent to do good, could teach industry and individuality to his Indian charges, thereby placing the tribe well on the road to recovery from barbarism.[39]

For the Board of Indian Commissioners, 1874 was a year of great turmoil. In February it was rumored in Washington that the board might be abolished, with the management of Indian Affairs soon to be restored to the War Department. Then, sensing that respect for their views on Indian policy might be dwindling, six of the original appointees to the board announced their resignations in May. They cited as reasons for their decision the failure of the Secretary of the Interior to urge upon Congress the legislation recommended by the board and the reluctance of board members to move their residence, as required by a new directive, to Washington, D.C. to conduct their business. Expressing regret at the departure of these men, a writer in the *New York Times* called for a closing of the ranks among all Christian men to show continued support for the Peace Policy. The work of the commissioners had resulted in a general improvement in the moral condition of the Indians who were now eager for the "appliances of civilization." Of course, the board deserved great credit for this achievement, but the writer admitted that the satisfactory condition of Indian affairs must also be credited to the plan adopted by the president to place the nomination of Indian agents in the hands of various religious bodies. After the board was reorganized with new appointees, the members in their annual report applauded the continued cooperation of the churches in the Peace Policy. Relying once again on a rather simplistic prediction for the future, the board concluded that "his [pagan Indian] conversion to Christianity brings him at once to understand that he must lead a new life, and, under the instruction of his religious teachers, his elevation to the plane of comparative civilization is easy and rapid."[40]

Secretary of the Interior Columbus Delano shared these anticipations for elevating the Indians to a civilized position in society. With the help of the Christian mission boards, the intellectual, moral, and religious aspects of tribal cultures were changing as rapidly as could be expected. The wise application by these boards of the right to nominate agents had resulted in a noticeable improvement in the records of these employees. Happily, each year more experienced and intelligent men were accepting assignments to these critical positions. An increase in salary for these dedicated individuals would be warranted because they had to surrender the advantages and comforts of civilized life to endure hardships and privations which were not often understood. Regarding the overall operations of the Indian Bureau in 1874, Delano was sure that the gratifying results would simply insure that the success of the Peace Policy initiated by the present administration was no longer in doubt.[41]

The esteemed leader of the present administration had little to say about Indian policy in his annual address to Congress in December. President Grant simply noted that his Peace Policy had been carefully adhered to during the year with very beneficial results. Confident that the nation was now on the right track with this issue, he was sure that the continuation of the policy for a few more years would relieve the frontiers from all dangers of Indian depredations. Clearly the President saw no reason to alter his views expressed at the beginning of the year when he defended his program from those who had criticized easterners with "broad-brimmed-hat ideas" about Indian policy. For W. F. M. Arny and the Navajos, the differences between the rhetoric of distant administrators and the reality of controversial local issues may have become blurred while the agent and his tribal delegation were traveling in the East. But many practical problems related to the conduct of agency affairs at Fort Defiance had accumulated in Arny's absence, and, as always, the path leading to solution of these problems would not be entirely free from unanticipated obstacles.[42]

8

A Fallen Idol, 1875

The retarding influences which prevent civilization,
moral, religious, and physical training of the Navajo
Indians . . . arises from the want of the co-operation of
the military in this country and the interference of the
squaw-men.
—W. F. M. Arny, Annual Report
October 19, 1875

While the wandering Navajos and their agent concluded their visit
in the East and started on their return journey to Fort Defiance, the
Board of Indian Commissioners convened, once again, a conference
of those churchmen and government officials who were concerned
with the ongoing development of the Peace Policy. When the dignitaries gathered at the Arlington Hotel in Washington, D.C. on January
13, Clinton B. Fisk, who had succeeded Felix Brunot as chairman of
the Board of Indian Commissioners, opened the meeting by calling
on John Lowrie to give his views on the current position of the Presbyterian Church and its association with the administration's experiment in reforming Indian policy. Lowrie admitted that he had received
little encouragement thus far from the program's progress. Nevertheless, he reiterated his strong belief that there was still one hope
and that was the influence of the Christian religion at all levels of
policymaking. Since the power of religion was the main motivation
in changing the condition of men, the Indians would eventually progress beyond their savage state much as the forefathers of Americans
had passed from darkness into light in years gone by. At the conclusion of the convocation, the participants found no cause to disagree
with Lowrie's continuing admiration of the president's conduct "in
standing firm as a rock against the effort to turn this matter back into
the hands of the politicians."[1]

In New Mexico a writer in a Santa Fe newspaper, choosing to
comment on matters of local interest pertaining to Indian affairs rather
than lofty religious platitudes, announced the triumphant return of

the Arny delegation on February 1, 1875. The uneventful return trip, retracing the same route used on the journey to the East, attracted little attention this time in the cities along the way. However, in Santa Fe the words of welcome for the travelers emphasized expectations for numerous benefits which would surely accrue to the Navajos from the efforts of their indefatigable agent. Reportedly Arny's lectures to eastern audiences had accomplished much to correct false impressions about New Mexico and its people. In addition, important contacts made by Arny along the way would surely result in untold advantages for the Indians. An immediate benefit derived from the trip was per-ceived in the presence in the return party of two new employees for the agency at Fort Defiance. While in the East, Arny had recruited Dr. Walter Whitney of Washington, D.C. to serve as physician at the agency. He had also ordered several looms, spinning wheels, and other devices to aid the Navajos in the manufacture of blankets and articles of clothing. To instruct the Indians in the use of these items, Arny had hired Miss Harriet Cook, who had recently been employed teaching weaving to the Santee Sioux Indians in Nebraska. When the weary wayfarers finally reached Fort Defiance on February 13, Arny noted, with obvious gratification, that the Indians had returned in good health and were pleased with their visit to the Great Father.[2]

If Arny believed all the glowing reports about his journey, he must have felt confident that the pages of history would report his expe-dition with the Navajo chiefs as an unqualified success. This expec-tation was not fulfilled. The first revelation of unsatisfactory conditions encountered on the trip came from an unexpected source. During Arny's absence, William Truax began to pressure John Lowrie for an appointment as Indian agent to some tribe allotted to the Presbyterian Church in the Southwest. Truax professed a great desire to be reunited with his wife, who still resided at their former home in Chicago. Of course, this was financially impossible, since his annual salary as farmer at the Navajo agency was only $750. However, by earning twice that amount as an agent he could summon Mrs. Truax to join him in trying to achieve his long-standing goal to enlighten and civ-ilize the Indians. Responding sympathetically to this touching plea, Lowrie recommended Truax for the vacant position of agent to the Hopi Indians in northern Arizona. When Truax acknowledged Low-rie's action on the Hopi appointment at the end of March, he told the mission board secretary, in utmost confidence, that he was also sending an important letter "respecting the agent here and the un-satisfactory condition of things."[3]

When Lowrie read the communication from Truax regarding Arny's conduct, he must have been greatly distressed. Abandoning his for-mer position as a staunch supporter of the Navajo agent, Truax now presented a picture of Arny as a person whose reputation as a good Christian was irrevocably tarnished. According to Truax, evidence now indicated that Arny had not been a good shepherd to his Indian flock during their stopovers in eastern cities. On the contrary, the Indians were intoxicated most of the time. Arny also took them to houses of prostitution where they had contracted syphilis. On one despicable occasion, he allegedly took one of the interpreters to a bawdy house where he spent twenty dollars among the women for wine and other alcoholic beverages. And not once during the entire journey did he take the Indians to a place of worship, although he frequently accompanied them to "low comique theatres." Faced with these shocking accusations, Lowrie could only carry out his painful duty and request a statement from Arny about the veracity of the charges brought against him.[4]

Surprised, no doubt, by Lowrie's knowledge of these charges, Arny decided to tell the whole story, from his viewpoint, about the events described by his accusers. First, he indignantly identified the inform-ant as the interpreter Henry Easton, sometimes known as Wild Hank. Defending his actions in each instance as well-meant, Arny asserted that he had taken all reasonable precautions to keep the Indians shielded from temptations. Despite his vigilant attitude, he admitted there were a few times when he had unfortunately lost contact with the Navajos. During his efforts to find the Indians, he and Easton had sometimes visited barrooms and brothels. At one grog shop the interpreter had ordered wine and then demanded five dollars from Arny to pay for it. The agent had complied with this request to avoid trouble, but soon learned to his dismay that Easton had previously visited the place and spent sixty dollars for wine "and other things." On two occasions Arny did find the Indians in dens of iniquity and, regrettably, he could not deny that some of them apparently became infected with syphilis after their debauchery. With these candid ad-missions, Arny hoped that Lowrie and all others who doubted his integrity could understand how all his acts could be construed as motivated by the best of intentions.[5]

For the time being at least, Lowrie elected to accept this explanation

of the charges raised by Truax. At Fort Defiance Arny certainly welcomed this reprieve because he had to deal with other problems that
threatened to disrupt the orderly conduct of agency affairs. While the
arrival of Dr. Whitney and Miss Cook could have been regarded as
advantageous to the interests of the Indians, who presumably would
benefit from the application of their special skills, one veteran employee at the agency resented these additions to the staff. John Menaul
understandably interpreted these moves as intervention into his own
fields of responsibility as dispenser of medicines and instructor in
weaving. The missionary decided that Arny's decision to bring in the
new employees could only be viewed as a vote of no confidence in
his ability to carry out his duties. Arny admitted that Menaul's assumptions were correct. Regarding the weaving experiment, Arny
told John Lowrie quite frankly that this venture had not progressed
under Menaul's tutelage. As for his displeasure with Menaul's services as agency physician, Arny rather feebly declared that the missionary was simply not competent to make the reports required by
the Office of Indian Affairs. In any event, John and Charity Ann
Menaul, thoroughly disgusted with the turn of events, departed for
good from Fort Defiance in mid-February, intending to remain in
Santa Fe until the mission board decided on their future assignments.[6]

On February 15, Walter Whitney officially relieved John Menaul as
physician to the Navajos. Although Whitney was not a member of
the Presbyterian Church, Arny believed that his excellent deportment
would soon produce significant advances in the health and religious
training of the Indians. In fact, Whitney had gained the confidence
of the Navajos so quickly that several of them, who had been reluctant
to seek the services of Menaul, had come to him for treatment. Harriet
Cook's implementation of her role as instructor in weaving was more
difficult. Since the looms and other articles ordered by Arny were still
in transit, Miss Cook had to illustrate her resourcefulness by repairing
the one old loom at the agency which, according to Arny, had not
been used for several years. From the operations of that rehabilitated
loom, at the end of March Miss Cook reported production of ten
yards of cloth by four Indian trainees. From these humble beginnings,
Arny was sure that the Navajos would eventually benefit greatly from
the inspirational leadership of this competent and pious lady. Indeed,
Arny believed that if all of his employees would emulate her saintly
example, then "I would consider myself the happiest Indian Agent
on this continent."[7]

Another measure of Arny's happiness could well have been reports of the continuing efforts to educate Navajo children at the agency during his absence. He had left his daughter-in-law, Cecilia, in charge of the little boarding home started in the previous year by Catherine Stowe. Cecilia reported that during the months of December, January, and February, she had made twenty-nine garments for the children entrusted to her care. In her opinion, the home and the children were in better condition than at any other time during her residence at the agency. In his role as teacher in the school, Valentine Friese had mixed opinions about the results of his efforts in the classroom. His average attendance during February was nine pupils. Some of these children showed progress to the point where he hoped to include instruction in geography and astronomy in his curriculum. For this purpose he needed appropriate textbooks, a recent wall map of the United States, a small globe, and an orrery, a device used to study the solar system. He had his doubts, however, about his chances of securing these items because many of the basic school supplies that he had ordered when he arrived at the agency a year ago had never been received. Adding to his woes, the teaching conditions in the one small room allotted for this purpose remained very primitive. He finally had to beg Arny for some packing crates which he used to fabricate crude desks and benches. Fully aware of these problems, Arny promised his support to acquire a larger and better facility for the school and a more ample home to accommodate at least fifty boarding students as soon as he could obtain funds for this purpose.[8]

Besides lack of tangible support for his educational endeavors, Valentine Friese had other reasons to deprecate Arny's contribution to the civilizing and Christianizing of the Navajos. In a confidential letter to John Lowrie, Friese disclosed how he and William Truax had started a Sabbath School which they conducted each Sunday, aided by an agency interpreter. Encouraged by an attendance which sometimes reached fifty Indians, the teachers then started prayer meetings and Bible classes which met on Sunday evenings. In all of these services, the Navajos showed much interest and progress in singing Christian hymns. However, according to Friese, these achievements were to a great extent neutralized by the Sabbath breaking, profanity, and blasphemy of some of the agency employees. Regrettably, Arny made no effort to remedy this deplorable situation. In fact, he showed his lack of interest in these worthy projects by refusing to attend the Sabbath School and, even more discrediting, he had never appeared at Friese's day school to hear recitations or examine the work of the pupils. Friese concluded his plaintive comments with the thought that he might still be inclined to continue trying to do his Christian duty if Arny would just provide a bit more assistance and encouragement of the work.[9]

While the critical reports about Arny's conduct continued to multiply in Lowrie's office, the harassed agent tried to cope with other problems that threatened the well-being of his Indians. Since food supplies secured at the end of 1874 were now exhausted, Arny felt compelled to purchase beef and grain in the open market, giving the usual promise that he would pay for these commodities when funds for this purpose became available. Pursuing this policy, he continued issuing rations to the Navajos throughout the winter and early spring, although he admitted in June that he had regretfully advised the Indians to kill some of their sheep to supplement his inadequate food allotments. Regarding the renewed efforts of the Navajos to raise enough crops to feed themselves, Arny chose to believe the old adage that if at first you don't succeed, try, try again. He procured seed grain and garden seeds which the Navajos assiduously planted in the spring when the weather permitted. Striving almost desperately to identify causes for previous crop failures, Arny decided that this year he would try to increase the water supply to the farmers by expanding the network of dams and irrigation ditches throughout the reservation. Convinced that he had done all in his power to deal with this matter, Arny, like all of his predecessors, could only hope that this time the forces of nature would work favorably to bring an abundant harvest.[10]

With characteristic zeal, Arny also directed his attention to renewing his crusade against the men who were leading the Indians away from the path of righteousness. On several occasions he traveled to Santa Fe and Albuquerque where he testified against men who were charged with selling whiskey to Indians. And with a determination that seemed to surpass any of his other fixations regarding evildoers, he continued his efforts to prevent the Navajos from visiting Fort Wingate where, according to Arny, drunken Indians could be seen almost daily. Refusing to abandon his one-sided viewpoint on the question of transmittal of venereal disease, the angry agent repeatedly called for directives from the War Department that would terminate "the continued infamous debauchery of Indian women by United States soldiers, with the full knowledge of their officers. . . ."[11]

In addition to whiskey sellers and diseased soldiers, Arny placed the "squaw men" who lived in close proximity to the agency at the top of his list of depraved persons who were still setting bad examples for the Indians. Arny believed that the most influential of this group were former employees at the agency whom he had discharged for their scandalous lifestyle. Arny insisted that the power of these men was so great that they had previously forced the Navajo agents to submit to their dictation in the conduct of agency affairs. One solution to the problem, as suggested by Arny, would be passage of a law making it a criminal offense for a white man to cohabit with an Indian woman unless he was married to her under the laws of the United States. If the parties in question then elected to abide by this law, they should be prohibited henceforth from living on the reservation. Beneath this general indictment of immoral conduct, Arny had particular persons in mind whom he regarded as the principal troublemakers. When he referred later to two men, natives of England who were not naturalized citizens of the United States, who had defied his authority by living in open adultery near Fort Defiance with Indian "squaws," there was no doubt that his ire was directed at Thomas Keams and his brother William.[12]

Thomas Keams, the former adversary of James Roberts and William Hall, had left Fort Defiance in the spring of 1873, declaring his intent to visit family and friends in England. If he did make this journey, he had returned to the vicinity of Fort Defiance in the late summer of that year. His first encounter with the new Navajo agent W. F. M. Arny resulted in creation of a hostile rivalry between the two men that was never reconciled. When Keams applied for a license to trade with the Navajos, Arny's description of Keams to Commissioner of Indian Affairs Smith as a person unfit to do business with the Navajos on their reservation was surely instrumental in Smith's decision to deny the license. By the summer of 1875 Arny was firmly convinced that Keams and his friends, who were still eager to obtain lucrative trading privileges with the Navajos, were conspiring to alienate the Indians from their well-meaning agent who was determined to thwart the schemes of the would-be traders.[13]

Arny received his first intimation of unrest among leaders of the Navajos soon after his return from Washington, D.C. At a meeting with the tribal chiefs on February 24, Manuelito expressed his discontent at the meager results of their trip to Washington. Nothing had come of the great plan to revise the reservation boundaries and there was no indication that the tribe would receive any compensation for the killing of Navajos by the Mexicans and Mormons. Arny assured the disgruntled chiefs that these matters were still receiving serious consideration, and when the council disbanded he believed there would be no further trouble. However, not long after this meeting Arny thought he could detect more discontent among the chiefs than he had ever experienced before. He deduced, at first, that this dissatisfaction could be attributed to his vigorous prosecution of the parties who had been selling whiskey to the Indians, but he soon decided that the causes of the agitation could be traced to former immoral employees living nearby with Navajo women who were determined to undermine his position.[14]

Although Arny's assumptions, at this point, were derived from local gossip, his suppositions were not totally unwarranted. Thomas Keams was conducting a campaign to secure Arny's removal and replace him with a better qualified agent, namely, Thomas Keams. Early in June Keams told John Lowrie that the dissatisfied Navajos wanted him to be their agent. Since the Indians knew that he was thoroughly familiar with their habits, they had great confidence in his ability to work effectively in their behalf. The Navajos had even prepared a petition, signed by all the principal chiefs, calling for the discharge of Arny and especially requesting Keams's appointment as agent. Keams was thoroughly convinced that he could control the Navajos and greatly assist in civilizing and Christianizing them, thereby making them a credit to Lowrie and his mission board. If Lowrie would deem him a proper person for the job at Fort Defiance, Keams pledged he would work to the best of his ability to further the interests of all parties concerned with the welfare of the Navajos.[15]

The petition referred to by Keams had been prepared on May 28. It was directed to the Honorable Commissioner of Indian Affairs and it bore the marks of thirty-nine principal chiefs and captains of the Navajo tribe. Heading the list of signatories were the names of Manuelito and Ganado Mucho. The Indians called for Arny's removal, citing three specific charges against the agent. First, they could not rely on his word as he was "a great prevaricator of the truth." Second, he used threats and coercion to make the chiefs sign numerous papers which were completely unfamiliar to them, telling them that they would get no more presents or annuities until they complied with his orders. Third, at the last issue of annuity goods, they believed that Arny had withheld a great part of the material rightfully due to them. When they wanted to examine the storeroom after the issue to see that all articles had actually been distributed, the agent had refused this request and locked the storeroom doors to prevent their entry. The unhappy chiefs then concluded their petition with the request that Thomas Keams, in whom they had great confidence, be appointed as their new agent.[16]

When Arny learned of the vote of no confidence in his actions as Navajo agent, he probably surmised that it was, to use later terminology, a put up job. Whether Keams and his allies did coach the Indians in the preparation of the petition remained unproven, but there was still an inescapable conclusion that could be drawn from the document. In one way or another, Arny had now succeeded in alienating just about everyone whom he depended on to sustain him in his position. Meanwhile, in New York John Lowrie continued to hear of the crisis brewing at Fort Defiance. In May William Truax, who was preparing to leave for his assignment as agent to the Hopi Indians, told Lowrie that conditions on the reservation were daily growing worse. Arny was rendering himself more and more obnoxious to the point where some of the desperate chiefs went to Fort Wingate to make their grievances known to the commanding officer at that post.[17]

In mid-June Lowrie and the mission board, fearing that an actual and violent rebellion by the Navajos was imminent, finally decided that Arny would have to go. Lowrie told the agent that the board, after careful consideration of the subject, had regretfully reached the conclusion that his connection with the Navajo agency should be terminated. Perceiving no need to discuss all the details leading to their decision, Lowrie simply told Arny that he must have already obtained a general idea of all of the unpleasant reports emanating from the agency at Fort Defiance. The Secretary of the Interior and the Commissioner of Indian Affairs sustained Lowrie when they learned of the mission board's action. Secretary Delano simply noted his agreement with a decision that was clearly taken in the best interest of the Navajos. Commissioner Smith admitted that he was actually relieved by the action. With no reason to doubt Arny's personal character and integrity, he still felt that the agent had greatly embarrassed his department by always creating deficiencies in his accounts.[18]

Arny's first reaction to the notice of his dismissal was one of passive submission to the wishes of his superiors. Near the end of July he sent a letter of resignation to Commissioner Smith requesting December 31, 1875, as the official date for termination of his duties. Then, after second thoughts about surrendering his post, he decided to leave Dr. Whitney in charge of the agency and go to Washington with hopes of summoning support from friends in the nation's capital who might secure his reinstatement in the good graces of the Office of Indian Affairs. This decision turned out disastrously for Arny and his friends and family who remained behind at Fort Defiance. By trying to prolong his tenure as agent, he only succeeded in inspiring further charges of dereliction of duty and, more serious, the Navajos vented their frustration about these matters by rebellious actions that could have escalated into a full-fledged Indian war in the Southwest.[19]

The Navajo chiefs, and those who may have used them to gain their own ends, continued to prepare petitions elaborating at greater length upon their grievances against Arny. On July 15 they sent one of these documents to Washington. This time they accused Arny of enriching himself at the expense of the Indians whom he was supposed to protect. Describing Arny as trifling, vacillating, and unreliable in his conduct of agency affairs, they deplored the "pomp and circumstance" of all his actions. Without mentioning specific charges, they insisted that Arny had wasted public property and misapplied public funds intended to be spent for the benefit of the Navajos. The chiefs then demanded appointment of a new agent whom they could trust, who would not waste the nation's money traveling over the country on personal business, and who would talk less and do more to bring justice to the long-suffering Navajo people. In short, they hoped that the president would appoint Thomas Keams, a man who possessed all of these good qualities, as their new agent.[20]

When the chiefs did not receive an immediate response to their request to the president, they decided to follow a suggestion from one of their advisors and direct a similar petition to John Lowrie and the Presbyterian Board of Foreign Missions. This epistle began with the explanation that the chiefs had learned of Lowrie's role in the selection of their agent from their "esteemed and respected friend," Reverend W. B. Truax. The chiefs had heard that Arny was in Washington, ostensibly on a mission to present, once again, the Navajos' wishes to exchange a certain portion of their reservation for another section of the public domain. Arny had no authority from the Indians to make this arrangement, according to the chiefs. They insisted that the land they would lose was the only area on the reservation that could be continuously cultivated by irrigation. It had always been their intent to establish large numbers of their people in this area as soon as they could be sure that the government could assure them of protection from the neighboring Ute Indians. In any event, no matter what Arny declared as the purpose of his visit, the Navajos, who wanted his immediate removal, hoped that Lowrie would recommend Thomas Keams, a man whom they all trusted, as his replacement.[21]

While Lowrie and others considered the Navajos request for immediate removal of Arny, the chiefs at Fort Defiance decided to force the issue by a course of action that was certainly more drastic than their previous attempts to gain their goals by writing petitions. On August 26, General William Sherman in St. Louis sent an urgent telegram to the Secretary of War. In this communique, Sherman included a startling report from Colonel J. Irwin Gregg, who commanded the 8th Cavalry in New Mexico, and an endorsement by General John Pope, commander of the Department of the Missouri. According to Gregg, he had received dispatches from Fort Wingate indicating that the Navajos, who were in a great state of excitement, had taken over their agency, driving off all the employees who resided there. Gregg believed there was no way to predict how the trouble would end, but the Navajos would probably return to their peaceful ways if they received assurance that Arny's resignation would be accepted immediately. Pope simply stated that he had instructed Gregg to tell Manuelito, the apparent leader of the rebels, that he would do all in his power to secure Arny's removal at once. In the meantime, the Indians should be warned that any acts of violence on their part would ruin their case and bring immediate reprisals from the garrison at Fort Wingate.[22]

Subsequent information received from Fort Wingate and Fort Defiance confirmed this alarming report. The trouble began on August 8 when Manuelito and several of his followers appeared at Fort Wingate. The excited Indians told the officer in charge that their agent, aware that he would soon be relieved, had plotted to steal the Indians' annuity goods. Some of these items were in wagons that had left the agency only a few days ago. In all fairness, the Navajos expected the soldiers to retrieve their property because the warriors of the Great Father always acted quickly to recover items allegedly stolen by the Indians. When the officer refused their request, explaining that the Indians had to address their complaints to their agent, the Navajos departed, bewildered by the strange suggestion that they should report thefts to the very man who was robbing them. Driven to despair by the lack of concern for their distress, on the morning of August 19 several of the Navajo chiefs rode into the agency at Fort Defiance and ordered all of the Navajo employees to leave. Frightened by these events, the members of Arny's family and other employees at the agency hurriedly prepared to flee to the safety of Fort Wingate. As they were departing, their fears intensified when the Indians broke into their baggage and seized part of the contents. Dr. Whitney, who refused to abandon his position as temporary agent during Arny's absence, then called for military assistance. Whitney was dismayed, however, when the commander at Fort Wingate refused to send troops to the agency because he had no orders that would have permitted him to take this drastic action. By this time, Whitney was completely terrified. Anticipating Arny's return any day from Washington, he sent a letter to Santa Fe warning the agent not to come to Fort Defiance unless he could obtain at least a company of soldiers to accompany him as bodyguards.[23]

If the Navajos based the decision to take over their agency on the assumption that only an open display of force would bring an acceptable response to their demands, they guessed correctly. On August 23, when Arny reached Santa Fe, he was shocked by the news from the Navajo reservation. He immediately asked Colonel Gregg to tell the chiefs that he had indeed resigned and his successor would be appointed as soon as possible. The Indians should also be reassured that no part of their present reservation would be taken from them. As for Arny, he only asked for a pledge from the chiefs that they would not interfere with him while he was concluding his affairs at the agency. When an officer from Fort Wingate conveyed this message to the rebels at Fort Defiance, the chiefs gave their assurance that Arny would not be in danger if he visited the agency for the purpose he had stated.[24]

In Washington and New York, Arny's assertion that he would be replaced as soon as possible was interpreted as the sooner the better. At the end of August the Secretary of the Interior informed Lowrie that the government expected an immediate nomination for Arny's successor from the mission board. Of course Lowrie was aware of the critical nature of the situation at Fort Defiance. Still, he was reluctant to move precipitously on a decision that might weigh heavily in restoring a balance of peaceful relations between the Navajos and their neighbors in the Southwest. Lowrie told Commissioner Smith that the immediate removal of Arny was obviously a necessity, although he could not believe that the beleaguered agent had been dishonest in any of his actions. Acknowledging that he had received petitions to nominate Thomas Keams for the position at Fort Defiance, Lowrie was still reluctant to support Keams's nomination. Certainly Keams had considerable influence with the Navajos, but Lowrie had heard that the applicant was still living with a Navajo woman who was not his wife. Until he could be sure that Keams was a man of correct conduct, he would prefer to wait a bit longer before submitting his nomination to the Office of Indian Affairs.[25]

John Lowrie's procrastination in New York left the situation at Fort Defiance in a rather precarious state. The immediate concern for govenrment officials was to find some way to induce the Navajos to peacefully relinquish their hold on the agency facilities. When the War Department suggested that an army officer assume the agent's duties until Arny's successor arrived, the Secretary of the Interior quickly accepted the offer. On September 9 Major William Redwood Price of the 8th Cavalry arrived at Fort Defiance from Fort Wingate with a contingent of soldiers to restore order to the conduct of agency affairs. The Navajos offered no opposition to Price's presence, but he encountered a major problem when Arny returned to the agency on September 23. Insisting that he was still officially employed by the Interior Department as Navajo agent, Arny questioned Price's authority. When the Major produced documents that defined his interim position, Arny then announced that it would probably be the end of the month before he could leave the agency for good.[26]

The relationship between Arny and Price did not improve while the departing agent tried to put the agency records in some semblance of order for his replacement, whomever that might be. Arny was determined to take many items which he claimed as his private property along with him when he left. When Arny included twenty-eight head of cattle from the agency herd and numerous other food and clothing items in the category of private property, Price was convinced that much of this material actually belonged to the government. The Navajos, who monitored the departure process closely, insisted on searching Arny's baggage wagons to make sure he had not taken any of their annuity goods. When Arny finally left Fort Defiance with his wagon train on September 30, the soldiers and the Navajos might well have limited their farewells to one emphatic declaration—good riddance.[27]

Unfortunately, as far as Arny was concerned, the acrimonious conditions created by the campaign to secure his ouster brought other revelations that tended to dim the luster on the one bright spot in his career as Navajo agent. He had returned from the trip to Washington with the Navajos with a reputation as a great friend of the Indians and a champion of their cause. However, in mid-September he had to defend himself again from reports that the Indians had become intoxicated on the journey. Arny had to admit that several of the Navajos had escaped from his supervision on the very day they were scheduled to meet with President Grant. This time Arny insisted that the culprit in the case was Thomas Keams, who was in Washington at the time. According to Arny, Keams had slipped into the hotel where the Navajo delegation was quartered and, with Manuelito and others, had led a tour of several drinking establishments. When the Indians finally found their way back that evening, they were so intoxicated they had to be confined to their rooms and the audience with the president had to be rescheduled. From another source, the reported satisfaction of the Indians with the trip was questioned. Major Price learned, during his stay at Fort Defiance, that the Navajos now complained that the whole trip was arranged for Arny's glorification. None of their requests were attended to or even talked about while they were transported around the country as some sort of traveling show.[28]

Embittered by these accusations, Arny availed himself of one last opportunity to vindicate his actions as he ended his association with the Navajos. From Santa Fe, where he rejoined his family, he submitted his final annual report to the Commissioner of Indian Affairs on October 19. He directed most of his comments in this document to damning the two groups who had been determined to obstruct his efforts to help the Indians. Anyone familiar with Arny's experiences could have guessed at the outset the identity of the opposing factions, but Arny made sure that all the readers would clearly understand who had betrayed him. "The retarding influences which prevent civilization, moral, religious, and physical training of the Navajo Indians . . . ," he wrote, "arises from the want of the co-operation of the military in this country and the interference of the squaw-men." After venting his anger on the evildoers, Arny concluded that the Navajos, whom he thought were good Indians except for a few chiefs, could become self-sustaining if their new agent would only be supported by those who sincerely wanted the Navajos to become civilized.[29]

While Arny was completing the arrangements for his departure from Fort Defiance, in New York John Lowrie finally reached a decision on his nomination for Arny's replacement. Aware of Lowrie's doubts about his marital status, Thomas Keams had hastened to assure the mission board secretary that he was no longer living with a Navajo woman. Keams now realized that he had committed a "gross wrong." He had learned his lesson, however, and with God's help he would never be tempted into that kind of sinful liaison again. Lowrie was not prepared to gamble on Keams's protestations of newly acquired virtue. In addition to the recommendations for Keams that he had received, he also had in his files several letters from Presbyterians in New Mexico who could not endorse the Keams candidacy. The Reverend George G. Smith, who succeeded David McFarland as pastor of the Presbyterian church in Santa Fe, warned that Keams could easily fall from grace again despite his declaration that he was now a good Christian. William Truax agreed that Keams was a better man in every respect than Arny, but surely Lowrie would want, if at all possible, to select bona fide Christian men as agents. Since Lowrie did have a decent Christian man available for the post at Fort Defiance, he decided to inform Keams that he could not recommend him for the Navajo appointment.[30]

The Christian man selected by Lowrie was Alexander Irvine of Peoria, Illinois. At the end of the summer 1875, Irvine was in Cimarron, New Mexico, serving as agent to the Jicarilla Apaches and the Moache Utes. Lowrie had selected him for that position in the summer of the previous year on the basis of a strong letter of recommendation asserting that Irvine would undoubtedly be the "right man in the right place" at any agency assignment. Impressed by Irvine's record of good work as agent at Cimarron, Lowrie and Commissioner Smith agreed to transfer him to the Navajo position and leave the conduct of agency affairs at Cimarron, for the present, in the hands of another agency employee. Smith was particularly anxious to obtain a good man with agency experience at Fort Defiance because "between Arny's impulsive and somewhat erratic disposition and methods, and the mischievous meddling of the military, the affairs of that agency are in a critical state."[31]

Irvine arrived at the Navajo agency on October 3, missing the turmoil caused by Arny's departure by only a few days. The new agent found Major Price still in charge at the agency, and he also discovered the magnitude of the problem awaiting him. He observed that a great deal of confusion seemed to have previously existed regarding division of responsibility among the employees, each of whom seemed to have created a separate establishment of his own. Like every other new agent who viewed the agency facilities for the first time, Irvine disconsolately agreed that all the buildings were going to ruin. When he learned that there would be a considerable delay before Price could obtain the necessary authority permitting him to relinquish command at the agency, Irvine returned to Cimarron, noting that the still had a few reports to complete there before he could move to Fort Defiance permanently.[32]

While he completed all the paperwork required of an Indian agent moving on to another assignment, Irvine had an opportunity to review the situation at the Indian agency. During this reassessment, he found some positive elements that tended to modify his first gloomy impressions. He was still discouraged by the dilapidated state of the agency buildings, but he recalled an abundance of material at the agency that could be used to rehabilitate these structures. And he did appreciate the qualities of the Navajo Indians. He concluded that they were largely self-supporting, raising many sheep and selling a great deal of wool. With the help of his wife, who would serve as teacher and also instruct the girls in sewing and housekeeping, he hoped to educate the Navajos to the point where they would abandon their old superstitious beliefs. All things considered, he thought the opportunities for making constructive changes at Fort Defiance made it one of the best fields in the whole Indian service.[33]

Unfortunately, Irvine's renewed confidence in his ability to serve effectively as an Indian agent in the spirit of the Peace Policy received a shattering blow from an unexpected outburst of violence at the Cimarron agency. On November 16, while Irvine was supervising the distribution of rations to the Indians, a drunken Apache, dissatisfied with his allotment of beef, threw the piece of meat in Irvine's face. The angry agent drew his revolver and shot the Indian, severely wounding him in the arm. When several friends of the injured man then began firing at the issue house, Irvine received a minor wound in his hand. The exchange of gunfire quickly ceased when other armed agency employees came to Irvine's rescue. Although Irvine's injury was not serious, the aftershock of this encounter completely unnerved him. He wrote to Commissioner Smith in Washington and Major Price at Fort Defiance announcing his resignation as Navajo agent and his intent to sever all connections with the Indian service as soon as possible. Apologizing to Price for any inconvenience that might result from his abrupt action, Irvine explained that "my reasons for resigning are varied. One good and sufficient one is that I am tired of the service, it is too vexatious."[34]

From the tone of this statement, one might have concluded that Irvine's mind was definitely made up on this matter. However, Commissioner Smith certainly did not wish to reopen the case of the Navajo appointment, thereby prolonging the interference by the military in matters at Fort Defiance that properly belonged to the jurisdiction of the Interior Department. On November 27, Smith telegraphed to Irvine urging him to reconsider his resignation. Moved by the Commissioner's fervent appeal, Irvine changed his mind and decided that perhaps he could succeed, where others had failed, to civilize and Christianize the Navajos. After he officially relieved Major Price at the Navajo agency on December 6, he settled down to try and bring some semblance of order to a situation that had drifted dangerously close to anarchy.[35]

As the explosive situation at Fort Defiance gradually subsided at the end of 1875, high-ranking government officials looked back at the results of their efforts during the year to solve the Indian problem. Commissioner of Indian Affairs Edward Smith believed that adoption of a more thorough system of compiling statistics received from the Indian agencies showed unmistakable evidence of significant advances toward the goal of self-sufficiency. Increases in production of agricultural goods, acres under cultivation, families living in houses, and children attending school, all showed conclusively that the quest to civilize the Indians was not only practicable but functional. Smith also recorded his great satisfaction with the hearty goodwill with which the several religious bodies in the nation had aided in the great and worthy cause in 1875. The advantages derived from the nomination of Indian agents by the churches were particularly evident. This policy, which secured a better class of officers than could be obtained by political nominations, had brought to the aid of the government the services of a large number of the best citizens of the country. As for the Indians, Smith concluded that any continued advancement of their interests required "that they should be recognized and treated for what they are, an ignorant and helpless people. . . ."[36]

Commissioner Smith had hoped he would receive favorable public acceptance of the results of his efforts to implement programs that

147

would uplift the Indians. By the end of 1875, however, his critics in the press and in the Congress had raised questions about his personal competence and integrity. Faced with an investigation into his accounting for the expenditure of Indian funds, he angrily resigned on December 11. As one Smith left the Commissioner's office, another moved in to take his place when President Grant selected John Quincy Smith of Ohio for the position. The new appointee had served one term in the House of Representatives, but when he was defeated for reelection in 1875, his friend, Senator John Sherman of Ohio, convinced Grant to select him for the top position in the Office of Indian Affairs. Regarding the Peace Policy, it was generally understood that J. Q. Smith favored continuation of the alliance with religious organizations because the churchmen were obviously sympathetic to the needs of the Indians and they were setting good examples for the less fortunate to emulate.[37]

A new leader also assumed direction of the Department of the Interior late in 1875. When Columbus Delano found himself subjected to the same kind of abuse in the press and Congress that had resulted in the departure of the Commissioner of Indian Affairs, he decided to submit his resignation in October. For his replacement President Grant picked Zachariah Chandler of Michigan. Chandler, who was one of the founders of the Republican Party, was one of the wealthiest men in his state. He served in the U.S. Senate from 1857 until March 3, 1875, when he was defeated for reelection. In a typical gesture of rewarding staunch supporters in the political arena, Grant then offered a cabinet position to a loyal Republican who was temporarily at loose ends. In his first annual report, Chandler echoed the sentiments of Commissioner Edward Smith. Notable advances had been made during the year in perfecting and extending the Peace Policy. Schools were increasing in number and interest on the reservations. Wherever the soil was suitable, the Indians were farming vigorously and intelligently, and they generally preferred to live in comfortable and fixed homes. The religious leaders, who continued to cooperate harmoniously and satisfactorily in nominating Indian agents, had obviously been very careful in their selection of proper men for these positions. On the whole, the work accomplished during the year showed decided progress in maintaining peace on the frontier, encouraging habits of industry among the Indians, and attaining the primary goals of the Peace Policy, namely, "the protection, support, and improvement of the aborigines of the country, without impeding the westward progress of white settlement."[38]

The Board of Indian Commissioners found no reason to disagree with any of these optimistic observations. The board members agreed that the undeniable evidence of statistics accumulated in 1875 showed that the Indians were progressing in habits of industry, education, and religious and moral ideas. There had been no organized act of hostility by any tribe or band of Indians during the year. Responding to perennial rumors that the direction of Indian affairs would soon be transferred from the Interior Department to the War Department, the commissioners acknowledged their highest respect for the ability, courage, and humanity of Army officers. But they could not ignore the fact that men who enlisted in the army in time of peace "are among the most vicious of our population. . . ." There was abundant evidence to show that when these men came into close contact with the Indians, debauchery of the women and demoralization of the men soon followed. However, if the present humane policy of the government to the Indians continued, then there would surely be better days ahead for "these helpless children of the forest."[39]

For those dedicated to reforming the Indian service, concern for questions about continuity of the Peace Policy motivated several churchmen to call on President Grant on November 1. Aware that the election of 1876 would produce a new leader of the nation, the pastors expressed their fears that abandonment of the present Indian program by a new administration would greatly disappoint Christian people in all parts of the country, indeed throughout the world. Grant replied with words of reassurance. He declared that his policy would be so firmly established by the time of his departure that his successor would be obliged to continue it in all of its aspects. Grant reiterated his position on this subject in his annual address to Congress in December. He believed that the steady pursuit of the Indian policy adopted at the beginning of his first term had produced satisfactory and encouraging results. Since his program had exhibited evidence of improvement in the condition of the Indians, the policy would undoubtedly continue with only the few modifications required by further experience.[40]

As always, while the federal government elected to view with favor the broad picture of Indian-white relations throughout the country, at Fort Defiance, Arizona, references to notable advances, harmonious cooperation, hearty goodwill, and self-sufficiency had little meaning

for Alexander Irvine as he viewed the physical and emotional wreck-
age left in the wake of Arny's catastrophic departure. When Inspector
Edward C. Kemble of the Office of Indian Affairs visited the agency
on December 10 to examine its condition, he was appalled by what
he saw. He concluded that a radical change in the service there was
required, both in day-to-day methods of operation and in the selection
of employees. Of course these changes must be initiated by a man
who could seize a new broom and sweep the premises clean. Kemble
left with a faint glimmer of hope, sensing that the new agent Alexander Irvine might be the man who could succeed "in introducing a
better state of things."[41]

9

If at First You Don't Succeed, 1876

A policy has been adopted toward the Indian Tribes . . .
which has been humane and has substantially ended
Indian hostilities in the whole land. . . .
—Ulysses S. Grant
December 5, 1876

On July 4, 1876, many people in the United States celebrated the
centennial of their Declaration of Independence. Proud of their
achievements during the past hundred years that had elevated their
country to the rank of world power, these same Americans were
appalled when, a few days later, newspapers in the East carried the
first reports of the disaster experienced by General George Armstrong
Custer and his Seventh Cavalry in a confrontation with Indians on
the Litte Big Horn River in southern Montana. Those who had dis-
agreed with President Grant's benevolent policies toward the Indians
in the past lost no time in reviling the administration for its futile
efforts to civilize those who would never change their savage ways.
Sensing the need to provide an objective interpretation of these events,
an editor of the *New York Times* argued that the so-called Sioux War
could not be blamed on the president's humane approach to Indian-
white relations. Ulysses Grant would soon relinquish his high office,
but posterity would surely conclude that no act of his administration
deserved more approbation than his much abused Peace Policy. Since
he had intended to instill a spirit of moral rejuvenation in the Indian
service, he had naturally sought the cooperation of the "moral and
reformatory" elements of the population to achieve his goals. The
prominent religious associations that had rallied to his call had picked
"their best and most educated men" to help the Indians. The unfortunate situation encountered by the army in Montana could not be
attributed to any deficiencies in the Peace Policy, but it could only be

151

considered "one of the fruits of a long course of rapacity and injustice by the nation."[1]

Earlier in the year, following the precedent established in 1871, the Board of Indian Commissioners had called another annual conference of those concerned with the continuing development of the Peace Policy. With no way to predict the impending debacle in the West, the commissioners and representatives from the mission boards of churches participating in the program met on January 19 at the Calvary Baptist Church in Washington, D.C. John Lowrie's remarks at this gathering were not very encouraging. He attributed the lack of progress at Presbyterian agencies in the Southwest to their remote locations. It was particularly difficult to secure and retain teachers for the schools in these inaccessible areas. When courageous teachers did accept these assignments, they invariably encountered the powerful opposition of representatives of the Roman Catholic Church who were eager to maintain their own influence over the Indians.[2]

Lowrie recognized another deterrent to the good work in the detestable traffic by the Indians with whiskey dealers. Without mentioning W. F. M. Arny by name, Lowrie indicated his belief that unfounded charges brought against one of his agents by these men had forced his removal. Regarding the results to date of the agent selection process, Lowrie asserted that his board always recommended men of integrity and capability. This careful screening process was obviously beneficial to the Indians because they received as agents upright men who would not be bribed and who would not cheat the Indians. Finally, Lowrie urged all those present to continue their efforts to convince the public that the Peace Policy should not be disturbed. If any change at all was desirable, it should be to create a new department in the government headed by a Secretary of Indian Affairs who would have sole responsibility for carrying out programs designed to uplift the "wards of the nation."[3]

If John Lowrie had visited the Navajos early in 1876, he would certainly have found conditions that were hardly conducive to uplifting that particular segment of the nation's wards. After his visit to Fort Defiance in December of the previous year, Inspector Edward Kemble reported a state of affairs that could only be regarded as chaotic. He had never observed such disorder and wanton neglect of government property at any other agency that he had visited. The Indians had badly damaged the facilities in the interval between agents. There were no habitable rooms in any of the half dozen buildings comprising the old officers' quarters of the fort. The shops and storehouses were in even worse condition. On all sides he encountered crumbling walls and leaking roofs. Doors, windows, gates, and fences were out of repair. The so-called dwelling rooms were contaminated with dirt and smoke and filled with vermin. The foul condition of the outhouses poisoned the atmosphere and seriously affected the health of the place. The Indians, in general, were scattered on and off the reservation. Some of them appeared at the agency only on ration days when they received a handout of inferior beef along with corn and wheat which was in danger of spoiling because it was kept in damp storerooms.[4]

Turning to an assessment of other problems requiring the immediate attention of the new agent Alexander Irvine, Kemble observed that all the books, papers, and accounts of the agency had been removed by the previous agent. There were literally no official records of any kind available to show how he had transacted agency business. If one wished to thank God for small favors in this otherwise distressing situation, it could have been recalled that Irvine at least had some knowledge of an agent's duties based upon his previous experience at the Cimarron agency. As for educational achievements among the Navajo children, Kemble ruthlessly stated that the school at the agency had been only "a shallow pretense" for some time. Considering Irvine's challenge to rebuild a new staff of agency employees, the inspector believed that it was imperative to secure good men as soon as possible to serve as physician, clerk, farmer, carpenter, and blacksmith. Ten to twelve Indian laborers were also needed and two good teachers should be recruited to reopen the school. With some trepidation about what the future held in store for the Navajos and their new agent, Kemble concluded his report by noting that when he departed he had left Alexander Irvine not a little discouraged and undecided if he would remain.[5]

Sometimes the opportunity to begin anew when trying to solve a difficult problem presents a challenge that calls forth in some individuals a renewed sense of dedication to a worthy cause. Perhaps the contemplation of this possibility to succeed where others had failed convinced Irvine to stay on at his new post, at least until he had a chance to see if his approach to civilizing the Navajos might be a start in the right direction. Whatever his reasoning, he decided to begin at once to try and correct some of the deficiencies noted by Inspector Kemble. He could address the problem of reopening the school for the Navajo children immediately. Although the Commissioner of Indian Affairs doubted that previous small attendance figures at the school warranted this action, Irvine went ahead and designated his wife Kate as teacher, effective January 1. When Commissioner Smith finally approved this appointment with an annual salary of a thousand dollars for Mrs. Irvine, the pleased agent announced that school records now showed an increase in attendance and interest, and the chiefs, who visited the classroom frequently, were well satisfied.[6]

Irvine could not report the same degree of success with the experiment initiated by W. F. M. Arny and Harriet Cook in instructing Navajos on the use of the new looms that had been installed at the agency. He admitted that the Indians seemed to prefer their own crude ways of weaving blankets which were, nevertheless, still regarded as examples of high quality craftsmanship, sometimes commanding as much as $125 for a prime specimen. The weavers obtained the wool for these projects from their own sheep which, according to Irvine, now numbered about 400,000 scattered throughout the reservation. In addition to obtaining an income by marketing their blankets, the Navajos also carred on a profitable barter business by trading their surplus wool for trinkets, leather, and various kinds of cloth. Irvine was particularly surprised when he learned that some of the men of the tribe were as adept in the use of a needle as the women. On several occasions he watched while a man prepared a new set of clothes in less than half a day.[7]

Considering possibilities for missionary work among the Navajos, Irvine mistakenly assumed that no missionaries had labored among the Navajos in the past. Of course, James Roberts, William Truax, and John and Charity Ann Menaul would have taken issue with him in this respect. There is no way to ascertain if Irvine simply had no knowledge of the previous efforts to Christianize the Navajos, or if he chose to ignore the efforts of the Presbyterians because there were no tangible results of their work. In any event, he hoped that one or more missionaries would soon be assigned to his agency because the Mormons, who were endeavoring to extend their influence over his Indians, were already making noticeable advances. Many Navajos, who visited the Mormon settlements north and west of the reservation each year to trade, were inevitably subjected to the proselytizing efforts of the disciples of Brigham Young. In New York, John Lowrie was probably cognizant of these warning signals, but he was reluctant to renew Presbyterian missionary work among the Navajos until he had received some indication from Fort Defiance that the Indians there were really ready to receive the blessings of Christianity.[8]

Although decisions to renew missionary work among the Navajos were out of his hands, Irvine could act to try and redress another of the major deficiencies observed by Inspector Kemble at the Navajo agency. The accumulation of so many eyewitness accounts in the past several years about the deplorable state of the agency buildings left little doubt that these facilities were, in fact, badly in need of repair or replacement. Irvine knew that there was no possibility of obtaining funds to replace all the old buildings, so he tried to make the best of a bad situation by directing Navajo laborers in various repair and maintenance projects. During the year the workers replaced broken window glass, installed and painted new doors and windows, and made major repairs in the grain warehouse to make it as moisture proof as possible. On the agency grounds, the Indians repaired corral walls and built a new irrigation dam. The only thing stopping him from initiating major rehabilitation work, according to Irvine, was his inability to obtain the required lumber. Although a sawmill at Fort Wingate could have produced this material, the Secretary of War refused to authorize this service because whatever Irvine could pay for the lumber would, by law, go directly into the Treasury and be lost to the War Department. The disappointed Navajo agent could only urge the commissioner of Indian Affairs to secure a sawmill for Fort Defiance. This facility could not only supply the lumber for agency construction purposes, but it could also provide material for the Navajos to build a better class of homes than their primitive hogans.[9]

Another problem facing Irvine was the tedious task of reinstituting in his office work the proper agency management procedures required by the Office of Indian Affairs. Since his predecessor had left things in such a shambles, Irvine had to order new supplies of appropriate forms for preparing property returns, abstracts of bid proposals, estimates for supplies, expense vouchers, receipts, and a multitude of other reports that contributed to the burden of paperwork borne by any Indian agent. As part of his property accountability, the agent had to maintain records of animals and conveyances used in the conduct of agency affairs. Irvine soon realized that these items, like just about everything else at Fort Defiance, had outlived their usefulness. In the agency corral he had six horses, four mules, and two oxen which he believed were so worn out that they were practically useless. Irvine proposed to sell all of the animals except two of the best mules which could be retained for hauling wood. Then he hoped to receive permission to buy two new horses and a light wagon for the transportation requirements of the agent. Adept in the bureaucratic ways of justifying expenditures, Irvine showed how the decrease in numbers of livestock would result in reductions in feeding costs which would probably cover the expense of the new team and wagon.[10]

Although Irvine could devise a plan of sorts to reduce the cost of feeding the agency livestock, he could not find a way to reduce the cost of feeding the Indians. When he had taken charge of the Navajo agency in the fall of the preceding year, he had found that Major Price had maintained a reduced schedule for issuing beef rations by borrowing some cattle from Fort Wingate. Fortunately, as winter approached, Irvine was able to resume issuing full rations of beef, grain, and flour when, soon after his arrival at Fort Defiance, he began to receive shipments of these items based on contracts awarded at the end of the summer of 1875. Early in the spring Irvine followed the same pattern established by his predecessors when he obtained seed grain and other garden seeds for the Navajos to plant as soon as the soil could be cultivated. On April 3 Irvine issued the remainder of the annuity goods that he found in the agency warehouse. When the Indians complained that the amounts distributed seemed to be less than the totals of these items established by the terms of their treaty, Irvine quieted their concerns by assuring them that they would receive everything promised to them for the rest of the year. On the whole, the new agent was pleasantly surprised when he observed that the Navajos were the only Indians that he knew who would say "Thank you" when they received any supplies.[11]

When Irvine reported that the Navajos were determined, once again, to plant extensively in the spring, he pointed out that he was not aware of any unused arable land anywhere on the reservation. This subject became a matter of discussion when he had his first full council meeting with the chiefs on April 6. The Indians reopened the old issue of revising the reservation boundaries. This time they did not mention exchanging sections of land. Instead, they simply expressed their desire to add large tracts to the east, west, and south of the reservation as it now existed. When Irvine transmitted this news to the Office of Indian Affairs, he noted that the chiefs insisted that they really did not have an opportunity to explain their position while in Washington the previous year. What they really wanted was more land because the only remaining acreage suitable for farming was in the northeast corner of their reservation. Although this area was well watered by the San Juan River, the Navajos were reluctant to settle there because it was too close to their enemies, the Ute Indians. When Irvine learned more about the good qualities of the San Juan region, he decided that his Indians could be induced to settle there if he could also move the agency to that place. This move was both feasible and desirable, according to Irvine, because the army had already recommended establishment of a military post in the same location to control the Utes. With all this information available, the agent concluded that the best course of action would be to concentrate in the San Juan country, "which small corner is worth more than all of the rest of their reservation put together."[12]

As he slowly but surely worked to put his house back in order at the Navajo agency, Alexander Irvine knew that the ultimate success or failure of his plans to aid the Indians depended, in large part, on the role played by the agency employees in the whole process. Although Inspector Kemble had called for a "radical change" in the roster of those employed at Fort Defiance, neither he nor Irvine expected to alter the basic structure of positions authorized at the agency. The agent was determined, however, to select men to work for him who had not been associated with the Arny controversy. With this objective always in mind, Irvine succeeded in assembling a staff of respectable employees. At no time during his tenure as agent did he have to deal with charges that his people were corrupting the morals of the Indians by their own profligate lifestyles. The only time Irvine encountered difficulties in obtaining a good man for a critical position was in the selection of an agency physician. For several months after his arrival at Fort Defiance, Irvine procured occasional medical treatment for the Navajos from an army doctor stationed at Fort Wingate. This informal relationship continued until Irvine tried to obtain funds to pay the doctor of this service. The Commissioner of Indian Affairs not only refused the request, but he also told Irvine that the impromptu arrangement itself was not permissible under the law. Faced with this rejection of what he had considered a very sensible and economical procedure, the disappointed agent could only continue to try and recruit a full-time physician to serve at Fort Defiance.[13]

While the Navajos and their new agent were endeavoring to establish a good working relationship at Fort Defiance, politicians in the nation's capital prepared for that greatest of all quadrennial exercises, a presidential election. Shaken by disclosures of corruption in several departments of the government during his second term, Ulysses Grant decided to accept the advice of leaders in the Republican Party who urged him to resist the temptation to run again. At their nominating convention, the Republican delegates finally selected Rutherford B. Hayes as their nominee for the presidency. Hayes, recently elected for a third term as governor of Ohio, ran against the standard bearer of the Democratic Party, Samuel J. Tilden, who had attained a reputation as a reformer in his position as governor of New York. Both parties chose not to address the Indian problem when preparing their party platforms. The Republicans, in essence, urged the voters to select a president, once again, from the party that saved the Union. The Democrats, delighted to exploit the revelations of corruption during the Grant administration, urged the electorate to throw the rascals out, replacing them with men who were pledged to reform the civil service.[14]

The results of the election in November precipitated a crisis that threatened to destroy the whole framework of constitutional government in the United States. The returns showed 184 electoral votes for Tilden, 165 for Hayes, and twenty contested and undecided. Republican strategists immediately realized that if they could secure those votes for their candidate, then Hayes would be elected by one vote. With no precedent to guide them in this incredible situation, leaders from both parties finally agreed that a commission comprised of five Senators, five Representatives, and five Supreme Court justices would examine the evidence pertaining to the disputed votes and then decide whether they would go to Hayes or Tilden. Days and weeks passed while apprehensive Americans wondered, as the end of the year approached, who would occupy the White House in 1877, and what policies and programs would be encounterd during the next administration.[15]

At Fort Defiance, Arizona, the Navajos and their agent may have been concerned about these issues, but in many respects it was business as usual on the reservation during the latter half of 1876. Irvine's efforts to bring a return to normalcy in his relations with his Indians had succeeded so well by mid-summer that he did not hestitate to ask for a sixty-day leave of absence from August 1 to September 30. During this vacation, he and his wife intended to visit friends and relatives in the East and also attend the great Centennial celebrations in Philadelphia and Washington, D.C. When he explained to his superiors in the Office of Indian Affairs that his issue clerk at the agency was perfectly competent to handle routine business in his absence, Commissioner Smith approved his request and Irvine departed feeling confident that the kind of rebellion that had unseated W. F. M. Arny would not occur while he was away.[16]

When Irvine returned to his agency at the end of September, he was pleased when he learned that the Navajos were expecting a good harvest. Although the wheat had been badly damaged by grasshoppers, the corn crop was better than in previous years. The Indians had obtained large amounts of pumpkins and melons, and in the Canon de Chelly area of the reservation they had harvested a bumper crop of delicious peaches. In October Irvine received permission to award contracts for enough beef and corn to continue issuing these items to the Navajos until the spring of 1877. From all indications, for the first time since 1871 when the first agent appointed under the Peace Policy arrived at Fort Defiance, the food problem would not become a desperate issue for the Navajos as they faced the possibility of another severe winter on their reservation.[17]

Efforts to educate Navajo children at the agency presented a more perplexing problem for Irvine. He had terminated the school conducted by his wife in April, when the children were needed by their parents to help with the spring planting. At that time, Irvine had expressed his displeasure with the classroom facilities provided at Fort Defiance for the children and their teacher. The only room available, which measured twelve feet by twelve feet, was entirely too small for its intended purpose. There were not enough desks and chairs, and it seemed almost impossible to keep the room warm enough to provide an environment that came even close to being comfortable. Concerned about the possible deterioration of his wife's health under these adverse conditions, Irvine insisted that he would not reopen the school under her supervision in the fall unless the deficiencies were corrected. In August John Lowrie learned that Irvine was considering abandoning the school entirely because he did not feel that previous and anticipated results warranted continued expenditures for this purpose. When Irvine returned in the fall from his vacation, he apparently changed his mind on this matter, because his register of employees for October 1 showed two men employed as teachers. In his annual report, however, the agent strongly recommended relocation of the school in an area on the reservation known as the Chusca Valley. Since this region was more densely populated by the

Navajos than others on the reservation, Irvine believed attendance figures at that location would show significant improvement over those recorded at Fort Defiance.[18]

At the end of 1876, Irvine must have felt very satisfied with his record as Navajo agent during the year. His success in restoring among the Indians a sense of respect for their agent could have been attributed to his readiness to at least try and resolve some of the major problems that had caused strife between the Navajos and W. F. M. Arny in the previous year. The healing process was also expedited by Irvine's ability to impress the Indians, when possible, with small but noticeable and appreciated gestures. For example, when it was obvious that the Indians did not want to use the expensive looms imported by Arny, Irvine simply decided to distribute the supplies of brightly colored yarn which had been purchased for lessons on the looms to the Indians to use as they saw fit. On another occasion, when a Mexican killed a Navajo suspected of stealing sheep, Irvine effectively cooperated with the army officer in charge at Fort Wingate in obtaining an agreement whereby the Navajos received 450 sheep in settlement of the case. Although Irvine did not like the practice of equating a certain number of sheep with a man's life, he did believe that the incident convinced the Indians that "they will be justly dealt with and must not try to right their own wrongs but submit to authority."[19]

There were other Indians in the West at this time, however, who refused to submit peaceably to the white man's authority. Writers in the eastern press late in 1876 directed much of their attention to analysis of causes and results of the summer campaigns conducted by the army against the Sioux and their allies in the Dakota and Montana Territories. The shock waves of the Custer debacle at the Little Big Horn spread all the way to the banks of the Potomac in the nation's capital where officials concerned with aiding the Indians had to assess the results of their well-meaning efforts in the year just passed. Not surprisingly, top administrators in the Department of the Interior concluded, first, that the so-called Sioux War was rather inconsequential when weighed in the balance of Indian-white relations nationwide and then, that the warfare on the northern plains could not be blamed on the Peace Policy.

Secretary of Interior Chandler led the way in adopting this defensive posture. He pointed out that practically all the Indians under the control of his department, except the hostile Sioux, were making commendable improvements in their lifestyles. Their success in cultivating their own fields and producing their own food had instilled in them a taste for such pursuits and a relinquishment of their natural desire to roam at will. Credit for these good results should be properly bestowed upon the officers in charge of the Indian agencies whose sense of purpose and integrity should be recognized and rewarded. It was rather remarkable that such men could sacrifice home comforts and other former advantages to endure hardships on the frontier for inadequate salaries. Certainly the nation was indebted to the various Christian organizations that had secured such intelligent and capable men for this otherwise thankless service.[20]

Commissioner of Indian Affairs J. Q. Smith went even further in lauding the work of the Christian agents and the success they had achieved in guiding their wards along the path to civilization. It was well known, of course, that one of the goals of the Peace Policy was to place employees of good moral and Christian character at the agencies. From this commendable policy, much had been accomplished toward establishing and maintaining peace, toward protecting Indians from evil influences, and toward awakening in the Indians the desire for a better mode of life. These achievements were not attained without overcoming obstacles unique to the Indian service. In other departments of the government, employees conducted business primarily with civilized and intelligent men. Not so in the Office of Indian Affairs. There, the agents had to deal with uncivilized and unintelligent people whose ignorance and suspicion naturally increased the difficulty of controlling and assisting them. With this handicap in mind, Smith called for a new schedule of graduated compensation for Indian agents to reward those who were responsible for the most important and difficult agencies.[21]

The Board of Indian Commissioners continued to rely on statistics to measure the degree of success achieved by the Peace Policy in 1876. Using a comparison with data available eight years previously, the rather awesome array of these figures presented in the annual report of the commissioners seemed to prove conclusively that efforts to uplift the Indians were making great strides in the right direction. Among the more impressive achievements, the commissioners noted that of 266,000 Indians in the United States, 104,818 were now wearing "citizen's dress." There were now 55,717 houses occupied by Indians, compared to only 7,476 in 1868. In 1868 the number of students attending reservation schools was 4,718, but in 1876 this figure increased to 11,328. There were now 177 church buildings on Indian reservations, and 27,215 Indians were church members. The figure of 54,207 acres of land cultivated by Indians in 1868 had increased by 1876 to 318,194 acres. From all this evidence, the commissioners could only conclude that the Indians could be civilized. In fact, many who were recently savage and warlike were well on the way to adopting habits of civilized life. The only thing required to finish this great endeavor was the patient continuance of present policies to complete what had been well begun.[22]

Ulysses Grant certainly hoped to convey the impression that present policies would continue in his final annual message to the Congress and the nation. While acknowledging that armed conflict with Indians had occurred during that year in parts of Nebraska, and in the Dakota, Wyoming, and Montana Territories, the departing president contended that these mishaps had been caused by greedy white men who had violated solemn treaty stipulations in the quest for gold. Actually, adherence to the principles of the Peace Policy during his presidency had, with only a few exceptions, brought peace on the frontier. "A policy has been adopted toward the Indian tribes . . . ," Grant asserted, "which has been humane and has substantially ended Indian hostilities in the whole land."[23]

Thankfully, peace reigned, for the moment, on the Navajo reservation. Alexander Irvine had heard rumors near the end of the year that a delegation of Utes had visited some of the Navajo chiefs, urging them to join in a war against the Americans who were trying to take their land. Irvine discounted the threat, recalling that the Navajos still remembered the Utes as traditional enemies. Besides, the Navajos, who had too much to lose by war, preferred to "seek for quiet."[24] While Irvine may not have been too concerned by the alleged Ute overtures, he knew that it would be fatuous indeed to assume that the Indians would not rebel again if they felt deceived by the government. Along with all Americans, Irvine could only watch and wait while deliberations continued in Washington at the end of the year to select a new President who might or might not favor a humane policy toward the Indians.

10

Where Do We Go from Here? 1877

Earnest efforts are being made to purify the Indian
service. . . .
—President Rutherford B. Hayes
December 3, 1877

John Lowrie was worried. Like most Americans, he grew impatient as the weeks passed early in 1877 and there was still no decision on the final tabulation of electoral votes cast in the previous fall for the presidency. The mission board secretary finally concluded that regardless of the outcome, the changes occurring in Washington on inauguration day in March would also bring changes in existing arrangements for recommending good churchmen to Indian agency positions. This pessimistic outlook did not deter Lowrie, however, from attending the now traditional annual meeting called by the Board of Indian Commissioners at the beginning of the year to discuss the Peace Policy in the context of results in the past year, along with future expectations. On February 5 those attending the conference assembled at Willard's Hotel in Washington, D.C. In his report to the delegates, Lowrie focused his remarks on Presbyterian interests in the work at several agencies entrusted to his mission board, but he omitted any specific comments about conditions at agencies in the Southwest. For the future he hoped that his church could find the financial resources to expand missionary work among the Indians. Since the sacred duty to bring the gospel to the nation's wards had been fulfilled to only a limited extent, it was now more important than ever to use vigorous measures for their proper religious instruction, "and to offer prayer on their behalf to Him who is able to save them."[1]

A primary concern, of course, for those gathering in Washington was to reaffirm their fervent hope that the principles of the Peace

Policy would still serve as a beacon to guide new decision makers in the formulation of Indian policy in the days ahead. The delegates formalized their position on this matter in a lengthy farewell memorial to President Grant. Prominent in the wording of the memorial was recognition of the good results experienced in securing the services of upright men as Indian agents. The commendable results were identified more precisely by citing the establishment of peace with tribes formerly regarded as warlike, by the remarkable advance of Indians on some reservations in habits of industry and self-support, by the education of Indian children, and through many examples of adoption by the Indians of the characteristics of Christian life and worship. Anticipating difficulties yet to be encountered in the way of Indian improvement, the memorialists hoped that "the work now happily in progress may go forward until the Indians all become a civilized and Christian people, prepared to become good citizens of our common country."[2]

While mission boards and government officials worried about possibilities of abandoning or seriously modifying the Peace Policy, Presbyterians in the church at large also directed their attention to this controversial issue. One concerned writer in a leading Presbyterian periodical acknowledged the criticism sometimes encountered about permitting mission boards to nominate Indian agents. Occasionally unsuitable and unworthy men had been selected, but in most cases their deficiencies were soon detected and they were dismissed. On the whole the arrangement had secured the services of men of higher character than most of those appointed under the old system. In the great majority of cases, the agents were now sincerely seeking the welfare of the Indians. The writer concluded his analysis by calling for continuation of the Peace Policy, "a policy not to be abandoned, as we trust, so long as any Indians are uncivilized and untaught."[3]

At long last, on March 2 the president of the Senate announced to both houses of Congress that the twenty disputed votes had been awarded by the investigating commission to Rutherford B. Hayes, thereby making him the duly elected next president of the United States, with a total of 185 electoral votes to 184 for Samuel Tilden. In his inaugural address on March 5, Hayes directed most of his attention to emphasizing the great need to reconcile all remaining differences between North and South. Those waiting to hear his position on the Peace Policy were disappointed when the new president chose not to comment on Indian policy, past, present, or future. However, he did call for reform in the civil service. When he endorsed a "thorough, radical, and complete" change in the appointment system compelling public officers to owe their service entirely to the government, advocates of the Peace Policy could only suspect that the framework of the great program initiated by President Grant would soon be dismantled. Hoping that these fears were groundless, members of the Board of Indian Commissioners soon obtained an audience with the new president to solicit his views on the Indian problem. Knowing full well that he could ill afford to alienate the many prominent Americans who were pledged to a benevolent program that would civilize and Christianize the Indians, Hayes carefully noted that, for the time being, he would simply carry forward the present Indian policy.[4]

As his Secretary of the Interior, replacing Zachariah Chandler, Hayes selected Carl Schurz, a liberal Republican who had attained the rank of Major General in the Union Army during the Civil War and who was known to favor a competitive merit system for appointment and promotion in the civil service. Soon after the announcement of his selection in the spring of 1877, an editor in the *New York Times* decided to lecture the new appointee on the proper course to follow in managing his Indian wards. Noting that in a recent address Schurz had not commented on that "most important branch" of his administrative responsibilities, the writer proceeded to tell the new department head how he should deal with the Indian problem. He should continue programs that provided training in techniques of agriculture, civilized arts, and industry on the reservations. He should prevent the illegal importation of firearms and liquor, and he should expel all "mischievous whites" who tried to settle among the Indians. He should locate and then dismiss all Indian agents who were not attentive to their job responsibilities. Finally, he should make it clear to the Indians that they must work or starve, as the "public distribution of alms every year among these tribes degrades the recipient and corrupts the givers. . . ."[5]

It would probably be safe to say that the *Times* editor had little knowledge from personal experience of actual conditions pertaining to the "public distribution of alms" to destitute Indians on a reservation in the West. Certainly at Fort Defiance, Arizona, the Navajo agent knew very well that he had to continue supplying rations during the winter and spring until the Indians could, hopefully, provide for at least part of their subsistence from crops planted, as always, in an environmental situation that was hardly conducive to setting new records for yields per acre. The beef and corn distributed by Alexander Irvine in the early months of 1877 sufficed to sustain the Navajos, at least to the point where their agent could feel rather confident that he would not have to deal with the dreaded problem of actual and widespread starvation. And again, as soon as the weather permitted, the industrious Navajos planted cereal grains and other garden seeds on every available piece of land except the attractive area in the north bordering on the Ute reservation. Still convinced that this latter region watered by the San Juan River could be used to raise all the corn, wheat, and vegetables needed by the Navajos, Irvine was determined to continue bringing this issue to the attention of his superiors during the year with the hope that he would eventually receive permission to move his agency to that choice location.[6]

In addition to the distribution of rations as "alms" to the Indians, Irvine also conducted periodic issues of the annuity goods promised in the treaty of 1868. His estimates of supplies needed to complete the annuity issue for the fiscal year ending on June 30, 1877, illustrated the kinds of items that could be best utilized, in his opinion, by the Navajos. Among the articles included in this list were calico, coffee, tin cups, indigo, men's hats, camp kettles, knives and forks, leather harness, shovels, spades, sugar, and tobacco. Anticipating a question about his request for a rather large amount of tobacco, Irvine explained that many Indians, who actually cared nothing about obtaining food rations, came from the farthest extremities of the reservation just to renew their supplies of tobacco. Pursuing a concern that he had previously noted, the agent rather audaciously included a request for a steam sawmill expected to cost approximately $3,500.[7]

Irvine scheduled the spring annuity issue for April 10–12. Lieutenant Thomas Blair of the 15th Infantry stationed at Fort Wingate was present with some of his men to witness the events and to ensure that everything would proceed in an orderly fashion. From his official report of the occasion, one can obtain a revealing insight into the process whereby the Navajos received some of the "alms" pledged to them by the federal government. When he arrived at Fort Defiance on the evening of April 9, Blair observed that a large number of the Indians had already arrived on the agency grounds. Early in the morning of the next day, Irvine began to issue tickets to the Navajos who passed single file into the confines of the agency corral. Men received red tickets, women blue, and children pink. To keep the Indians from going through the line two or more times, Irvine required all of them to remain in the corral as this process continued through the day. Commenting on the unusually severe weather on that date, with snow and sleet falling all day, Blair was surprised that the Indians, huddled together like sheep in a pen with no shelter, accepted their situation with excellent behavior and good humor.[8]

On April 11 actual issue of goods began. Along the whole front of the agency storehouse, employees had fenced in a pathway about three feet wide. At the entrance to this path, Blair had stationed two of his soldiers, one to take tickets and the other to put the tickets in a tin box with a slot in the lid. Each Indian passing through the line received one or more articles as he or she passed by the doors and windows of the storehouse. At the exit a soldier prevented any return of those who had already gone through the line. Among the articles issued were hatchets, axes, butcher knives, hoes, tin cups, tin pans, frying pans, wool cards, sieves, needles, gloves, common thread, combs, indigo, woolen yarn, white and colored cotton cloth, sheeting, calico, and colored handkerchiefs. This process continued on the following day until in the evening when the chiefs provided an estimate of the numbers from their bands who could not attend. Irvine did not have enough remaining supplies to give a full issue to the absentee claimants, but he made a pro rata distribution of everything remaining and the chiefs all seemed pleased as they departed from the agency.[9]

Lieutenant Blair concluded his report on the annuity issue with a word of approval for the Navajo agent who conducted the whole business—in Blair's opinion, in an open and aboveboard fashion. If Irvine was satisfied with his supervision of the annuity issue, he was less pleased with arrangements for the more numerous issues of food rations. His requests for the purchase of the beef and corn used for these rations showed the difficulty encountered in making accurate estimates to contractors for these food items. While many Navajos lived on the results of their harvests in late summer, by early fall from 100 to 200 of them began to arrive at the agency for a weekly ration issue. These numbers gradually increased until, during the winter months, an average of 1,500 Indians expected to be fed from his larder. These numbers escalated dramatically during the occasional annuity issues when at least 9,000 Navajos expected a ration issue along with their annuity items. Compounding his problems in this area of concern, Irvine complained about a new edict requiring him to issue rations only to heads of families. This seemingly harmless stipulation apparently anticipated the beginning of a more orderly enrollment of the Indians and their family status in the records of the agency. However, Irvine declared that many of the Navajos refused to give their names because they suspected that this action was a first step toward revising all issue procedures in a manner detrimental to their interests. Although Irvine did not expect any major problems as he tried to convince the recalcitrant Navajos that the government intended to remain firm on this new policy, he did intend to request the presence of one or more soldiers from Fort Wingate on all issue days to show support from the military for his position.[10]

On one major point related to the selection and issue of annuity goods, Irvine had some rather strong views that were probably not shared by very many of the Navajos. He was convinced that the addition of still more sheep to the large numbers already present on the reservation, and a wider distribution of those animals among the members of the tribe would be critical factors in creating a viable economic base that would ensure the tribe's future prosperity. Although statistics showed that the Navajos had many sheep in the aggregate, many of the Indians had none. Each family should have a chance to own a flock of sheep, and a good start to this end could be achieved by including 15,000 ewes in the selection of next year's annuity goods. While the Indians may have endorsed this recommendation, they were sure to take exception to Irvine's next proposal to the Commissioner of Indian Affairs regarding the livestock owned by the Navajos. The agent believed that the possession of horses by the Indians should be discouraged or perhaps even prohibited. Since the horses were used for riding and not work, they contributed little or nothing to the goal of training the Navajos in agricultural and industrial pursuits. Besides, in Irvine's reasoning, if the Indians had no horses, then they would be more inclined to remain in one place where they could be better controlled.[11]

There is no indication that Irvine pursued his campaign to deprive the Navajos of their horses beyond the point of making his position on the subject a matter of record in the Office of Indian Affairs. On another important issue pertaining to the conduct of his agency, Irvine displayed a more tactful approach to a nagging problem. He had little hope of obtaining a sawmill for the agency unless he could justify the need for such a large expenditure. Aware of the great accumulation of complaints in the commissioner's office from all of his predecessors about the deplorable condition of agency buildings, Irvine provided still more reasons why a major rehabilitation program for agency facilities was long overdue. Constant drifting of sand against the buildings over the years had raised the ground level around some structures as much as two feet higher than the interior floors. This sad state of affairs was a major cause of the generally damp and unhealthy living conditions inside the buildings. The accumulation of snow after recent storms now had to be shoveled off the roofs of all buildings at once. If this were not done, the occupants of rooms below would be constantly drenched from the melting snow dripping through the innumerable holes in the roofs. Decision makers in the nation's capital were finally convinced that an on-site rehabilitation program made possible with lumber provided by an agency sawmill would be the least expensive of all alternatives to remedy this situation. Accordingly, they finally ordered the mill Irvine requested, which was to be delivered sometime during the summer.[12]

Pleased, no doubt, by his success with the sawmill venture, Irvine was less than satisfied with the status of the school for Navajo children. He frankly acknowledged that if there was any change worth noting in the results of this educational endeavor, he would have to rate the achievements in the first part of 1877 as less significant than those of the year before. To maintain some semblance of a school at the agency, he would often ask one or more of the reasonably intelligent and literate employees to combine the teaching responsibility with other duties. Irvine saw no real hope for significant progress in this respect unless schoolhouses were built at several of the more densely populated locations throughout the reservation where full-time teachers and their families could establish permanent residences among the Indians. When the new sawmill became operational, Irvine believed that adequate supplies of lumber would be available to construct any number of schoolhouses and teachers' residences at a nominal cost. Until then the Navajo school at Fort Defiance would have to be considered, in all honesty, as a school in name only.[13]

Somehow in his busy schedule Alexander Irvine found the time to take on another responsibility that was certainly unanticipated and probably unwelcome. In the summer of 1875, William Truax had relinquished his position as farmer at the Navajo agency to accept an assignment as agent to the Hopi Indians in northern Arizona. Near the end of 1876, Truax learned from the Office of Indian Affairs that continuance of the Hopi position as a separate agency was no longer practicable. In the future the Navajo agent could easily look after the very minimal needs of the Hopi. Irvine did not contest this arbitrary

Chapter 10

extension of his duties that would require him to travel almost 100 miles from his base of operations at Fort Defiance to reach the remote Hopi villages. Perhaps he regarded the new assignment as an indication that the Commissioner of Indian Affairs believed that everything on the Navajo reservation was running so smoothly that he could be spared occasionally to maintain contact between the government and other Indians in the vicinity. In any event, Irvine did make several trips to the Hopi communities. From his reports of these visits one can sense his appreciation for these encounters with Indians who were, in fact, self-sufficient.[14]

Irvine was particularly impressed by the Hopi farming practices. Although these Indians also lived on barren land that appeared, at first glance, unfit for cultivation, the Navajo agent discovered that the Hopi could always retain in their granaries a year's supply of corn. In this manner, they never suffered except in an unlikely situation where two crops failed in succession. The Indians attributed their success with the corn harvests to unusually deep planting of the seed to take advantage of even the smallest amount of subsurface moisture. Although corn was a staple part of their diet, the Hopi were not vegetarians. They obtained meat by organizing rabbit hunts when every able-bodied man in the villages turned out to pursue the plentiful animals across the countryside. In addition to the meat secured from these expeditions, the Hopi also skillfully wove the rabbit skins into warm blankets. Irvine was somewhat shocked to learn that the Hopi children went completely naked, except in exceedingly cold weather, until they were six or seven years old. Concerned about hardening their children to the elements, in the winter the parents washed the boys and girls in cold water or snow and then let them find a place in the sun to thaw out. Irvine concluded from these visits that the Hopi were so attached to their homes and their lifestyle that they would strongly resist any efforts to move them to a more accessible location.[15]

At this stage of his career as an Indian agent, Alexander Irvine's performance record was certainly regarded as satisfactory if not superior. It must have come as a surprise, then, to officials in the Office of Indian Affairs when the Navajo agent suddenly submitted his resignation in July to take effect on September 30, 1877. In his notice of resignation, Irvine did not give any reason for his abrupt decision, but a later report in a Santa Fe newspaper stated that he had accumulated business interests in that city that now required his attention.

In any event, Irvine assumed that the preparation of his annual report on September 1 would probably be one of his last official acts as agent to the Navajos. Among the positive factors in his report, he noted that the crops on that date were all in satisfactory condition. If there was not an exceptionally early frost, the Indians could expect a good harvest. However, even with this unusually good news regarding anticipated agricultural production, Irvine repeated and strongly endorsed his previous recommendation to relocate the agency to some point on the San Juan River where it would be possible to raise enough corn, wheat, and vegetables to feed twice the number of Navajos then in the tribe. The only difficulty that he experienced in the previous year, according to the departing agent, was the Navajos' reluctance to give their names and other information about their families on issue days. Assuming that the majority of the Indians would not have resisted unless directed to do so, Irvine concluded that some of the chiefs had instigated this opposition led by their ringleader Manuelito, "who has been a disturber ever since the Navajoes [sic] were placed upon the present reservation."[16]

If the Navajos did resent the invasion of their privacy by Irvine's efforts to obtain personal information from them on issue days, their ill feeling was apparently directed to other policymakers in the Indian service and not to their agent. At least this was the impression received by Inspector William Vandever, who visited the agency in October. He reported that the Navajos spoke very well of their agent and seemed to sincerely regret his decision to leave them. Regarding conditions at Fort Defiance, the inspector's examination of Irvine's records showed that he had "fairly administered the affairs of this agency." Noting the industrious habits of the Indians, Vandever was impressed when Irvine told him that the Navajos supplied nine-tenths of their own subsistence and clothing by their own labor. The inspector was less pleased with his other observations about agency affairs. He could not discern that the Indians had advanced toward civilization in any appreciable degree since he visited them in 1873. They had certainly not improved in their morals. Efforts to establish schools among them had also not been successful. Irvine admitted he had tried four times that fall to reopen the school, but without success. Succumbing, perhaps, to the persuasive talents of the departing agent, Vandever concluded his report by endorsing Irvine's proposal to move the agency to a site on the San Juan River where the Navajos would be withdrawn "from the vicinity of men whose influence over them is bad."[17]

One revealing bit of information included in Inspector Vandever's report of October 23 had nothing to do with conditions at the agency, but it did reflect upon Alexander Irvine's status at Fort Defiance. When the inspector mentioned that Irvine was still waiting to be relieved, it was obvious that the departing agent's hopes to vacate his post by September 30 had not been fulfilled. Moving quickly on Irvine's resignation, Secretary of the Interior Carl Schurz notified John Lowrie of the impending vacancy and requested Lowrie's nomination of a replacement as soon as possible. Among those interested in the post was the perennial contender, Thomas Keams. Inspector Vandever had pointed out that the Navajos would like to have Keams as Irvine's successor, because he would not be a complete stranger to their needs and he was familiar with their language. Keams had renewed his application for the agent's position in a letter to President Hayes on May 1, 1877. Supporting the application were letters testifying to his honesty, industry, sobriety, and trustworthiness. When copies of this correspondence reached Lowrie, any change of heart on his part about accepting Keams was probably short-lived when he received notice that one of Keams's supporters was now withdrawing his endorsement because the applicant had returned to his old ways of living with a Navajo woman who was not his wife. With this disturbing revelation before him, Lowrie decided to follow the pattern that had worked so well with Irvine's assignment, that is, transfer a former agent at the Cimarron agency to fill the Navajo vacancy. Acting on this decision, the mission board secretary notified John Pyle of his nomination to the position soon to be vacated at Fort Defiance.[18]

Lowrie had selected Pyle to replace Irvine at Cimarron when the latter moved over to the Navajo agency at the end of 1875. Pyle was employed as a bookkeeper for a lumber business in Helena, Montana, when he decided to apply for an agency position early in 1873. Those who supported his application described him as a highly esteemed elder of the local Presbyterian church with a wife who was also a thoroughly conscientious and earnest Christian. Although Lowrie had no job opening for Pyle in 1873, when the Cimarron position became available after Irvine's transfer, he asked Pyle if he was still interested in an appointment as Indian agent. Pyle accepted at once and he served effectively at Cimarron until the Office of Indian Affairs, as an economy measure, decided to turn the agency business at Cimarron over to the Pueblo Indian agent in Santa Fe in the fall of 1876. Pyle continued his employment at the Cimarron agency as Farmer-

In-Charge until he received and accepted Lowrie's offer of the Navajo agency in the summer of 1877. The Office of Indian Affairs approved the transfer when Inspector Edward Kemble, who had recently visited Cimarron, reported that the residents of that community spoke very highly of Pyle. In Kemble's opinion, he had the material within him to make as good an agent for the Navajos as Alexander Irvine.[19]

Although everything was apparently proceeding smoothly in the appointment of a new agent, days and weeks passed and Alexander Irvine was still unrelieved at Fort Defiance. Certainly John Pyle was ready to move at once, but he was experiencing difficulty in obtaining co-signers on the surety bond required of all Indian agents. Reluctantly accepting the responsibility to carry out his duties until officially relieved, Irvine could only continue as Navajo agent on a day-to-day basis until his successor appeared. Meanwhile, back at the headquarters of the Presbyterian Church, a very serious crisis had arisen concerning the role of the mission boards of that denomination. A manifestation of this critical situation had appeared at Fort Defiance earlier in the year. When Irvine reported on the annuity issue to the Navajos in April, he mentioned a visitor who had helped in compiling the records for that event. His assistant was the Reverend Sheldon Jackson, self-styled Superintendent of Presbyterian Missions for the Rocky Mountain West. Jackson was an extraordinary individual. He had obtained his appointment to establish home mission stations for his church in the West in 1869. In the span of a few years, the dynamic leader had organized many new congregations all across the vast expanse of his assigned territory. By 1877 Jackson was ready to lead a movement among prominent Presbyterians interested in mission work to transfer responsibility for civilizing and Christianizing the Indians from the Board of Foreign Missions to his employer, the Board of Home Missions.[20]

Jackson's position on these potentially divisive considerations was not without foundation. In his tour of the Southwest, he had observed the absence of missionary work by his church at most of the Indian reservations he visited. This neglect was very visible at Fort Defiance. Since the departure of W. F. M. Arny two years ago, no missionaries had been assigned to preach and teach among the Navajos. In fact, John Lowrie seemed to have little interest in any of the activities of Alexander Irvine. During the administrations of previous agents selected by Lowrie, there was considerable evidence of a perceived need for regular exchanges of information between agents and the mission board secretary. But while Irvine held the Navajo position, communication between Fort Defiance and board headquarters in New York drastically declined. Lowrie did make one attempt to recruit a missionary for the Navajos in the summer of 1877. His advertisement announcing this opportunity carried within it unmistakable evidence that the original expectations of the Peace Policy had not been forgotten. Applicants should be men of earnest missionary purpose. Preferably, they should be young men who could readily learn the native language. If the candidates were married, their wives should share the same spirit of dedication to a righteous cause. Although the church would provide moderate but sufficient support, the main motives, of course, for accepting this challenge, should be spiritual rather than monetary. Finally, Lowrie assured those reading the notice that there was no finer field for useful labor for Christ than the opening at Fort Defiance, Arizona. Unfortunately, this call to arms in the service of the Lord went unheeded. At the end of the year, the great field for Christian usefulness among the Navajos remained unoccupied.[21]

There were no indications that Alexander Irvine was overly concerned about the absence of good Presbyterian missionaries at his agency in the fall of 1877. He wanted to leave that field for useful labor, however, as soon as possible. Meanwhile, his time was occupied with the usual tasks. He resumed the issuance of rations to the Indians in October. From supplies received under new contracts, he distributed beef, corn or wheat, and small amounts of coffee, sugar, and tobacco. A new element of concern in this otherwise routine procedure was a source of irritation to the Navajo chiefs. Either by oversight or intent, the contract for supplying beef to the agency did not stipulate that the Indians could have the hides from the slaughtered cattle. Accustomed to using these hides for moccasins and other articles of clothing, the angry Navajos talked of using force, if necessary, to retain this traditional prerogative. Irvine managed to quell this incipient rebellion by convincing the Office of Indian Affairs to let him buy the hides for the Indians from the contractors at the same price per pound quoted for beef in the contract.[22]

Irvine was less successful in his efforts to deal with the constant problem of illegal sale of alcoholic beverages to the Navajos. While he realized that these transactions were prevalent at settlements all around the reservation, his greatest concern was with the reports of transgressions at Fort Wingate. He had received complaints that the soldiers were openly selling whiskey to the Indians. When Irvine conveyed these accusations to the commanding officer at the fort, he was disappointed by the officer's apparent lack of interest. The officer insisted that these charges were derived, at that point, from suspicions only. Even if any evidence could be found to support the allegations, the result would doubtlessly show that only one case in hundreds was substantiated. Recalling his cordial and cooperative relationship with the military in agency affairs, Irvine decided to let the matter rest, assuming perhaps that there was little more he could do without formidable support from his superiors.[23]

Earlier in the year, Irvine had great difficulty persuading the Navajos to give him their names and other personal information on issue days. He experienced this same resistance when he tried to comply with instructions to conduct a formal census of the tribe. When he issued some annuity goods in October, he tried again to compile some sort of tribal roster. When the Navajos continued their stubborn unwillingness to give their names, Irvine could only confirm his previous conclusion that many of the Indians either had a superstitious dread of having their names recorded, or else they were afraid that other members of the tribe would laugh at them when they revealed their names. The frustrated agent also tried to explain to Commissioner Smith that at least half the Navajos did not have distinguishable names, at least in the context accepted by white society. Many of them shared simple identifying appellations such as "tall man" or "short man." While this was a pleasantly informal system, it was hardly one that could be readily translated into a meaningful census.[24]

While Irvine fretted at the end of the year about the delay in relieving him of his responsibilities as agent to the Navajos, in eastern cities many Americans who were proud to be identified with the goals of the Peace Policy had an opportunity to reassess their commitment to the principles espoused by that benevolent program. In the Presbyterian Church, a spokesman for the Board of Foreign Missions assigned great importance to continued selection of upright and religious men as Indian agents. There was every reason to be thankful that so few of the Presbyterian nominees had failed to give satisfaction in the fulfillment of their duties. However, the board felt that it must also comment on the controversy between the Foreign Board and the Home Board regarding the superintendence of the work among the Indians. It was common knowledge that some well-meaning brethren had already taken practical steps to transfer the Indian mission program to the Home Board. With a warning that any precipitous action on this matter outside the usual channels of church governance could only be harmful to the cause, the Foreign Board spokesman called for the General Assembly of the church to consider the pros and cons of the arguments presented by both sides in the dispute before abandoning long-standing procedures.[25]

Without naming names in their report, members of the Board of Foreign Missions knew very well who had taken "practical steps" to force this issue in New Mexico. In September, Sheldon Jackson made another tour of the Southwest. Accompanying him on this journey was Henry Kendall, secretary of the Presbyterian Board of Home Missions. The two men spent several days visiting leaders of their church in Santa Fe. Soon after their departure, Presbyterians in New Mexico who were concerned with the apparent neglect of missionary work among Indian tribes in the Southwest began a letter-writing compaign to bring this problem to the attention of those eastern decision makers who directed the course of Indian policy. In November, the Commissioner of Indian Affairs received one of these petitions from members of the Presbytery of Santa Fe. The writers noted with pride that their Presbytery was in better condition than ever before to cooperate in the work of educating and civilizing the Indians residing in their vicinity. Expressing particular concern about increasing the number of Indian schools operating on these reservations, the authors of the document hoped that the commissioner would appoint a Superintendent of Indian Schools in New Mexico who would not only assist the agents in procuring competent teachers, but would also consult with the agents and teachers about ways to improve school facilities. Assuring the commissioner that adoption of this course of action would greatly increase the efficiency of educational work among the tribes, the petitioners concluded by suggesting the name of Sheldon Jackson for this new and badly needed position. Heading the list of signatures on this petition was the name of James Roberts, one-time teacher for the Navajos at Fort Defiance and now moderator of the Presbytery of Santa Fe.[26]

Roberts and his associates directed their next attempt at reorganizing the Indian mission work to John Lowrie. In this communication they took a very bold step indeed. The malcontents declared that they had gone ahead and placed all the work with Mexicans and Indians within the bounds of their Presbytery under the care of the Board of Home Missions, because that organization was now conducting the work of evangelization in the territory with great vigor. Lowrie was surely astounded by this drastic action of the brethren in New Mexico. Assuming that he was dealing with a fait accompli, he only sought to remind Roberts and the others that they had clearly exceeded their authority. On numerous occasions the General Assembly of their church had recognized the Foreign Board as in charge of the Indians in New Mexico and Arizona. Although the entire matter of responsibility for Christianizing the Indians would probably be debated at length in the next Assembly meeting, the members of the Presbytery of Santa Fe had hardly done the right thing by unilaterally closing the door against the legitimate rights of the Foreign Board. The dejected board secretary then concluded his reply to the rebels with announcement of a momentous decision. "Our board takes no formal action on the minute of your Presbytery," Lowrie asserted, "but I think it will decline to take further steps in New Mexico and Arizona."[27]

While it appeared, at least momentarily, that the Presbyterian Church was undergoing a period of serious soul searching regarding its association with the Peace Policy, there were warning signals in the nation's capital at the end of 1877, indicating that the new administration was also ready to move cautiously toward reassessment of the government's Indian policy. Secretary of the Interior Carl Schurz was not pleased with the general condition of Indian affairs. He believed that the present policy permitting religious societies to nominate candidates for positions as Indian agents was, in some respects, an improvement over the old political patronage system. However, the frequent necessity of changes among Indian agents demonstrated that the program was by no means perfect. Customary recommendations of good character obviously could not be relied upon to obtain men well-fitted for the discharge of complicated and delicate duties and responsibilities. From these deductions Schurz concluded that the greatest need of the Indian service, as a new year approached, was the element of stability.[28]

In the Office of Indian Affairs, the customary removal of carry-over administrators from an outgoing administration did not occur until September 1877. At that time President Hayes dismissed Commissioner J. Q. Smith, replacing him with Ezra A. Hayt. Hayt was a wealthy businessman from New York who had previously served on the Board of Indian Commissioners. In his annual report, the new commissioner revealed his thoughts on the present status of the Indians and their anticipated role in American society. "The Indian, in his savage state, is the only born aristocrat on American soil," the commissioner proclaimed. "He despises labor and looks upon it as an indignity." Hayt strongly believed that the Indian's "natural repugnance" to work could only be overcome by requiring agents to demand some form of physical labor from their wards before furnishing them with any rations. Indians must also appear civilized. "The blanket must give way," Hayt insisted. "It is only tolerable in the rudest savage life. It is unfitted to be the garment of civilization. . . ." To this end, the commissioner called for adoption of a uniform style of clothing, consisting of a coat and pantaloons, for all Indians. This costume would surely be more comfortable for the wearers, and it would simplify the bidding process among competitors for clothing contracts. Finally, Hayt believed that in considering any comprehensive scheme for the civilization of the Indian race, "it is indispensable at the outset to throw aside the sentimentality that is so fashionable in our day, and to treat the subject in a practical and commonsense way."[29]

For advocates of the Peace Policy, these were ominous words indeed from the Secretary of the Interior and the Commissioner of Indian Affairs. Without explicitly announcing abandonment of the old policy, these officials left little doubt that they would proceed to find solutions for the Indian problem in a "practical and common-sense way." Meanwhile, there was still one bastion of support among government agencies for President Grant's Indian program. The members of the Board of Indian Commissioners, reflecting their non-partisan position, continued to applaud the results of the Peace Policy. Relying again on comprehensive use of statistics, the commissioners in their annual report pointed to increases in all categories of Indian response to government support programs in 1877. Reports from religious societies affiliated in the past with the Peace Policy also continued to show an increasing interest on the part of all Christian people in the nation in the moral elevation of the Indians. "These results in industry, education, and Christianity in the short span of nine years confirm our belief . . . ," the commissioners concluded, "that the peace policy is the only right policy, and there should be no longer any doubt as to its continuance as the permanent policy of the government."[30]

Despite these reassurances from the Board of Indian Commissioners, doubts about the continuation of the Peace Policy were not dispelled by President Hayes in his first annual message to the Congress in December. In presenting his views on Indian policy, he began by rejoicing that a series of "most deplorable conflicts" had been successfully concluded, and the nation was now at peace with all the Indian tribes. Without citing specific incidents, it was still quite clear that the president referred to several Indian wars that broke out in 1877, most notable being the war with the Nez Perce Indians in the Northwest which culminated in the gallant but futile attempt of Chief Joseph to lead his people to sanctuary in Canada. Searching for causes of these and other Indian wars in the past, Hayes contended that many, if not most, of these conflicts had their origin in broken promises by the United States. Many of these promises were included in formal treaties, but other commitments had been derived from adoption of certain general policies designed to civilize the "aboriginal occupants of the land we now possess." Regrettably, the advance of Indians in civilization had not been as rapid as anticipated, because the treatment they received "did not permit it to be faster and more general." Announcing his support for all policies outlined by his Secretary of the Interior and Commissioner of Indian Affairs, the president then ended his remarks on this issue by promising renewed endeavors to improve the work of the Office of Indian Affairs. "Earnest efforts are being made to purify the Indian service," Hayes assured, "so that every dollar appropriated by Congress shall redound to the benefit of the Indians, as intended."[31]

At the end of 1877, several provocative questions had been raised regarding the future course of the nation's Indian policy. At the national level, concerned citizens hoped to receive early in the coming year more precise definitions for a policy that would "purify" in a "practical and common-sense way." What exactly did that mean in terms of actual programs? In the Presbyterian Church, one might have expected to witness a continued tug-of-war between the Board of Home Missions and the Board of Foreign Missions for control of the Church's efforts to Christianize the Indians. In New Mexico, Presbyterian leaders surely wondered if John Lowrie really meant it when he said his board would not want to be involved in this work in Arizona and New Mexico in the future. Finally, at Fort Defiance, while the Indians were probably oblivious to the portent of all of these matters as they struggled to survive through another winter, Alexander Irvine had one paramount concern—when do I get out of here?

11

Conclusion

"The Old, Sad Story"

It is, we repeat, the old, sad story. From a distance the
world looks at the case [Indian policy] in its sentimental
aspect; close at hand it is seen in the light of hard facts.
The theory of the business is one thing, the practice
another.
—*New York Times*
November 9, 1871

"I would gladly withdraw from further connection with Indian affairs
in Washington, but I hope I shall never cease to feel a deep concern
for the spiritual interests of the Indians. I think no people on the face
of the earth have stronger claims on the churches of our country."[1]
In these comments to the pastor of the Presbyterian Church in Santa
Fe in June 1878, John Lowrie candidly revealed his growing disen-
chantment with the direction of Indian policy in the nation's capital.
For Lowrie and other prominent churchmen who had been closely
associated with ex-President Grant's Peace Policy, the sands of time
measuring the life span of this innovative program started to run
down soon after Rutherford B. Hayes took office in 1877. The new
president and other officials concerned with the administration of
Indian affairs in the Department of the Interior carefully refrained
from open disavowal of the church/state relationship that had produced programs designed to solve the Indian problem in the previous
eight years. Nevertheless, in the matter of agency appointments,
Lowrie and the members of his mission board soon suspected that
the Office of Indian Affairs intended to gradually change the role of
churchmen from that of active recruiting of Presbyterians to one of
passive endorsement of candidates presented by the commissioner.
Disturbed by this foreboding premonition, Lowrie still decided to
accept his usual invitation to attend the annual meeting with the
Board of Indian Commissioners called for January 10, 1878, in Washington, D.C.[2]

In his report to this convocation, Lowrie carefully noted that his

181

mission board was still quite certain that the Peace Policy pursued by the government for the last several years had produced good results. He then admitted that he had been unable to assign any additional missionaries to Indian agencies in the past year because the funds needed to sustain these appointments were simply not available. If good men and the means for their support could be secured, his board would gladly make commitments to new evangelizing endeavors, particularly among one of the largest of the tribes, the Navajos. These and other Indians should not be allowed to pass from this life, according to Lowrie, without encountering the path to salvation. Anxious to speak to Rutherford Hayes about their concerns, the delegates at the conference adjourned to the White House where the president reportedly "received each one with marked cordiality. . . ." Lowrie and others seized the opportunity to show their support for continuation of the goals established by the Peace Policy. After expressing "full sympathy" with all of the recommendations, Hayes assured his audience that "there was no just cause to fear any material change in the present humane policy of the government."[3]

At Fort Defiance, Arizona, Alexander Irvine would certainly have appreciated a "material change" in his position as Navajo agent. As the harsh winter weeks passed and spring returned to the Navajo reservation, Irvine faithfully continued his administration of agency affairs while he hoped each day to receive news that John Pyle was en route to take over the agency. At long last, at the end of March a notice appeared in a Santa Fe newspaper announcing that Mr. J. E. Pyle, formerly agent for the Utes and Apaches at Cimarron, was on his way to relieve Alexander Irvine at Fort Defiance. With his bonding requirements finally satisfied, Pyle officially relieved Irvine as agent to the Navajos on April 1. The new agent's first impressions of his agency coincided with those of all of his predecessors. He was shocked by the condition of the agency facilities. Referring to the squalid buildings as hovels, he was sure that the dirt walls, dirt floors, and dirt roofs of these structures created an unhealthy environment that was simply intolerable. In addition, there was apparently no effort underway at the time to operate a school at the agency. Reflecting upon the futile expenditures of thousands of dollars in past years on transient teachers and transient pupils, he doubted that there was a single Navajo on the reservation who could read or write. With these and other problems facing him, Pyle understandably wondered why the agency had been allowed to function for so long under conditions that were "most unfortunate in every respect. . . ."[4]

The continued involvement of the Presbyterian Church for a few more years in the conduct of affairs at the Navajo agency could have been described by critics at the time as "unfortunate in every respect." John Pyle struggled to cope with the usual problems encountered by all the men who had preceded him as Navajo agent, but his brief tenure in this position ended before he could really follow through with any of his own theories for improving the condition of the Indians. The incident leading to his departure from Fort Defiance occurred on September 8 when General William T. Sherman visited the agency to confer with the chiefs regarding their relationship with the government. At this meeting, which Pyle attended, the Indians asked for two things: a larger reservation and dismissal of their agent, who isolated himself at the agency and refused to listen to them when they came to visit him. Sherman did not reveal his thoughts on these issues to Pyle at the time, but in his report to the Secretary of War on the meeting, the General recommended Pyle's transfer to another position. According to Sherman, a good replacement for Pyle would be Thomas Keams, a man held in high regard by the chiefs, or possibly one of the Navajo chiefs, perhaps his old friend Manuelito, to serve as agent. Pyle's suspicions that Sherman would reach these conclusions prompted him to defend himself to the Commissioner of Indian Affairs. He told Ezra Hayt that the chiefs may have felt ignored at times by their agent, but "my time is too valuable to be thrown away in listening to the begging appeals of selfish chiefs for extraordinary allowances to themselves of goods and supplies."[5]

Distressed by these indications of dissatisfaction with the conduct of his agency and concerned about the deterioration of his health, at the end of 1878 Pyle obtained a sixty-day lease of absence, commencing December 1, to visit his home in Helena, Montana. During this recuperative interlude, he learned that the Commissioner of Indian Affairs had decided to terminate his appointment as Indian agent. Although Pyle did not understand the reason for this action, he must have assumed that General Sherman's negative report and his own health problems had been instrumental in the decision. Soon after receiving his dismissal notice, Pyle heard from John Lowrie that his replacement had already been selected. If the process used for choosing the new agent had been submitted to close scrutiny at the time, the procedures utilized could only have confirmed the fears of Lowrie and others that the time had indeed arrived when the role of the churches in initiating the selection of Indian agents had been noticeably altered. Senator Thomas W. Ferry of Michigan had written to Secretary of the Interior Carl Schurz recommending Ferry's brother-in-law, Galen Eastman, a businessman from Grand Haven, Michigan, for an appointment as Indian agent. Schurz now submitted Eastman's name to Lowrie for the post at Fort Defiance. After examining several testimonials in his behalf gathered by Eastman, Lowrie then dutifully announced to Schurz that he approved the appointment, although "the members of the [Mission] Board have not the pleasure of being personally acquainted with Mr. Eastman."[6]

If John Lowrie harbored any resentment for his relegation to a rubber stamp position in the Eastman selection process, he kept these thoughts to himself as the new agent traveled in the spring of 1879 to assume his duties as agent to the Navajos at Fort Defiance. For about a year, Eastman tried to carry out his responsibilities as Navajo agent as he viewed them. Following procedures utilized by previous agents, he conducted annuity issues to the Navajos without incident. When a severe drought badly damaged crops throughout the reservation, he quickly called for an increase in the amount appropriated for rations for the Indians in the coming winter. Then, in mid-April of 1880, Eastman left Fort Defiance on a buying trip for agency supplies in the East. On April 23 several of the Navajo chiefs, including Manuelito and Ganado Mucho, appeared at Fort Wingate requesting the commanding officer at that post to tell the president they wanted Eastman's removal because he had refused to continue the special gifts customarily bestowed on them as chiefs. When the report of this incident was augmented by stories of threats to the safety of employees at Fort Defiance, the Office of Indian Affairs quickly authorized Eastman's suspension while the charges against him could be evaluated.[7]

In an ironic turn of events, the designation of a temporary agent for the Navajos during Eastman's suspension brought the story of agency appointments under the Grant Peace Policy full circle at Fort Defiance. Captain Frank Bennett, who served as agent until relieved by James Miller under the terms of the new Peace Policy in 1871, had been reassigned by the army to duty with the Ninth Cavalry at Fort Wingate. Knowing of his past experience working with the Navajos, the War Department, with the concurrence of the Office of Indian Affairs, ordered Bennett to oversee agency affairs while Eastman waited in Albuquerque for a decision in the disposition of his case. Bennett arrived at Fort Defiance to take charge of the Navajo agency on June 13, 1880. Although he held this position for over a year, his temporary custody of the post could best be described as a holding action, as he knew full well that the Department of the Interior would eventually reclaim its prerogative to again appoint a civilian agent to the Navajos.[8]

When the announcement finally appeared disclosing the name of the person who would take over from Bennett as agent to the Navajos, the revelation must have come as a surprise, to say the least, to the Indians and white employees at Fort Defiance. After examining numerous statements both condemning and supporting Galen Eastman's record, and yielding, perhaps, to pressure from Senator Ferry, the Commissioner of Indian Affairs declared that Eastman would be reinstated, effective July 1, 1881, as the Navajo agent. When Eastman returned to Fort Defiance, he was surprised to encounter opposition from Frank Bennett, who insisted he had no instructions from his superiors to relinquish the agency. However, an exchange of telegrams with officials in Washington soon confirmed Eastman's position, and he resumed his plans to aid the Navajos who, he believed, were friendly and glad to see him again.[9]

Not all observers of the reunion of Galen Eastman with the Navajos shared his opinion that the Indians rejoiced at his return. Referring to information received from Santa Fe, a writer in the *New York Times* concluded that the Navajos were ready to revolt because they had wanted Frank Bennett to remain as their agent. Soon after this report, another writer in the *Times* noted that the Secretary of the Interior would soon send an impartial inspector to Fort Defiance to confirm or deny the stories of impending revolt. Inspector J. M. Haworth arrived at the Navajo agency to conduct this investigation early in August. He concluded from interviews with Navajo chiefs, agency employees, and officers at Fort Wingate that the danger of immediate rebellion was greatly exaggerated. However, according to Haworth, Eastman's position was precarious at best. He did not really enjoy the respect of the Navajos, who had placed him in the position of "having to appear in a pleading attitude before the Indians which they are quick to notice and puts him in a great disadvantage with them."[10]

There were others besides the Navajos who had lost any respect they may have had for the beleaguered agent. In his lengthy report, Inspector Haworth observed that the missionary teachers residing at the agency had also concluded that Eastman, who would never become an acceptable agent for the Indians, was certainly not sympathetic to their plans for conducting a school for the Navajo children. The resumption of missionary appointments to the incipient Navajo school occurred in the fall of 1879. An examination of the steps taken to appoint the Reverend Alexander Donaldson as missionary to the Navajos at that time would have revealed an accommodation of sorts between the Home and Foreign Mission Boards of the Presbyterian Church in carrying on the missionary efforts with the Indians of the Southwest. Acting for the Board of Home Missions, it was Sheldon Jackson who had convinced the recent graduate of Allegheny Seminary in Pennsylvania and his wife to accept the Navajo assignment. When Jackson then proceeded without opposition to designate other missionaries to tribes originally allotted to the Presbyterians in Arizona and New Mexico under the Peace Policy, it was evident that John Lowrie meant what he said earlier about the Board of Foreign Missions relinquishing the responsibility for missionary work among these Indians. While the General Assembly of the church continued to debate the question of jurisdiction in this matter in the larger context of national church polity, on the Navajo reservation it appeared that Lowrie and his board would continue to pay lip service to the agent selection process, while Jackson and his superiors on the Board of Home Missions would try to find ways and means to bring knowledge and the message of salvation to the Indians.[11]

Perhaps influenced by the renewed commitment by the Presbyterians to assign teachers to the Navajo agency, Commissioner of Indian Affairs Hayt agreed in the fall of 1879 to take immediate steps to provide funds for erection of a new and commodious school building at Fort Defiance. While plans for this construction project gradually materialized, the Donaldsons, who arrived at the agency on October 13, maintained a small school in their crude living quarters until January, when Eastman asked the missionary to examine the affairs at the vacated Hopi agency. Soon after he returned from this unwelcome task, Donaldson contracted pneumonia, and on April 30 he died. Although Sheldon Jackson tried at once to recruit replacements for the Donaldsons, it was not until February 1881 that he finally convinced Mr. J. D. Perkins and his wife, who had been conducting a school in Santa Fe, to take charge of the Navajo school. The Perkins family found their brief association with Frank Bennett tolerable. However, they had much to criticize later in their treatment by Galen

Eastman when he returned to the agency. The teachers complained incessantly about petty grievances which offended their Christian sensibilities. Eastman's use of the agency wagon to gather firewood on the Sabbath was, perhaps, hardly noteworthy, but the accusation by Mrs. Perkins that the agent and his family were diverting supplies intended for the Navajos to their own use was obviously a more serious matter. On one occasion, after listing several of her complaints against the agent, Mrs. Perkins vehemently told Sheldon Jackson that "Mr. Eastman has no friends here, he is hated by everyone."[12]

Surprisingly, Eastman managed to weather the gathering storm of complaints about his mismanagement of agency affairs until the summer of 1882 when another inspector from the Office of Indian Affairs visited Fort Defiance. From his observations and interviews, Inspector C. H. Howard concluded that the agency, as operated by Eastman, was utterly useless for two obvious reasons, a want of funds and the inefficiency of the agent. Anticipating a notice of dismissal based on these findings, Eastman decided to go ahead and submit his resignation effective December 31, 1882. When that date arrived, D. M. Riordan, a California politician and Civil War veteran residing at the time in Arizona for his health, took charge of the Navajo agency with no indication that John Lowrie or anyone else connected with the Presbyterian Church was involved in the selection process for the new agent. In the summer of 1883, a writer in an eastern newspaper ventured the opinion that the Navajos had finally received the leadership they so desperately needed in the person of D. M. Riordan, "a man of wisdom, force, and great personal experience, who six months ago replaced the last of a series of incompetent or at least unsuccessful men."[13]

At the same time incompetent or unsuccessful men struggled to help the Navajos in the Southwest during the waning years of the Peace Policy, their counterparts in the East who were associated with formulating and implementing Indian policy had their own difficulties. These well-meaning gentlemen suffered from the perhaps inevitable dilemmas identified with a transition period when one government program is shelved in favor of a new approach to solving a problem that seemed to offer no easy solution. In the reports of these government officials, much of the pious rhetoric used in former years when the Peace Policy was in vogue disappeared. In its place, a new panacea for solving the Indian problem attracted much attention. For example, in his last annual report prepared on November

1, 1879, Commissioner of Indian Affairs Ezra Hayt referred to widespread support for allotment in severalty of land on Indian reservations to the individual members of the tribes residing there. Adoption of this concept would presumably carry with it all the incentives and advantages of private property ownership. When the Indians eventually obtained title to a tract of their reservation land, the reservations themselves and their frequently criticized tribal lifestyles would surely fade away.[14]

Secretary of the Interior Carl Schurz also became convinced that adoption of some plan leading to ownership of private property by Indians was a very desirable goal to pursue. In the preparation of his annual report on November 1, 1880, he declared that any Indian would soon cease wanting to lead the life of a nomad and abandon all thoughts of war when he could live in a house he could call his own; cultivate his own acres, fenced in by his own labor, with his own plow; and feast upon the bounties derived from his own herds of cows and swine and his own flocks of poultry. This fortunate individual could then send his children to school, with the assurance "that they may become as civilized and prosperous as white people."[15]

Members of the Board of Indian Commissioners and churchmen concerned with Indian policy were aware of the growing support for still another approach to solving the Indian problem. At their annual meetings, which continued in the 1880s, these men discussed at length their ongoing role, if any, as participants in any new master plan which might eventually evolve for civilizing and Christianizing the Indians. John Lowrie voiced the concerns of all at the meeting on January 8, 1880, when he called for a forceful statement to Secretary Schurz and President Hayes regarding the critical condition of the Peace Policy. Lowrie wanted the president and secretary to know that the mission boards of the various churches contemplated withdrawal from a program that now bore little resemblance to the principles espoused by President Grant a decade earlier. Concluding his remarks on this subject, Lowrie hoped that Hayes could be made to understand that "we are all of one mind as to getting back to the original basis—that we ought to go back to the original plan of carrying on this work without the politicians."[16]

Unfortunately for the distressed churchmen, the politicians were, by this time, ready to proclaim rest in peace over the expiring corpse of the Peace Policy. President Hayes and his successors had little to say about Indian affairs in their annual messages. When they did mention the subject, they echoed the sentiment of the times by calling for Congress to move ahead with enactment of appropriate legislation for allotment of land in severalty to the nation's Indian wards. During the four years from 1881 to 1885 when James Garfield and Chester Arthur occupied the White House, the men holding the positions of Commissioner of Indian Affairs and Secretary of the Interior carefully completed the dismantling or revising of the associations established under the old Peace Policy.

Was there no place for the churches of America in the new scheme of things? Commissioner of Indian Affairs Hiram Price, writing in 1882, answered this question affirmatively with the assurance that the role of the churches in the years ahead was quite obvious. The religious societies should continue to provide Christian men and women to serve as educators and missionaries to the Indians. These people, who would go among the Indians for higher and nobler purposes than pecuniary gain, would provide the only means to reclaim the Indians from lives of barbarism, idolatry, and savagery. The Christian teaching, which would educate the Indians to be sober, industrious, and self-reliant, would surely elevate "these untutored and unciliv-ized people to a higher plane of existence."[17]

But what about the expectations that selection by the churches of Christian men to serve as Indian agents would bring "New Hope for the Indians"? Secretary of the Interior Henry Teller confirmed the termination of this supposedly enlightened concept in a letter to the secretary of the missionary society of the Methodist Episcopal Church on August 5, 1882. Teller bluntly declared that he would no longer ask religious bodies to recommend nominees for posts as Indian agents. Speaking rather callously, he insisted that he saw no reason why government officials should be selected for one class of government employment by religious bodies and not for all. Since the Indian agent was, essentially, the business manager of the Indians, he must be a good businessman as well as a man with notable Christian qualities. Without mentioning specific cases, Teller charged that some of the grossest frauds in the history of Indian affairs had been perpetrated on the Indians and the government since the religious bodies had been allowed to select agents. The secretary concluded that the record of frequent changes in these appointments was sufficient evidence of many mistakes, "and my own observation has convinced me that no benefit accrued to the service by this method of selection."[18]

Those attending the annual meeting of churchmen and the Board of Indian Commissioners on January 16, 1883, read Secretary Teller's letter with dismay. One delegate then dejectedly expressed the feelings shared by all by simply noting, "After receiving this communication, we considered ourselves mustered out of service. . . ."[19] John Lowrie, who had attended the meeting as usual, conveyed the sad news to members of the Presbyterian Church in his annual report of the Board of Foreign Missions in 1883. His words might well have reflected the feelings of all the disappointed Americans who had originally seen in the Peace Policy a compassionate and effective vehicle for uplifting the Indians. "The influence of the manner of making appointments," Lowrie wrote,

in use from 1870 to 1877, and less completely in use from 1877 to 1881, can not but remain in the public mind. The Missionary Boards are now relieved from a difficult and delicate duty; and while mistakes have sometimes been made by them, particularly as to the efficiency of some of their nominees, it is yet true that there was a great improvement over the plans previously followed; and the attention of the country was turned to the importance of having good and able men in these agencies. The great abuses so common in former times, are not likely to be generally tolerated hereafter.[20]

The great experiment was over. What went wrong? Any analysis of the reasons why the Peace Policy did not live up to expectations in its application to the Navajo tribe might begin with an examination of the records of the men who received appointments as Indian agents at Fort Defiance. Obviously, those selected were not the saints described in the rhetoric of their recommendations. They could not speak the Indians' language, and they had little or no advance knowledge of the history and culture of the tribe entrusted to their care. But their employers did not expect the applicants to have these qualifications. Employment of local interpreters would overcome the language barrier and the agent could soon obtain a minimal but adequate understanding of the tribal culture. Since one goal of the Peace Policy was to replace old tribal societies with something called the white man's civilization, it was simply not regarded as worthwhile for an agent to spend much time plumbing the depths of tribal ethnohistory at his agency. Even with an objective understanding of these conditions, one would probably have still agreed with William Truax when he told John Lowrie in 1873, "I fear this Indian Agency business is giving you more anxiety than any other department of your work.

Too many persons want to be Agents. But, alas, how few really comprehend the duties and responsibilities of the position."[21]

The Presbyterian agents assigned to the Navajo reservation, who had formerly resided in small towns in the East, were woefully ignorant of the simple realities of day-to-day living at a remote Indian agency. The $1,500 annual salary soon proved inadequate for the cost of living on the frontier. If other agencies usually provided acceptable housing for the agent and his family, at Fort Defiance the overwhelming testimony about the deplorable condition of the agent's living quarters left no doubt that these were the crudest kind of ramshackle structures imaginable. If an agent refused to subject his wife and children to such outrageous living conditions, then his financial burden was increased by the requirement to support his family back home. Without denying that religious zeal may have contributed to the initial desire of the Presbyterians to help the Indians, certainly none of the agents would have agreed with John Lowrie when, defending the agent's salary as adequate, he declared that all Indian agents should cheerfully carry out their tasks with a higher motive than monetary considerations.[22]

The sense of frustration, experienced at one time or another by all the Presbyterians assigned as Navajo agents, must have been intensified by the inability of these well-meaning men to attain objectives anticipated in directives received from their employer. When the agents tried to end the nefarious whiskey trade with the Indians, their attempts were thwarted by only token efforts to enforce existing laws prohibiting such activity. There were occasions when the Navajos, always described by the agents as peaceful and law abiding, committed depredations on their neighbors. The agents invariably reported these incidents as arising from extreme provocations, but the Office of Indian Affairs was usually inclined to regard the agent at fault, in some manner, for not keeping his charges under control. And what could be more exasperating to an agent than to report continued crop failures from Indians who were trying to achieve self-sufficiency. Although the crop failures on the Navajo reservation could have been correctly attributed to the vagaries of weather and barren soil conditions, the government still expected the Indians to accept the agricultural panacea offered to cure all their ills.

Turning from these rather negative observations, other more positive aspects of Presbyterian endeavors with the Navajos should also be acknowledged. To help the Indians develop their skills in agricultural pursuits, the agents could suggest improvements in irrigation practices, utilization of more efficient farming implements, and adoption of more productive strains of seed grains. On the Navajo reservation, support for the introduction of greater numbers of sheep and goats brought lasting and diverse benefits to the tribe. Some of the agents, or the missionaries assigned to the agency, used their medical ability to treat a variety of illnesses. Though not always successful, and probably reaching only a small fraction of the Navajo population, the medical treatment must have helped, in some cases, to alleviate suffering and disease. The agents were, apparently, basically honest. Despite insinuations of wrongdoing by jealous critics, there were no charges sustained against the agents for fraudulent use of agency funds. Finally, the agents and missionaries felt compelled to establish a school for the Indians. If results did not initially measure up to expectations, no one at the time would have questioned the need to provide this opportunity for long-range benefits to the Indians who, presumably, could not advance beyond their degraded position without attaining some degree of literacy.

Regrettably, the inability of agents and missionaries to maintain the cordial and compatible relationships anticipated in the philosophy of the Peace Policy was a source of great disappointment to all parties concerned. At the beginning of President Grant's benevolent new program in 1870, a writer in the *New York Times* spoke of "The Duty of the Churches to the Indians." According to this analyst, "The heart of every wild people is especially open to the sentiment of religion. A missionary comes as if from above. He has no selfish aims."[23] Were the Presbyterian missionaries assigned to the Navajo agency selfish? If being selfish meant anticipating a financial remuneration that would enable them to subsist somewhere above the edge of poverty, then they were, perhaps understandably, selfish. On the other hand, if selfish meant being self-centered in their conduct at Fort Defiance, then they clearly had selfish aims. James Roberts and the other Presbyterian missionaries were always totally dogmatic in their understanding of the correctness of their beliefs. Right was right, and wrong was wrong, and there was no room for compromising on God's word. In the frontier society of the Southwest, evil was detected everywhere. But one wonders if it was really aiding the cause to belittle an agent's performance for applying practical as well as scriptural guidelines in decisions that would obviously benefit the Indians. Petty indictments of agents for their transgressions were quite common, and the longed-for harmony of purpose between men of kindred faith at an agency was seldom achieved.

In New York City, at the Offices of the Board of Foreign Missions of the Presbyterian Church, John Lowrie tried his best to make the Peace Policy work in his area of responsibility. Of course, problems associated with mission stations throughout the world often occupied much of his time. And there were other Indian tribes assigned to his jurisdiction besides the Navajos. With very limited funds for the financial support of all his missionaries in the field, he could do little more than act as a cheerleader on the sidelines for the churchmen and women at Fort Defiance, always assuring them that they were God's instruments in a divinely ordained enterprise. For the Presbyterian agents, Lowrie did try, in most cases, to at least support their viewpoints in differences of opinion with the Office of Indian Affairs. The emergence of differences of opinion, however, between the Board of Foreign Missions and the Board of Home Missions about responsibility for mission work among the Indians came at a time when a unified support group could surely have carried out the objectives of the church in this area of concern more effectively. If the Presbyterians really believed in the critical nature of the Indian problem at this time, then one might have hoped that their intradenominational rivalries could have been set aside in the interest of creating a clearly defined partnership arrangement between the two boards to provide "New Hope for the Indians."

Certainly administrators of Indian affairs in Washington had to share the blame for any shortcomings experienced in the development of the Peace Policy in the Southwest. Although the term "credibility gap" appeared much later in American history to describe controversial events occurring in the nation's capital, the same expression would have served well to characterize the words and deeds of federal officials who worked with the new Indian program. While government spokesmen poured forth their declarations of hearty and continuing support, unity of purpose among all branches of the government, and results beyond expectations, the agents at Fort Defiance tried to explain to the Indians why treaty obligations remained unfulfilled, why there was no money available to feed those who were starving, and why the president seemed to change his mind so often about his plans for helping the Indians. Regarding the alleged spirit of camaraderie prevalent among all government agencies participating in the Peace Policy, embarrassing incidents occurred all too often where manifestations of internal strife surfaced to disrupt the harmonious atmosphere. For example, the bickering between the Departments of the Army and the Interior about division of responsibility in implementing Indian policy had more far-reaching implications than rivalries between mission boards. In Washington, there were annual campaigns to return all these responsibilities to the War Department, from whence they were injudiciously removed in 1849. Regrettably, this very intense rivalry often affected Indian agencies in the West at critical times when Indian agents thought they needed, but could not secure, the cooperation of nearby army garrisons to maintain law and order on the reservations.[24]

In Congress, where decisions about allotment of funds in annual budgets had a decisive bearing on implementation of Indian policy, a spirit of division rather than unity was also evident in heated discussions of the Indian problem. In the Senate, during debate on the Indian appropriation bill in 1871, a spirited exchange between Senator William Stewart of Nevada and Senator Samuel Pomeroy of Kansas vividly illustrated the depth of feeling on this matter:

Mr. Stewart: I think we cannot discuss the Indian question too much. . . . I want to say right here that I believe every dollar appropriated by Indians tends to demoralize the Indians and the whites, tends to prevent the Indians from becoming civilized, teaches them to live in idleness, induces both parties to keep up Indian wars, and demoralizes the country. I do not believe that human nature, when fed, will labor, and I do not believe that Indians can ever become civilized without labor. I believe this system of appropriating money for Indians and taxing white men and making them to work and feed Indians is the radical evil at the bottom of this whole business. It is the source of all the corruption in the management of our Indian affairs. I am opposed to the whole bill.[25]

Senator Pomeroy, who hoped that Senator Stewart's remarks were not to be taken seriously, replied with a plea for compassionate understanding:

Mr. Pomeroy: When we were weak and the Indians were strong we were glad to make treaties with them and live up to those treaties. Now we have grown powerful and they have grown weak, and it does not become this great nation to turn around and trample upon the rights of the weak. . . . Now that these poor people are fast fading away from the earth, it is no time for us to put the heel of power, the heel of oppression upon them, and to say we will disregard our obligations and turn them out to perish.[26]

Unswayed by these comments, Senator Stewart continued with a sweeping indictment of the whole Indian policy and the evils derived from it:

You keep a few aristocratic big Indians, big Indian chiefs, drunk, swaggering and oppressing the weak. . . . I am utterly opposed to making treaties with a few drunken Indians, giving them large amounts of money to squander, men who enslave their wives, who enslave their children; brutes who are made so by your bounty. It is an outrage upon humanity; it is a disgrace to the country. The whole Indian policy of feeding drunken, worthless, vagabond Indians, giving them money to squander between them and their Indian agents, has been a growing disgrace to this country for years.[27]

In the Southwest, the Navajo chiefs would surely have resented Senator Stewart's outspoken denunciation of all Indians who were subjected to the white man's well-meaning efforts to solve the Indian problem. During the decade when the principles of the Peace Policy prevailed in the conduct of Indian affairs at Fort Defiance, leaders of the Navajo tribe reacted to government programs instituted in their behalf in a manner that was quite understandable under the circumstances. One might conclude, quite simply, that they learned to play the white man's game. Aware of numerous material advantages that could be secured for themselves and the rest of the Navajos from the government's largess, Manuelito and the other chiefs gladly accepted what was offered to "uplift" the tribe in the form of food rations and annuity goods. If they were less responsive to the teaching and preaching of Presbyterian missionaries, they did succeed in conveying the impression that a more positive reaction to these particular civilizing and Christianizing overtures would surely be obtained when adequate facilities and competent personnel were provided for these purposes. Like anyone else placed in their situation, the Navajos tolerated the government's efforts when those efforts came from reasonably competent and sincere agents. However, the Navajos soon found ways to bring about the removal of agents who clearly did not have the Indians's best interests at heart. If the Navajos did not make giant steps during this period toward the position assigned to them in the white man's society, they succeeded, sometimes in spite of directives that they must have regarded as absurd, in reacting with adaptive responses that at least ensured their survival.

Before dismissing the Presbyterian efforts to help the Navajos during the Peace Policy era as unproductive or even ridiculous, it would be helpful to call again for an understanding of the spirit of the times. In the desire to right past wrongs and lead a so-called degraded race to salvation, perhaps too much was expected. When W. F. M. Arny accepted appointment to the Navajo agency in September 1873, he hoped the results of his efforts would be as a "light placed upon a hill which will give light and Christian life under the blessing of God to all around."[28] One is struck at once by the similarity to the City Upon a Hill envisioned by John Winthrop for the Puritan experiment in Massachusetts in 1630. When the glittering vision began to tarnish, the churchmen gradually realized the goal as originally conceived would not be attained.

In the same year that the Navajo agent hoped to place his "light upon a hill," William Truax, the discouraged missionary at that agency, sounded an alarm. "The whole Christian Church is in great danger," he warned, "of having her garments soiled by this Indian business."[29] A decade later John Lowrie finally announced termination of the government's plan to look to missionary boards for recommendations for agency appointments. According to Lowrie, the old procedures in vogue before the Peace Policy would probably be renewed. Folloiwng this announcement, some of the Presbyterians might have breathed a sigh of relief as they questioned, with the benefit of hindsight, earlier decisions of church leaders to involve their church in matters properly identified with civil jurisdiction. Perhaps the Christian Church did, then, shake her garments, trying to remove any residual stains of this particular part of the "Indian business" as the churchmen moved on to support other avenues of approach to solution of the Indian problem.[30]

Epilogue

Following their tour of duty at Fort Defiance, the missionaries who served there during the period of the Grant Peace Policy moved on to other assignments in the West. From 1873 to 1881, when James Roberts maintained a mission station at Taos, New Mexico, he organized several Presbyterian churches for Mexican-Americans in small communities in northern New Mexico and southern Colorado. In 1881 he moved with his wife and six children to Anaheim, California, where he died on May 5, 1885. After leaving Fort Defiance in the spring of 1875, John Menaul resided briefly at the Southern Apache agency in New Mexico where he served as agency physician. In 1876 he opened a mission at the Laguna Indian Pueblo, about forty miles west of Albuquerque, where he and his wife labored with distinction until 1889. After various assignments at churches in and near Albuquerque, in 1903 the Menauls retired in Hinton, Oklahoma, where Charity Ann died on November 19, 1906, and John on January 9, 1912. William Truax's appointment in the spring of 1875 as Hopi agent lasted only until the Office of Indian Affairs decided to abolish the agency as a separate entity in the fall of 1876. Truax then accepted various teaching and preaching positions in the Midwest. He died at his retirement home in Perth Amboy, New Jersey, on February 23, 1885. John Lowrie, overseer of the work of these missionaries while they worked with the Navajos, finally retired in 1891 after serving for fifty-three years as assistant secretary and secretary of the Board of Foreign Missions. Honored as one of the most influential directors of the mission policy of his church in the late nineteenth century, he died May 31, 1900, in his ninety-second year.[1]

Of the men who served as agents to the Navajos during this period, two attracted the attention of the Office of Indian Affairs in later years. Embittered by the events leading to his dismissal in the fall of 1875, W. F. M. Arny petitioned Commissioner of Indian Affairs J. Q. Smith on several occasions early in 1876 for copies of all charges brought against him by the army. He also demanded reimbursement for food supplies retained by Major William R. Price at Fort Defiance, which Arny insisted were his private property purchased with his own funds. There is no indication that Arny ever obtained satisfaction in these matters, and he was in dire financial straits when, on September 18, 1881, he died in Topeka, Kansas, during a projected trip to England to claim an inheritance. The heirs of James Miller tried for over a year following his death in June 1872 to secure support from the Departments of the Army and Interior to pay for transporting the remains of the murdered agent to a cemetery near his wife's home in Pennsylvania. Apparently this goal was never achieved as a marker dedicated to Miller in this cemetery has been identified as a memorial only.[2]

Two other prominent members of the cast of characters who were involved in helping the Indians, albeit in differing roles, attained claims to fame after their experiences with the Navajos. Although his persistent attempts to receive an appointment as agent at Fort Defiance were continually rebuffed, Thomas Keams maintained his residence on or near the Navajo reservation long after the departure of the last Presbyterian agent. He eventually built a famous trading post in the canyon which now bears his name on the Hopi reservation, where he resided until his death at his family home in England on November 30, 1904. In his role as superintendent of Presbyterian home mission work in the Rocky Mountain West, Sheldon Jackson made numerous trips to New Mexico and Arizona, promoting the establishment of schools on Indian reservations. He took particular interest in 1880 in recruiting children from various tribes in the Southwest, including the Navajos, to attend the new government boarding school for Indians at Carlisle, Pennsylvania. He was also instrumental in opening a regional boarding school for Indian students in Albuquerque, New Mexico, in 1881. He devoted his later years to the task of organizing schools and missions for Indian tribes in Alaska. When he died on May 2, 1909, a writer in a Denver newspaper eulogized him as "a modern Zaccheaeus, in the double sense that he was short of stature and had a desire to see."[3]

The efforts by Jackson and his confederates in the Presbytery of Santa Fe to wrest control of Indian mission work from the Board of Foreign Missions continued to find support from those in the Presbyterian Church who had become convinced that, logically, the board of Home Missions should have this responsibility. Typical arguments advanced at the time for making this change appeared in two Presbyterian periodicals. Writing in *The Interior* in 1878, one of Jackson's missionaries stationed in southern Colorado spoke of "The Home Board for Home Fields." Referring specifically to the situation at the Navajo agency, he concluded that those Indians had advanced to the point where "they need but one more engine of good, the Home Missionary, to make them dwellers in settled habitations." In the same year, George G. Smith, pastor of the Presbyterian church in Santa Fe, penned an article for Jackson's newspaper, the *Rocky Mountain Presbyterian*. He argued that the Home Board could "surround and besiege the positions of all the tribes accessible to our labors as the Foreign Board, gauged for foreign work, can not hope ever to do. . . . The Indians lie in the great highways of the forward march of the army of the Board of Home Missions." Delegates to the annual General Assembly of the church debated this issue at length each year until 1884 when, yielding to this militant rhetoric, they finally declared that all missions conducted by the Foreign Board among the Indians should be transferred henceforth to the Home Mission Board.[4]

If the Presbyterians concerned with civilizing and Christianizing the Indians regarded the Assembly action of 1884 as a long-needed step in the right direction toward solving the Indian problem as it related to their particular interests, other churchmen, Christian laymen, and many government officials applauded a new approach adopted in Washington to deal with the perplexing issue of reforming Indian policy. New interest groups such as the Indian Rights Association, founded in 1882, and the Lake Mohonk Conference of the Friends of the Indian, convened annually from 1883, exerted pressure on Congress to pass legislation providing for allotment of land in severalty to Indians residing on reservations. These lobbying efforts helped to secure passage of a bill in 1887 which became identified with one of its sponsors, Senator Henry L. Dawes of Massachusetts. The Dawes Severalty Act authorized the president to permit allotments, generally in blocks of 160 acres, of reservation lands to tribal members who could receive final title to this land if they held it for twenty-five years. Interpreting this action as a truly enlightened response to the spirit of the times, Senator Dawes confidently described the new law as "a self-acting machine that we have set going, and if we only run it on the track it will work itself all out, and all these difficulties . . . will pass away like snow in the spring time, and we will never know when they go; we will only know they are gone."[5]

On the Navajo reservation, Chief Manuelito may not have appreciated the significance for his people of the new "self-acting machine." Despondent over the deaths of two of his sons, who were attending the Carlisle Indian School, he died in 1893 after suffering for several years from acute alcoholism. Some of the plans advanced by the Presbyterian agents for improving the lot of the Navajos did reach fruition, however. By executive order in 1878 and 1880, President Hayes authorized enlargements of the reservation which provided the Indians with more land east, west and south of the original reservation boundaries. The government also finally approved location of a subagency in the fertile San Juan River valley in 1903. As for the Presbyterian school for Navajo children at Fort Defiance, Sheldon Jackson managed to keep it staffed with teachers whom he recruited until 1885. After that date, Presbyterian involvement in school work on the reservation ceased until 1901 when the Home Mission Board authorized the reopening of a mission and school for the Navajos at Ganado, Arizona. This school operates today, with support from the Presbyterian Church, as the College of Ganado, an accredited junior college drawing much of its enrollment from Navajo students.[6]

The only current visible relic of the Presbyterian presence at the Navajo agency during the period of the Grant Peace Policy can be found in a tiny graveyard near the present community of Fort Defiance. Here an eroded stone marker, inscribed simply "Rev. A. H. Donaldson," identifies the final resting place of the young missionary teacher whose sudden death abruptly ended his efforts to work with the Navajos. When the grief-stricken Mrs. Donaldson prepared to leave the agency to return to her former home, she sent one last letter to Sheldon Jackson. "Oh, it is so hard to have to give up so soon," the bereaved widow wrote, "to go back in less than a year and to go alone, is so hard."[7] The implications of this obviously heartfelt sentiment should not be ignored in analysis of this rather extraordinary episode in the history of American Indian policy. Despite records of inept administration, petty jealousies and insincere motivation, there were still many well-meaning men and women who fought the good fight, as they perceived it, and they were loath to have to retreat so soon in the face of insurmountable obstacles as they struggled to give "New Hope for the Indians."

Notes

Preface

1. "New Hope for the Indians," *The Record of the Presbyterian Church in the United States of America*, 21 (October 1870): 227.

2. The reference here is to the northern branch of the church, known at the time as the Presbyterian Church in the United States of America.

Chapter 1

1. For a useful and objective account of the tragedy at Sand Creek, see Stan Hoig, *The Sand Creek Massacre* (Norman: The University of Oklahoma Press, 1961).

2. Report of the Commissioner of Indian Affairs, 1850, *Senate Executive Document No. 1*, 31 Congress, 2 session, serial 587, pp. 35–36. For the development of antebellum reservation policy, see Robert A. Trennert, Jr., *Alternative to Extinction: Federal Indian Policy and the Beginnings of the Reservation System, 1846–1851* (Philadelphia: Temple University Press, 1975).

3. Treaty with the Arapahoe and Cheyenne, February 15, 1861, in Charles J. Kappler, ed., *Indian Treaties, 1778–1883* (New York: Interland Publishing Co., 1972, reprint of 1904 edition), p. 809.

4. Francis Paul Prucha, *American Indian Policy in Crisis: Christian Reformers and the Indian, 1865–1900* (Norman: The University of Oklahoma Press, 1976), p. 13.

5. For identification of those dedicated to reform of Indian policy and the story of their activities, see Robert W. Mardock, *The Reformers and the American Indian* (Columbia: The University of Missouri Press, 1971).

6. *United States Statutes at Large*, XIII, 572–73. Other members of the Dool-

ittle Committee were Senators Lafayette S. Foster of Connecticut and James W. Nesmith of Oregon, and Representatives Asahel W. Hubbard of Iowa, William Highby of California, Lewis W. Ross of Illinois, and William Windom of Minnesota. For the complete record of the testimony presented at the Sand Creek hearings, see Massacre of the Cheyenne Indians in Report of the Joint Committee on the Conduct of the War, *Senate Report No. 142*, 38 Congress, 2 session, serial 1214, pp. I–VI, 1–108 and Proceedings of a Military Commission Convened by Special Orders 23, Headquarters District of Colorado, Denver, Colorado Territory, February 1, 1865, in the Case of Colonel J. M. Chivington, First Colorado Cavalry, *Senate Executive Documents No. 26*, 39 Congress, 2 session, serial 1277, pp. 1–228.

7. Condition of the Indian Tribes, Report of the Joint Special Committee Appointed Under Joint Resolution of March 3, 1865, with an Appendix, *Senate Report No. 156*, 39 Congress, 2 session, serial 1279, pp. 3–10. Defending the historical significance of the Doolittle Report is Donald Chaput, "Generals, Indian Agents, Politicians: The Doolittle Survey of 1865," *Western Historical Quarterly*, 3 (July 1972): 269–82. Taking issue with Chaput on the value of the report to historians is Harry Kelsey, "The Doolittle Report of 1867: Its Preparation and Shortcomings," *Arizona and the West*, 17 (Summer 1975): 107–20.

8. *United States Statutes at Large*, XV, 17–18. Along with Commissioner Taylor, who was a former Methodist minister, the other civilian members of the commission were Samuel F. Tappan of Colorado, a well-known advocate of Indian rights; Senator John B. Henderson of Missouri, chairman of the Senate Committee on Indian Affairs; and John B. Sanborn, a lawyer from Washington, D.C. Appointees from the army were Generals William T. Sherman, Afred H. Terry, William S. Harney, and Christopher C. Augur. The complete texts of the eight treaties are in Kappler, *Treaties*, pp. 977–89, 998–1023.

9. Report of the Indian Peace Commissioners, *House Executive Document No. 97*, 40 Congress, 2 session, serial 1337, pp. 16, 20–22. A spokesman for the Board of Foreign Missions of the Presbyterian Church expressed general approval of the report, although "the remarks . . . about so much money being sent to Asia and Africa might well have been omitted." "Report of the Indian Peace Commission," *The Record of the Presbyterian Church in the United States of America*, 19 (March 1868): 66.

10. A somewhat outdated but still adequate general discussion of the involvement of the Quakers with the Peace Policy is Rayner W. Kelsey, *Friends and the Indians, 1655–1917* (Philadelphia: Associated Executive Committee of Friends on Indian Affairs, 1917). For a thoughtful case study of more recent vintage on this topic, see Clyde A. Milner II, *With Good Intentions: Quaker Work Among the Pawnees, Otos, and Omahas in the 1870s* (Lincoln: University of Nebraska Press, 1982).

11. James D. Richardson, ed., *A Compilation of the Messages and Papers of the Presidents*, 11 vols. (Washington: Bureau of National Literature and Art, 1911), 6:3962.

12. President Grant's authority to appoint the army officers was derived from an act of 1834 providing for the organization of the Department of Indian Affairs. Section four of that act included the statement: "And it shall be competent for the President to require any military officer of the United States to execute the duties of Indian agent." *United States Statutes at Large*, IV, 736.

13. Ibid., XVI, 40.

14. J. D. Cox, Secretary of the Interior to Felix R. Brunot, Esq., July 5, 1869, Letters Sent, Indian Division, Office of the Secretary of the Interior [OSI] 1849–1903, Record Group [RG] 48, National Archives [NA], Microcopy M606, Roll 8; Report of the Commissioner of Indian Affairs, 1869, *House Executive Document No. 1, Part 3*, 41 Congress, 2 session, serial 1414, pp. 486–93. The first appointees to the board were William Welsh, Philadelphia; John V. Farwell, Chicago; George H. Stuart, Philadelphia; Robert Campbell, St. Louis; William E. Dodge, New York; Edward S. Tobey, Boston; Felix R. Brunot, Pittsburgh; Nathan Bishop, New York; and Henry S. Lane, Indiana. Vincent Colyer, New York, was added in July 1869.

15. Report of the Secretary of the Interior, 1869, serial 1414, pp. X–XI. Francis Paul Prucha described the Peace Policy as, basically, "a state of mind, a determination that since the old ways of dealing with the Indians had not worked, new ways which emphasized kindness and justice must be tried." Prucha, *Indian Policy*, p. 30.

16. Report of the Commissioner of Indian Affairs, 1869, serial 1414, pp. 446–47. For an excellent biography of Parker, see William H. Armstrong, *Warrior in Two Camps: Ely S. Parker, Union General and Seneca Chief* (Syracuse: Syracuse University Press, 1978).

17. Richardson, *Messages and Papers of the Presidents*, 6:3992–93.

Chapter 2

1. The Presbyterian Church had divided into Old School and New School factions in 1837. The Old School group insisted on the use of Presbyterian mission boards to operate the mission program within the church. The New School adherents saw wider appeal in working with national mission societies supported by all good Christians. The coming of the Civil War compounded the problems of fragmentation in the church. In 1857 the New School faction split into northern and southern branches, and in 1861 the Old School also divided. McFarland's missionary commission was from the Old School faction of the northern branch of the church. The complex issues related to this process of fragmentation are discussed in Earl R. MacCormac, "The Development of Presbyterian Missionary Organizations: 1790–1870," *Journal of Presbyterian History*, 43 (September 1965): 149–173.

2. Lonnie J. White, ed., *Chronicle of a Congressional Journey: The Doolittle Committee in the Southwest, 1865* (Boulder, Colorado: Pruett Publishing Co., 1975), pp. 46–51.

3. Cornelia Martin to Vincent Colyer, Secretary, Board of Indian Commissioners, May 30, 1871, Board of Indian Commissioners [BIC] Letters Received, 1870–1872, 5 vols., RG75, NA, 2: 109. Bishop Jean Baptiste Lamy had arrived in New Mexico in 1851. In 1866 his inspired leadership of the Catholic community was well-illustrated in plans for construction of an imposing new cathedral in Santa Fe. Lamy's early experiences in New Mexico are thoroughly documented in Paul Horgan, *Lamy of Santa Fe: His Life and Times* (New York: Farrar, Straus, and Giroux, 1975). For a more critical appraisal of Lamy's career, see Fray Angelico Chavez, *But Time and Chance: The Story of Padre Martinez of Taos, 1793–1867* (Santa Fe, New Mexico: Sunstone Press, 1981).

4. Sandra L. Myres, ed., *Cavalry Wife: The Diary of Eveline M. Alexander, 1866–1867* (College Station, Texas: Texas A & M University Press, 1977), pp. 111–12.

5. *The Annual of Washington and Jefferson College, Washington, Pennsylvania* (Buffalo, New York: Gies and Co., 1889), pp. 99–100; *Santa Fe New Mexican,* January 12, 1867; Edith J. Agnew and Ruth K. Barber, "The Unique Presbyterian School System of New Mexico," *Journal of Presbyterian History,* 49 (Fall 1971): 202. Alice Blake, "Spanish Speaking Missions in New Mexico," manuscript, Presbyterian Historical Society [PHS], pp. 28–29. McFarland's little school was called the Santa Fe Collegiate Institute until December 6, 1870, when it was chartered under the laws of New Mexico in rather grandiose fashion as the Santa Fe University, Industrial, and Agricultural College. "Historical Narrative of the Presbytery of Santa Fe," October 19, 1871, Minutes, Synod of Colorado, 1871–1888, PHS, p. 7.

6. "A Plea for New Mexico," *The Presbyterian Banner* (Pittsburgh, Pennsylvania), April 3, 10, and 17, 1867.

7. Lowrie to McFarland, May 24, 1867, Board of Foreign Missions [BFM], Letterpress Copies of Letters Sent, PHS, RG31-42-8, pp. 210–12; Myres, *Cavalry Wife,* p. 160. In 1837, the General Assembly of the Presbyterian Church gave the care of American Indian missions to the Board of Foreign Missions, reasoning, perhaps, that Indian tribes were treated, in some respects, as foreign nations, and, of course, they did speak foreign languages. Sherman H. Doyle, *Presbyterian Home Missions* (Philadelphia: Presbyterian Board of Publications and Sabbath School Work, 1902), p. 74. For a useful analysis of Lowrie's work with Indian missions, see Henry G. Waltmann, "John C. Lowrie and Presbyterian Indian Administration, 1870–1882," *Journal of Presbyterian History,* 54 (Summer 1976): 259–76.

8. For a good account of the army's campaigns against the Navajos, see Frank D. Reeve, "The Federal Indian Policy in New Mexico, 1858–1880, Part I," *New Mexico Historical Review,* 12 (July 1937): 218–69.

9. White, *Chronicle,* p. 39. The experiences of the Navajos at the Bosque Redondo are fully discussed in Gerald E. Thompson, *The Army and the Navajo: The Bosque Redondo Reservation Experiment, 1863–68* (Tucson: University of Arizona Press, 1976).

10. Condition of the Indian Tribes, serial 1279, p. 433.

11. Lowrie to McFarland, May 24 and July 5, 1867, BFM, Letters Sent, RG31-42-8, pp. 210–12, 215–16.

12. Kappler, *Treaties*, pp. 1015–20.

13. Blake, "Spanish Speaking Missions," pp. 77–78. This author believed that the ladies of the mission association "had an idea that a large strong looking man would have a civilizing influence over the savages." James Roberts appeared to be the ideal type, so they offered him the position.

14. Lowrie to Roberts, July 15, 1868, BFM, Letters Sent, RG31-42-8, p. 241; O. H. Browning, Secretary of the Interior to the Secretary of War, October 13, 1868, OSI, M606, Roll 8; Browning to the Commissioner of Indian Affairs, October 19, 1868, OSI, M606, Roll 9; *The New Mexico, Arizona, and Colorado Missionary Association, Annual Report, 1869*, p. 11, bound as *Our Mission Field* in the Sheldon Jackson Collection, PHS.

15. *The Record of the Presbyterian Church in the United States of America*, 19 (December 1868): 281 and 20 (January 1869): 11. Actually the "Romanist priests" had exhibited great interest in developing an educational program for Navajo children at the Bosque Redondo. Bishop Lamy's plans included assigning a priest to teach at Fort Sumner and sending some of the Indian children to a Catholic school in Santa Fe. These plans came to naught with the collapse of Carleton's experiment. Conditions of the Indian Tribes, serial 1279, pp. 148–49, 187–88, 224.

16. Francis P. Prucha, *A Guide to the Military Posts of the United States, 1789–1895* (Madison: The State Historical Society of Wisconsin, 1944), p. 71; Lawrence C. Kelly, "Where Was Fort Canby?" *New Mexico Historical Review*, 42 (January 1967): 49–62. For an informative account of the early history of Fort Defiance, see Maurice Frink, *Fort Defiance and the Navajos* (Boulder, Colorado: Pruett Press, 1968).

17. Roberts to Lowrie, January 20, 1869, American Indian Correspondence [AIC], Letters Received, Record Group Ms In25, file B-1, document 148, PHS.

18. Ibid.

19. Mrs. James Roberts to Lowrie, January 29, 1869, AIC, B-1, 150; Roberts to Lowrie, March 4, 1869, AIC, B-1, 167.

20. French to J. M. Gallegos, Superintendent of Indian Affairs to New Mexico, March 26 and June 18, 1869, Office of Indian Affairs [OIA], Records of the New Mexico Superintendency of Indian Affairs, 1849–1880, RG75, NA, Microcopy T21, Roll 9.

21. Roberts to Lowrie, March 4, 1869, AIC, B-1, 167.

22. Report of the Secretary of the Interior, 1869, serial 1414, pp. 531–32. Vincent Colyer devoted much of his life to support of various reform movements. Active in the abolitionist cause in the antebellum years, he raised and commanded a black regiment during the war. In May 1868, when a group of private citizens formed the United States Indian Commission to publicize the need for reform in the Indian service, Colyer served as secretary of that

organization until he accepted a similar position with the Board of Indian Commissioners in July 1869. *The National Cyclopaedia of American Biography,* 58 vols. (New York: James T. White & Co., 1897), 7:541.

23. Roberts to Lowrie, July 10, 1869, AIC, B-1, 195.

24. Report of the Secretary of the Interior, 1869, serial 1414, p. 531.

25. Roberts to Lowrie, March 4 and April 8, 1869, AIC, B-1, 167, 176.

26. McFarland to Lowrie, April 6, 1869, AIC, B-1, 174.

27. *Missionary Association, 1869,* pp. 11–12 and *1870,* p. 11.

28. Ely Parker to Major William Clinton, Superintendent of Indian Affairs for New Mexico, November 2, 1869 with copies to McFarland and Roberts, OIA, T21, Roll 8.

29. Charity Ann Gaston to the Santa Fe Association, February 25, 1870, in *Missionary Association, 1870,* p. 15.

30. Roberts to Lowrie, April 15 and September 3, 1869, AIC, B-1, 179, 207.

31. Roberts to Lowrie, October 14, 1869, AIC, B-1, 217.

32. Bennett to Clinton, August 26, September 2, October 15 and October 20, 1869, OIA, T21, Roll 9.

33. Parker to Clinton, August 16, 1869, OIA, T21, Roll 8. The complete text of Governor Mitchell's extraordinary proclamation is in the State Records Center and Archives, Santa Fe, New Mexico.

34. Bennett to Clinton, September 9, 1869, OIA, T21, Roll 9; Parker to Clinton, December 17, 1869, OIA, Letters Sent, 1824–1882, RG75, NA, Microcopy M21, Roll 94; Bennett to Clinton, December 23, 1869, OIA, Letters Received, 1824–1880, New Mexico Superintendency, RG75, NA, Microcopy M234, Roll 557. Surveyors had started to define the boundaries of the Navajo Reservation in 1869, but the appropriation of $36,220 provided for this purpose proved to be inadequate for the vast project. The surveyors suspended their work at the end of the year pending a decision on supplemental funding to complete the task. Parker to Jacob D. Cox, Secretary of the Interior, November 25 and December 8, 1869, Report Books, OIA, 1838–1885, RG75, NA, Microcopy M348, Roll 19. Since the term "Mexican" was widely used at the time to refer to Americans of Mexican or Spanish descent, it will be used in like manner in this study.

35. Bennett to Clinton, September 17 and November 18, 1869, OIA, T21, Roll 9; Report of the Secretary of the Interior, 1869, serial 1414, p. 680. During Colyer's visit to Fort Defiance he had noticed "the usual story of useless goods purchased and forwarded at immense expense, by wagon, thousands of miles. . . ." Report of the Secretary of the Interior, 1869, serial 1414, p. 532.

36. Bennett to Clinton, November 18 and 25, December 1 and 30, 1869, OIA, T21, Roll 9; Bennett to Clinton, December 30, 1869, OIA, M234, Roll 557.

37. *Missionary Association, 1870,* p. 12.

38. Parker to Clinton, November 2, 1869, OIA, T21, Roll 8; Roberts to Lowrie, December 2, 1869, AIC, B-1, 230.

39. Bennett to Clinton, December 23, 1869, OIA, M234, Roll 557.

40. Roberts to Lowrie, July 10, 1869, AIC, B-1, 195.

41. Roberts to Lowrie, March 4 and December 2, 1869, AIC, B-1, 167, 230.

42. "Work for the United Church—A Campaign in the Rocky Mountains," [November, 1869], The Scrapbooks of Sheldon Jackson, 64 vols., PHS, 59: 12.

Chapter 3

1. *United States Statutes at Large*, XVI, 319. For a penetrating analysis of President Grant's motives in expanding the Quaker experiment, see Henry G. Waltmann, "Circumstantial Reformer: President Grant and the Indian Problem," *Arizona and the West*, 13 (Winter 1971): 323–42. Waltmann regards the congressional action of July 15, 1870, as the key factor in extending the program, with Grant's role best defined as "accidental" or "incidental."

2. Vincent Colyer to Felix Brunot, April 13, 1870, BIC, Letters Sent, 1870–1891, 1893–1909, 14 vols., RG75, NA, 1: 54–56.

3. Ibid., June 22, 1870, 104–7 and Colyer to Lowrie, June 6, 1870, 92–94.

4. *Minutes of the General Assembly of the Presbyterian Church in the United States of America* (New York: Presbyterian Board of Publications, 1870), p. 37.

5. Minutes, June 20, 1870, BFM, PHS; Lowrie to Colyer, June 22, 1870, BIC, Letters Received, 1: 68.

6. Cox to Reverend J. B. Treat, July 19, 1870, and Cox to Grenville M. Weeks, Secretary, United States Indian Commission, July 23, 1870, OSI, M606, Roll 10.

7. Bishop to Colyer, June 28, 1870, BIC, Letters Received, 1: 70; Minutes, July 27, 1870, BIC, 3 vols., RG75, NA, 1: 38.

8. Report of the Board of Indian Commissioners, 1870 in *Senate Executive Document No. 39*, 41 Congress, 3 session, serial 1440, pp. 4–5, 97–100; Colyer to Cox, August 11, 1870, BIC, Letters Sent, 1: 151–53.

9. Cox to Brunot, August 20, 1870, BIC, Letters Received, 1869–1899, 5 trays, RG75, NA, tray 1; Cox to Lowrie, August 19 and September 8, 1870, and Colyer to Lowrie, December 16, 1870, AIC, B-2, 276, 277.5, 259. In addition to the five agencies in the Southwest, the Presbyterian Church received the Uintah Valley agency for the Ute Indians in Utah, the Seminole and Choctaw agencies in the Indian Territory, and the Nez Perce agency in Idaho. For a sympathetic history of the work of the Catholic Church with Indian missions at the time, see Peter J. Rahill, *The Catholic Indian Missions and Grant's Peace Policy, 1870–1884* (Washington, D.C.: The Catholic University of America Press, 1953).

10. Roberts to Parker, March 18, 1870, OIA, M234, Roll 557.

11. Bennett to Clinton, March 9, 1870, ibid.

12. Roberts to Parker, March 18, 1870, ibid.; Colyer to Dear Christian Friend, March 22, 1870, BIC, Letters Sent, 1: 33–35.

13. Parker to Clinton, March 26, 1870, OIA, M21, Roll 94; Roberts to Brunot

[June 1870], BIC, Letters Received, 1: 71. Bennett revealed his continuing animosity toward Roberts in a letter transmitting the annual reports from the agency to Clinton. "As the Rev. J. M. Roberts missionary here is doing nothing," Bennett charged, "and as he notified me in my office a few days ago that he had nothing to do with the Government, I considered that no report from him was necessary. . . ." Bennett to Clinton, August 24, 1870, OIA, T21, Roll 12.

14. Roberts to Lowrie, January 11 and June 23, 1870, AIC, B-2, 4, 34; *Missionary Association, 1870*, p. 15; Report of the Commissioner of Indian Affairs, 1870, *House Executive Document, No. 1, Part 4*, 41 Congress, 3 session, serial 1449, pp. 617–18.

15. Roberts to Lowrie, January 11 and June 23, 1870, AIC, B-2, 4, 34.

16. Roberts to Lowrie, January 11, March 1, and April 25, 1870, AIC, B-2, 4, 17, 24.

17. Conditions of the Indian Tribes, serial 1279, p. 357.

18. Clinton to Parker, January 18, 1870, OIA, M234, Roll 557.

19. Parker to Clinton, March 5, 1870, OIA, T21, Roll 11; Report of the Commissioner of Indian Affairs, 1870, serial 1449, pp. 615–16.

20. Parker to Clinton, January 15, 1870, OIA, T21, Roll 11; Report of the Commissioner of Indian Affairs, 1870, serial 1449, p. 613.

21. Parker to Clinton, February 12, 1870, OIA, M21, Roll 93; Report of the Commissioner of Indian Affairs, 1870, serial 1449, pp. 612–13.

22. Report of the Secretary of the Interior, 1869, serial 1414, p. 699; Clinton to Parker, May 30, 1870, Hamilton Fish, Secretary of State, to Cox, June 11, 1870, and Captain S. B. M. Young to Lieutenant John W. Pullman, Post Adjutant, Fort Wingate, New Mexico, August 26, 1870, OIA, M234, Roll 557.

23. Major W. R. Price to Bennett, August 26, 1870, and Clinton to Parker, September 3, 1870, OIA, M234, Roll 557.

24. Circular Letter, Department of the Interior, May 20, 1870, OIA, T21, Roll 12; Report of the Commissioner of Indian Affairs, 1870, serial 1449, pp. 614, 616–17; Clinton to Parker, January 17, 1870, OIA, M234, Roll 557.

25. Major W. R. Price to Parker, September 16, 1870, OSI, Appointment Papers, New Mexico, 1850–1907, RG48, NA, Microcopy M750, Roll 14.

26. *The Presbyterian* (Philadelphia), September 3, 1870.

27. George Ainslie to Lowrie, September 6, 1870, and George McKinley to Lowrie [September 1870], AIC, B-2, 96, 180.

28. McFarland to Lowrie, September 9 and October 10, 1870, AIC, B-2, 106, 203; Lowrie to Cox, August 22, 1870, Lowrie to Parker, September 14, 1870, and Lowrie to Parker, September 20, 1870, BFM, Letters Sent, RG31-43-2, pp. 34, 41, 44. Members of the Board of Indian Commissioners had rejected all suggestions to appoint ministers of the gospel as Indian agents because "persons of that class could not always be found possessed of sufficient mercantile experience or commercial education to make them efficient

officers." Report of the Board of Indian Commissioners, 1870, serial 1440, p. 112.

29. J. P. Newman, Chaplain of the Senate to Lowrie, July 25, 1870; Samuel D. Williamson to Lowrie, September 3, 1870; W. T. Otto, Acting Secretary of the Interior to Lowrie, October 15, 1870; William Rankin to Otto, October 17, 1870; Cox to Lowrie, October 22, 1870; AIC, B-2, 43, 80, 278, 279, 280.

30. Williamson to Parker, November 9, 1870, and A. J. White, Acting Chief Clerk, Department of the Interior to Parker, November 23, 1870, OIA, M234, Roll 557; J. C. Geyer to Lowrie, September 10, 1870; John M. Brown to Lowrie, undated; Parker to Lowrie, November 10, 1870; Miller to Lowrie, December 3, 1870; AIC, B-2, 120, 124, 250, 283; James H. Miller, Service Record, Navy and Old Army Branch, Military Archives Division, NA.

31. "New Hope for the Indians," *The Record of the Presbyterian Church in the United States of America*, 21 (October 1870): 227.

32. Parker to Clinton, May 27, 1870, OIA, M21, Roll 95; Jules Le Carpentier, Acting Assistant Surgeon, U.S. Army to Clinton, October 10, 1870, and Le Carpentier to Nathaniel Pope, December 19, 1870, OIA, M234, Roll 557; *Necrological Reports and Annual Proceedings of Princeton Theological Seminary*, 4 vols. (Princeton, New Jersey: C. S. Robinson and Co., 1891, 1899, 1909, 1919), 4: 165–66; Lowrie to Roberts, August 17 and October 6, 1870, BFM, Letters Sent, RG31-43-2, pp. 29–48.

33. Roberts to Menual, October 23, 1870, AIC, B-2, 211.

34. Menaul to Lowrie, October 31 and November 21, 1870, AIC, B-2, 219, 246.

35. Roberts to Lowrie, November 2 and December 12, 1870, AIC, B-2, 224, 257.

36. Menaul to Lowrie, December 21, 1870, AIC, B-2, 264.

37. Francis B. Heitman, *Historical Register and Dictionary of the United States Army* (Washington, D.C.: Government Printing Office, 1903), p. 798; Pope to Parker, November 30 and December 2, 1870, OIA, M234, Roll 557; H. R. Clum to Pope, December 14, 1870, OIA, M21, Roll 97; *Report of the Commissioner of Indian Affairs to the Secretary of the Interior, 1871* (Washington, D.C.: Government Printing Office, 1872), p. 367.

38. Dumas Malone, ed., *Dictionary of American Biography*, 10 vols. (New York: Charles Scribner's Sons, 1933), 2: 477; Delano to the Acting Commissioner of Indian Affairs, December 8, 1870, OSI, M606, Roll 11. One of Columbus Delano's biographers admitted that Delano had certain deficiencies as an administrator with the statement: "It is impossible to avoid the conclusion that though he was personally honest, he was woefully lacking in high ideals of public service or an appreciation of the responsibility of a department chief." Malone, ed., *Dictionary of American Biography*, 3: 218.

39. Report of the Commissioner of Indian Affairs, 1870, serial 1449, p. 474; Richardson, *Messages and Papers of the Presidents*, 6:4063–64.

40. Miller to Lowrie, December 3, 1870, AIC, B-2, 250.

Chapter 4

1. A comprehensive account of this meeting appears in Report of the Board of Indian Commissioners, 1870, serial 1440, pp. 110–13.

2. Minutes, January 13, 1871, BIC, 1:40–43. One report of the gathering noted that Delano "laid great stress on the fact that to President Grant, and to no other person, belongs all the credit for having inaugurated the successful policy. . . ." *New York Times*, January 14, 1871.

3. Compiled from H. R. Clum, Acting Commissioner of Indian Affairs to John S. Armstrong, Esq., August 23, 1871, OIA, M21, Roll 102. Armstrong was the Presbyterian nominee for the agency at Abiquiu, New Mexico, serving the Capote and Weminuche Ute Indians.

4. Roberts to Lowrie, January 11, 1871, AIC, RG31-40-7, 18; Lowrie to Roberts, January 28, 1871, BFM, Letters Sent, RG31-43-2, pp. 62–64; Roberts to Lowrie, February 16, 1871, AIC, RG31-40-6, 59.

5. Ninth Census, 1870, Town of Neosho, Neosho Township, Neosho County, Missouri. Frank Bennett left the agency to join the Ninth Cavalry Regiment stationed in Texas. His work with the Navajos received commendation in a Santa Fe newspaper with the statement that "he has succeeded better than any of his predecessors in restraining the thieving propensities of this tribe of Indians and recovering stolen property from them." *Santa Fe New Mexican,* February 14, 1871.

6. *Report of the Commissioner of Indian Affairs, 1871*, p. 377; Miller to Pope, February 14, 1871, OIA, M234, Roll 558.

7. Roberts to Lowrie, February 7, 1871, AIC, RG31-40-6, 51$^{1}/_{2}$.

8. Lowrie to George McKinley, April 22, 1871, BFM, Letters Sent, RG31-43-2, p. 78. Charity Ann Gaston agreed with Roberts on this issue. In her view, not one of the government employees at the agency was a Christian or even moral man. She felt that "if God would send the Holy Spirit to their hearts to convince them of sin and lead them to Jesus, how much they might help our work." *Missionary Association, 1870*, p. 15.

9. Lowrie to Miller and Roberts, April 25, 1871, BFM, Letters Sent, RG31-43-2, pp. 79–80; Miller to Lowrie, June 5, 1871, AIC, RG31-40-6, 118.

10. Menaul to Lowrie, January 10, 1871, AIC, RG31-40-7, 16; *Menaul School, Albuquerque, New Mexico: Seventy-Five Years of Service, 1881–1956* (Albuquerque, New Mexico: privately published, 1956), p. 8; Menaul to Lowrie, February 21, 1871, AIC, RG31-40-6, 59.

11. Lowrie to Menaul, January 31, 1871, BFM, Letters Sent, RG31-43-2, p. 65. Menaul concluded, finally, that "it is the opinion of all . . . except Brother Roberts, that I should stay here." Menaul to Lowrie, April 26, 1871, AIC, RG31-40-6, 100.

12. Pope to Bennett, December 17, 1870, OIA, T21, Roll 29; Pope to Parker, February 22, 1871, OIA, M234, Roll 558; Menaul to Lowrie, February 21, 1871, AIC, RG31-40-6, 59.

13. Miller to Pope, February 6, 11, and 22, 1871, OIA, T21, Roll 14; Pope to Parker, February 24 and April 6, 1871, OIA, T21, Roll 29; H. R. Clum to Pope, March 8, 1871, OIA, T21, Roll 13.

14. H. R. Clum to Pope, June 3, 1871, OIA, M21, Roll 102; Miller to Pope, June 23, 1871, OIA, T21, Roll 14; *Report of the Commissioner of Indian Affairs, 1871*, pp. 376–77; *Santa Fe New Mexican*, May 13, 1871.

15. Miller to Lowrie, August 5, 1871, AIC, RG31-40-9, 160.

16. Roberts to Lowrie, November 8, 1871, AIC, RG31-40-8, 228.

17. *Report of the Commissioner of Indian Affairs, 1871*, pp. 375–76.

18. Miller to Lowrie, August 5, 1871, AIC, RG31-40-9, 160; Roberts to Lowrie, May 3, 1871, AIC, RG31-40-6, 106. Williamson D. Crothers, Lowrie's appointee as agent to the Hopi Indians in Arizona, was also impressed with the record of Charity Ann Menaul. He attributed her ability to master the Navajo language to her sincere dedication to her job. On the other hand, Crothers viewed the results of Roberts's efforts as an "unparalleled failure." Crothers to Lowrie, June 20, 1871, AIC, RG31-40-6, 126.

19. Menaul to Lowrie, June 6, 1871, AIC, RG31-40-6, 119.

20. Roberts to Parker, August 7, 1871, OIA, M234, Roll 558; Miller to Lowrie, August 5, 1871, AIC, RG31-40-9, 160; Lowrie to Menaul and Roberts, July 25, 1871, BFM, Letters Sent, RG31-43-2, pp. 92–93.

21. H. R. Clum to Miller, October 21, 1871, OIA, M21, Roll 103; Roberts to Lowrie, October 25, November 8, and November 30, 1871, AIC, RG31-40-8, 223, 228, 241.

22. Miller to Pope, April 30, August 5, and October 1, 1871, OIA, T21, Roll 14; Miller to Pope, October 24, 1871, OIA, M234, Roll 558; *Report of the Commissioner of Indian Affairs, 1871*, pp. 377–78.

23. Pope to Parker, July 16, 1871, and Miller to Pope, July 20, 1871, OIA, M234, Roll 558. For a definitive account of the development of the Navajo sheep enterprise, see John O. Baxter, "Restocking the Navajo Reservation After Bosque Redondo," *New Mexico Historical Review*, 58 (October 1983): 325–45.

24. Miller to Pope, September 1 and November 30, 1871, OIA, T21, Roll 14; Pope to Francis A. Walker, December 11, 1871, OIA, M234, Roll 558; Walker to Columbus Delano, December 15, 1871, OIA, M348, Roll 21; B. R. Cowen, Acting Secretary of the Interior to Honorable James G. Blaine, Speaker, House of Representatives, December 16, 1871, OSI, M606, Roll 10.

25. Frank McNitt, *The Indian Traders* (Norman: University of Oklahoma Press, 1962), pp. 126–27; Pope to Miller, November 10, 1871, OIA, T21, Roll 29; Miller to Pope, November 30, 1871, OIA, M234, Roll 558.

26. Menaul to Lowrie and Miller to Lowrie, August 31, 1871, AIC, RG31-40-9, 182, 184; Walker to Pope, December 26, 1871, OIA, M21, Roll 103; McNitt, *The Indian Traders*, pp. 69, 124–41, 246. According to McNitt, the correct spelling for the surname of the agency clerk was Keam, in accord with the usage by his family at their home in England. However, in the Southwest, he was commonly cited as Keams.

27. Parker to Pope, March 17, 1871, and Clum to Pope, May 17 and July 28, 1871, OIA, T21, Roll 13; Miller to Pope, August 21, 1871, OIA, T21, Roll 14; Benjamin M. Thomas to Lowrie, May 1, 1872, AIC, L-1, 156; Menaul to Lowrie, no date, AIC, B-2, 174¹/₂; Miller to Lowrie, March 4, 1872, AIC, L-1, 76. Thomas's appointment was not officially confirmed until March 1, 1872. A friend of Thomas described him as "a modest yet very active Christian young man, leading when at home in young people's meetings, Christian associations, etc." W. J. Essick to Lowrie, July 2, 1872, AIC, L-1, 209. For more on Thomas's interesting life in New Mexico, see Reba Benge, "Benjamin M. Thomas: Career in the Southwest, 1870–1892," Ph.D. dissertation, University of New Mexico, Albuquerque, New Mexico, 1979.

28. Miller to Pope, March 17 and June 12, 1871, OIA, T21, Roll 14; Ruth Underhill, *The Navajos* (Norman: University of Oklahoma Press, 1956), pp. 161–62.

29. Roberts to Lowrie, July 3 and 5, August 15, 1871, AIC, RG31-40-9, 132, 133, 170.

30. Report of Employees at the Navajo Agency, Second Quarter, 1871, OIA, T21, Roll 14; Menaul to Lowrie, March 9 and June 6, 1871, AIC, RG31-40-6, 74, 119; Menaul to Lowrie, December 12, 1871, AIC, RG31-40-8, 257.

31. Armstrong, *Warrior in Two Camps*, pp. 138, 160; H. Craig Miner, "Francis Walker" in Robert M. Kvasnicka and Herman J. Viola, eds., *The Commissioners of Indian Affairs, 1824–1977* (Lincoln: University of Nebraska Press, 1979), pp. 135–40. Although assuming active control of the Office of Indian Affairs in November, Walker did not receive his official appointment until December 16. According to Miner, when a lapse in appropriations for salaries in the census bureau coincided with a vacancy in the Indian office, Walker received the appointment to the latter post to keep him on the government payroll until the census work could be completed.

32. *Report of the Commissioner of Indian Affairs, 1871*, pp. 1–8.

33. "Report of the Secretary of the Interior, 1871," *House Executive Documents*, 42 Congress, 2 session, serial 1505, pp. 3–11.

34. "Third Annual Report of the Board of Indian Commissioners" in *Report of the Commissioner of Indian Affairs, 1871*, pp. 12–22.

35. Richardson, *Messages and Papers of the Presidents*, 6:4106.

36. Miller to Pope, December 29, 1871, OIA, T21, Roll 14; Miller to Lowrie, August 5, 1871, AIC, RG31-40-9, 160.

Chapter 5

1. *Report of the Commissioner of Indian Affairs, 1871*, pp. 167–68.

2. Ibid., pp. 177–78, 190.

3. Miller to Pope, January 1 and 22, 1872, OIA, T21, Roll 16; *Santa Fe New Mexican*, February 5, 1872.

4. Miller to Pope, February 21, 1872, OIA, T21, Roll 16; Walker to Pope,

February 27, 1872, OIA, M21, Roll 105; Miller to Pope, March 19 and April 3, 1872, OIA, M234, Roll 559; *Santa Fe New Mexican,* April 4, 1872. Near the end of April, a writer in the *New Mexican* reasoned that "the Indians are not much to blame if they steal merely to satisfy hunger, but at the same time the owners of the stock thus taken cannot be expected to quietly submit to the thefts and sooner or later trouble will ensue." *Santa Fe New Mexican,* April 26, 1872.

5. *Report of the Board of Indian Commissioners, 1872* (Washington, D.C.: Government Printing Office, 1872), pp. 140–41; unidentified newspaper clipping, OIA, M234, Roll 559. "Braying donkey," "treacherous black-hearted dog," and "miserable fizzle," were among the other demeaning labels applied to Colyer in southwestern newspapers at the time. Richard N. Ellis, "Vincent Colyer and the New Mexico Press, 1871" in Albert H. Schroeder, ed., *The Changing Ways of Southwestern Indians: A Historic Perspective* (Glorieta, New Mexico: The Rio Grande Press, Inc., 1973), pp. 205–9.

6. *Report of the Commissioner of Indian Affairs to the Secretary of the Interior, 1872* (Washington, D.C.: Government Printing Office, 1872), p. 296; Menaul to Lowrie, May 21, 1872, AIC, L-1, 169; Miller to Pope, May 23, 1872, OIA, T21, Roll 16; *Santa Fe New Mexican,* June 4, 1872. The report of one hundred children dying from starvation was unconfirmed. An employee at the Navajo agency recalled only a few deaths in the tribe in 1872, and those were generally from old age. *Report of the Commissioner of Indian Affairs, 1872,* p. 304.

7. Miller to Pope, March 2, 1872, OIA, M234, Roll 559; Walker to Pope, March 21, 1872, OIA, M21, Roll 105.

8. Menaul to Miller, February 27, 1872, OIA, T21, Roll 16; Pope to Walker, April 2, 1872, OIA, M234, Roll 559; Miller to Lowrie, January 18, 1872, AIC, L-1, 18.

9. Miller to Pope, January 26, 1872, and Menaul to Pope, July 5, 1872, OIA, T21, Roll 16; Pope to Walker, March 9, 1872, OIA, T21, Roll 29; Walker to Pope, May 4, 1872, OIA, M21, Roll 107; Menaul to Lowrie, May 4, 1872, AIC, L-1, 158. Among the diseases that he treated, Menaul found syphilis, rheumatism, and sore eyes most prevalent. In his excellent study on the history of Navajo weaving, Charles Amsden credits women captives taken from the Pueblo tribes of the Southwest with the introduction of weaving skills among the Navajos about the middle of the eighteenth century. Charles A. Amsden, *Navajo Weaving: Its Technic and Its History* (Glorieta, New Mexico: The Rio Grande Press, 1971), p. iii. During his travels through the Southwest in the 1830s, Josiah Gregg found the Navajos producing blankets of a very high quality which commanded high prices from the Mexican population. Josiah Gregg, *Commerce of the Prairies,* Max L. Moorhead, ed. (Norman: University of Oklahoma Press, 1954, edition of 1844), p. 199.

10. Miller to Lowrie, January 18, 1872, AIC, L-1, 18; *Santa Fe New Mexican,* April 10, 1872; *Report of the Commissioner of Indian Affairs, 1872,* p. 296.

11. Miller to Lowrie, January 18, 1872, AIC, L-1, 18.

12. Roberts to Lowrie [no date], AIC, L-1, 311; Roberts to Lowrie, January 24, 1872, AIC, L-1, 23; Roberts to Lowrie, February 20, 1872, AIC, L-1, 58.

13. Roberts to Lowrie, March 1, 1872, AIC, L-1, 70; Miller to Lowrie, March 4, 1872, AIC, L-1, 76.

14. Roberts to Lowrie, March 6, 1872, AIC, L-1, 81.

15. Menaul to Lowrie, March 7, 1872, AIC, L-1, 84.

16. Lowrie to Roberts, March 23, 1872, BFM, Letters Sent, RG31-43-2, p. 175; Miller to Lowrie, April 10, 1872, AIC, L-1, 124. Lowrie admitted that his decision to recall Roberts was greatly influenced by the missionary's inability to learn either the Spanish or Navajo language.

17. Pope to Miller, February 29, 1872, OIA, T21, Roll 29; Miller to Pope, May 28, 1872, OIA, T21, Roll 16; *Santa Fe New Mexican,* June 17, 1872; Keams to Pope, June 13, 1872, OIA, M234, Roll 559.

18. *Santa Fe New Mexican,* June 17, 1872.

19. Menaul to Lowrie, June 13, 1872, AIC, L-1, 166. Andrew Curtis, Presbyterian agent to the Mescalero Apaches in New Mexico, was convinced that Miller's murderers were not Utes, but Navajos driven to desperate acts by their own destitution. Curtis to Lowrie, June 27, 1872, AIC, L-1, 200.

20. *Santa Fe New Mexican,* July 9, 1872; Pope to Keams, June 20, 1872, OIA, T21, Roll 29; Keams to Pope, June 25, 1872, and Pope to Walker, August 15, 1872, OIA, M234, Roll 559; Keams to Pope, July 6, 1872, OIA, T21, Roll 16.

21. Columbus Delano to General O. O. Howard, March 4, 1872, OSI, M606, Roll 10; Pope to Colonel Gordon Granger, August 10, 1872, OIA, T21, Roll 29; Walker to Delano, September 3, 1872, OIA, M348, Roll 22. A transcript of the discussions at this famous meeting with General Howard is included in Pope to Walker, August 16, 1872, OIA, M234, Roll 559. For Howard's Report of his extensive travels through Arizona and New Mexico, see *Report of the Commissioner of Indian Affairs, 1872,* pp. 148–78.

22. Lowrie to Delano, March 7 and 30, 1872, BFM, Letters Sent, RG31-43-2, pp. 165, 171; Delano to Lowrie, March 9, 1872, and Walker to Lowrie, March 18, 1872, AIC, L-1, 326, 330. Frank McNitt credits Frank Bennett, James Roberts's old nemesis, with originating the plan for a Navajo police force in 1869. McNitt, *Indian Traders,* p. 137. Oakah L. Jones, Jr. discusses this subject at length in "The Origins of the Navajo Indian Police, 1872–1873," *Arizona and the West,* 8 (Autumn 1966): 225–38.

23. Keams to Pope, August 21, 1872, OIA, T21, Roll 16; Walker to Delano, September 17, 1872, OIA, M348, Roll 22; *Santa Fe New Mexican,* August 28, 1872; Walker to Pope, September 7, 1872, and H. R. Clum to Pope, October 2, 1872, OIA, M21, Roll 107; *Report of the Commissioner of Indian Affairs, 1872,* p. 303.

24. Keams to Pope, August 15, 1872, OIA, T21, Roll 16. Frank McNitt felt sure that Howard's informant was W. F. M. Arny, agent at Santa Fe to the Pueblo Indians who would accept an appointment as agent to the Navajos in 1873. McNitt, *Indian Traders,* p. 136.

25. B. Sunderland, pastor, First Presbyterian Church, Washington, D.C. to Lowrie, December 7, 1870, and Hall to Lowrie, December 8, 1870, AIC, B-2, 254, 253; Hall to Lowrie, June 28, 1872, AIC, L-1, 204; J. Casey, U.S. Court of Claims to Lowrie, July 6, 1872, OSI, M750, Roll 14.

26. *Report of the Commissioner of Indian Affairs, 1872*, pp. 296, 303–4.

27. Ibid., pp. 296, 304; Keams to Pope, September 6, 1872, OIA, T21, Roll 16; Walker to Pope, September 25, 1872, M21, Roll 107; Keams to Pope, October 5, 1872, and Pope to Walker, October 17, 1872, OIA, M234, Roll 559.

28. Crothers to Lowrie, June 9, 1872, and McFarland to Lowrie, June 17, 1872, AIC, L-1, 182, 192; Lowrie to Truax, June 18, 1872, BFM, Letters Sent, RG31-43-2, p. 221.

29. *Santa Fe New Mexican*, October 19, 1872; Menaul to Dr. Ellinwood, August 20, 1872, and Roberts to Lowrie, June 14, 1872, AIC, L-1, 245, 188.

30. Roberts to Lowrie, September 17, 1872, AIC, L-1, 256.

31. Lowrie to Roberts, September 26 and October 5, 1872, BFM, Letters Sent, RG31-43-2, pp. 234, 242.

32. *Santa Fe New Mexican*, November 14, 1872. For reasons not revealed, the Pueblo agency was the only agency in New Mexico that was not assigned by Vincent Colyer to the Presbyterians. The Christian Church had responsibility for this agency, although David McFarland insisted that the agent, John Cole, was, in fact, a Methodist who had received his appointment, not by any church, "but by the Secretary [of the Interior] or higher official of one of the Departments in Washington who was a personal and intimate friend of Mr. Cole's father in Ohio. . . ." McFarland to Lowrie, March 13, 1873, AIC, M, 78.

33. Truax and Roberts to Lowrie, November 27, 1872, AIC, L-1, 289.

34. W. F. M. Arny to Lowrie, November 22, 1872, and Roberts to Lowrie, December 17, 1872, AIC, L-1, 290, 306.

35. Hall to Lowrie, November 9, 1872, AIC, L-1, 283; *Report of the Commissioner of Indian Affairs, 1872*, pp. 296, 302.

36. *Santa Fe New Mexican*, November 19 and December 14, 1872; McFarland to General O. O. Howard, December 10, 1872, AIC, M, 4.

37. Dudley to Walker, December 16, 1872, OIA, M234, Roll 559; Hall to Lowrie, November 9, 1872, AIC, L-1, 283.

38. Hall to Lowrie, November 20 and 29, 1872, AIC, L-1, 288, 296.

39. Hall to Lowrie, November 29, 1872, AIC, L-1, 296; Chief Clerk, Department of the Interior to Commissioner of Indian Affairs, November 1, 1872, and Hall to Dudley, December 16, 1872, OIA, M234, Roll 559.

40. *Report of the Commissioner of Indian Affairs, 1872*, pp. 3–14.

41. *Report of the Board of Indian Commissioners, 1872*, pp. 3–6; *New York Times*, November 5, 1872. Thomas Cree, who had replaced Vincent Colyer as secretary of the Board of Indian Commissioners, indicated his unqualified support for the Peace Policy in an article in a Presbyterian newspaper. "This system," Cree insisted, "so humane and just . . . cannot fail of success." *The*

Presbyterian Banner, March 20, 1872. Commenting on the report of the Board of Indian Commissioners for 1872, a writer in a Presbyterian periodical thought that the government was now on the right course with its humane policy because "we have always believed that the American Indian is possessed of very much the same kind of human nature as other people." *Herald and Presbyter*, February 13, 1873.

42. "The New Indian Policy," *The Record of the Presbyterian Church in the United States of America*, 23 (November 1872): 347–48. When John Lowrie mentioned to the Secretary of the Interior that he had noted statements in the press predicting abandonment of the program, he received immediate assurance that there was not the slightest danger of any change in policy, "especially so long as the present seems to be working with such good results." B. R. Cowen to Lowrie, October 25, 1872, AIC, L-1, 357.

43. "Report of the Secretary of the Interior, 1872," *House Executive Documents*, 42 Congress, 3 session, serial 1560, pp. 3–10. In distributing credit for the success of the Peace Policy, Secretary Delano pointed out that "the aid and cooperation of the various religious associations of the country have been of the highest value. In no case has there been the slightest misunderstanding between them and the Department. . . ." Ibid., p. 8.

44. Richardson, *Messages and Papers of the Presidents*, 6:4154.

45. Pope to Walker, July 7, 1872, OIA, M234, Roll 559; George W. Dodge to Walker, July 26, 1872, ibid.; Charles Adams to Commanding Officer, Fort Garland, Colorado, July 31, 1872, ibid.; *Report of the Board of Indian Commissioners, 1872*, pp. 110–11, 147–50.

Chapter 6

1. *New York Times*, January 16, 1873.

2. *New York Times*, January 16 and 17, 1873; *National Republican*, January 16, 1873, in BIC, Scrapbooks of Newspaper Clippings, 5 vols., RG75, NA, 1: unpaginated.

3. Hall to Honorable Columbus Delano, February 5, 1873, AIC, M, 40.

4. Hall to Dudley, January 31, 1873, OIA, T21, Roll 19; Truax to Lowrie, March 22 and April 9, 1873, AIC, M, 95, 113; Hall to Lowrie, April 29, 1873, AIC, M, 126. The list of school supplies ordered by Hall included six dozen slate pencils, four boxes of crayons or chalk, one large atlas of the United States, seven spelling books for beginners, and twelve pictorial primers.

5. Lowrie to Hall, April 24, 1873, BFM, Letters Sent, RG31-43-2, pp. 327–28; John Menaul to Lowrie, May 20, 1873, and Charity Ann Menaul to Lowrie, June 19, 1873, AIC, M, 139, 157.

6. Menaul to Hall, January 21, April 16, and July 16, 1873, OIA, T21, Roll 19; Menaul to Agent for Navajo Indians, September 1, 1873, AIC, M, 230. In the latter annual report, Menaul recorded ninety-three visits to the sick in

their hogans, fifty-seven teeth extracted, 1,540 patients who applied for medicine, and 754 prescriptions filled.

7. Truax to Lowrie, April 10 and May 27, 1873, AIC, M, 115, 144; Truax to Dudley, April 10, 1873, OIA, T21, Roll 21; *Santa Fe New Mexican*, May 14, 1873. Writing to Lowrie from his mission at Taos, New Mexico, James Roberts, dogmatic as always, found no cause for regret in Truax's departure, as he had discovered that his erstwhile companion was a Mason, and many of the friends whom he had cultivated in the territory were of the same way of thinking. Roberts to Lowrie, July 23, 1873, AIC, M, 192.

8. Hall to Dudley, January 28 and March 6, 1873, OIA, T21, Roll 19; Commissioner E. P. Smith to Dudley, April 5, 1873, OIA, M21, Roll 109.

9. Richard Crawford, "Edward Parmelee Smith," in Kvasnicka and Viola, *Commissioners of Indian Affairs*, pp. 141–47.

10. Smith to Dudley, April 5, 1873, OIA, M21, Roll 109; Hall to Dudley, May 28, 1873, OIA, T21, Roll 19; Smith to Dudley, May 24 and May 29, 1873, OIA, M21, Roll 111.

11. Lowrie to Hall, February 14, 1873, BFM, Letters Sent, RG31-43-2, p. 293; Hall to Lowrie, March 10, 1873, AIC, M, 76.

12. Hall to Lowrie, March 10, 1873, AIC, M, 76.

13. Charles Adams, Agent, Los Pinos Agency, Colorado to Hon. E. P. Smith, April 28, 1873, OIA, M234, Roll 560; *Report of the Board of Indian Commissioners, 1873* (Washington, D.C.: Government Printing Office, 1873), p. 154; *Report of the Commissioner of Indian Affairs, 1873* (Washington, D.C.: Government Printing Office, 1874), pp. 111–12; *New York Times*, May 21, 1873.

14. Hall to Lowrie, March 10, 1873, AIC, M, 76; H. R. Clum to Dudley, January 2, 1873, OIA, M21, Roll 110; Crothers to Lowrie, February 7, 1873, AIC, M, 50.

15. Lowrie to Delano, April 22, 1873, BFM, Letters Sent, RG31-43-2, p. 323; Dudley to Smith, May 5, 1873; OIA, M234, Roll 560; Delano to Commissioner of Indian Affairs, May 13, 1873, OIA, M234, Roll 561; *Santa Fe New Mexican*, June 27 and September 16, 1873.

16. Truax to Lowrie, March 22 and April 9, 1873, AIC, M, 95, 113; Lowrie to Arny, April 24, 1873, and Lowrie to Delano, June 7, 1873, BFM, Letters Sent, RG31-43-2, pp. 331 and 351; Lowrie to Delano, June 12, 1873, OSI, M750, Roll 14.

17. Hall to Lowrie, June 21 and June 28, 1873, AIC, M, 159, 166.

18. Perry E. Brocchus to Lowrie, May 10, 1873, AIC, M, 355; Menaul to Lowrie, June 21, 1873, AIC, M, 160; McFarland to Lowrie, March 8, 1873, AIC, M, 74; Truax to Lowrie, May 27, 1873, AIC, M, 144; Delano to Lowrie, June 9, 1873, AIC, M, 360. Arny had served previously in New Mexico as agent to two bands of Ute Indians and to the Pueblo Indians. For an excellent and objective biography of Arny, see Lawrence R. Murphy, *William F. M. Arny, Frontier Crusader* (Tucson, Arizona: University of Arizona Press, 1972).

19. H. R. Clum to Hall, July 19, 1873, OIA, M21, Roll 112; Arny to Lowrie,

August 6, 1873, AIC, M, 205; Arny to Smith, August 13, 1873, OIA, M234, Roll 560; Smith to Hall, August 30, 1873, OIA, M21, Roll 114.

20. Arny to Dudley, September 1, 1873, OIA, T21, Roll 19; Arny to Lowrie, August 14 and 29, 1873, AIC, M, 214, 227. Eager to show that his dismissal was not an unfavorable reflection on his character, Hall insisted in a public statement that the action resulted only from a difference of opinion between himself and John Lowrie regarding educational programs for the Navajos. *Santa Fe New Mexican*, September 13, 1873.

21. *United States Statutes at Large*, XVI, 360; E. P. Smith to Vandever, July 12, 1873, OIA, M21, Roll 111; Vandever to Smith, September 25, 1873, OIA, Reports of Inspection of the Field Jurisdiction of the Office of Indian Affairs, 1873–1890, RG75, NA, Microcopy M1070, Roll 29. The Congress anticipated appointment of five regional inspectors with the intent to gradually phase out the positions of resident regional superintendents.

22. Arny to Smith, September 6, 1873, and Arny to Dudley, September 6 and 27, 1873, OIA, T21, Roll 19. William Hall had formed a different opinion about Anson Damon. He came to regard him as "an intelligent and efficient man from Boston and naturally a good man, but his good qualities have been somewhat perverted by residence among the worst class of people since his youth." Hall to Lowrie, April 29, 1873, AIC, M, 126.

23. Arny to Smith, September 6, 1873, OIA, T21, Roll 19; Arny to Lowrie, September 8 and 23, 1873, AIC, M, 238, 249. Mentioning John and Charity Ann Menaul in his report, Inspector Vandever described them as exerting "a very salutary influence upon the Indians by whom they are held in great esteem." Vandever to Smith, September 25, 1873, OIA, M1070, Roll 29.

24. Dudley to Smith, July 29, 1873, OIA, M234, Roll 561; Arny to Lowrie, September 23, 1873, AIC, M, 249; Arny to Dudley, September 23, 1873, OIA, T21, Roll 19; H. R. Clum to Dudley, November 5, 1873, OIA, M21, Roll 114.

25. Hall to Lowrie, April 29, 1873, AIC, M, 126; Arny to Smith, September 6, 1873, OIA, T21, Roll 19; *Report of the Commissioner of Indian Affairs, 1873*, pp. 272–73.

26. Lowrie to Arny, September 30, 1873, BFM, Letters Sent, K–L, pp. 2–3; *Report of the Commissioner of Indian Affairs, 1873*, p. 267.

27. Arny to Lowrie, September 8 and 27, 1873, AIC, M, 238, 259. Arny's friend Sheldon Jackson, superintendent of home mission work in the Rocky Mountain region, went ahead and advertised for a minister and his wife to accept an assignment at Fort Defiance. Calling on his many talents as a publicist, Jackson stated: "As Fort Defiance is one of the best sanitariums on the continent, health may be an inducement to some consecrated minister in the Presbyterian Church to offer himself for that service." Jackson Scrapbooks, no date, 58:107.

28. Arny to Dudley, October 8, 1873, OIA, T21, Roll 19; Arny to Miss Amanda Painter, October 28 and November 5, 1873, AIC, M, 275, 278; Arny to Lowrie, November 5, 1873, AIC, M, 279; Lowrie to Arny, November 20

and December 11, 1873, BFM, Letters Sent, K–L, pp. 24, 38; Dudley to Lowrie, November 18, 1873, AIC, M, 285.

29. *Report of the Commissioner of Indian Affairs, 1873,* p. 271; H. R. Clum to Second Comptroller of the Treasury, July 29, 1873, OIA, M21, Roll 111; Arny to Dudley, September 1, September 18, October 2, October 25, December 5, and December 13, 1873, OIA, T21, Roll 19.

30. Arny to Captain W. A. Elderkin, October 13, 1873; Frank Chapman to Arny, October 14, 1873; Arny to Dudley, October 24, 1873; Arny to Commissioner Smith, November 1, 1873; Elderkin to Arny, November 11, 1873; OIA, T21, Roll 19. William Hall and Dudley had tried to substitute sheep, in large part, for these annuity goods, but their requests arrived too late in the Office of Indian Affairs to achieve this objective in the arrangements made for fiscal year 1873–1874. Dudley to Smith, May 28, 1873, OIA, M234, Roll 560; Smith to Dudley, June 13, 1873 and H. R. Clum to Dudley, July 16, 1873, OIA, M21, Roll 111.

31. H. R. Clum to Dudley, January 2, 1873, OIA, M21, Roll 110; Hall to Dudley, February 14, 1873, OIA, T21, Roll 19; Hall to Dudley, July 19, 1873, and Arny to Smith, September 5, 1873, OIA, M234, Roll 561; Clum to Dudley, August 13, 1873, OIA, M21, Roll 114.

32. McFarland to Lowrie, March 20, 1873, AIC, M, 88; Arny to Smith, September 6, 1873, and Gould to Dudley, August 31, 1873, OIA, T21, Roll 19; *Report of the Commissioner of Indian Affairs, 1873,* p. 271; Gould to Dudley, September 29 and October 3, 1873, and Arny to Dudley, October 13 and October 27, 1873, OIA, T21, Roll 19; H. R. Clum to Dudley, October 15, 1873, OIA, M21, Roll 114.

33. Williamson Crothers to Lowrie, December 18, 1872, AIC, L-1, 307; Arny to Dudley, October 2, 1873, Defrees to Dudley, October 11, 1873, Dudley to Smith, October 22, 1873, OIA, M234, Roll 561; H. R. Clum to Defrees, October 13, 1873, OIA, M21, Roll 113. Regarding Arny's stated need for the Defrees's habitation to house teachers for the school, Dudley bluntly noted that "no teachers have arrived nor do I know that any soon are expected." Dudley to Smith, November 19, 1873, OIA, M234, Roll 561.

34. Menaul to Lowrie, December 2, 1873, M. A. Breeden to Lowrie [December 1873], and Defrees to Lowrie, November 10, 1873, AIC, M, 299, 297, 280. Lowrie called for a more rational approach from Defrees in his feud with Arny when he replied: "Whatever may be Mr. Arny's merits and demerits, it is evident that you have written this letter under too much excitement." Lowrie to Defrees, December 2, 1873, BFM, Letters Sent, K–L, p. 29.

35. Lowrie to Defrees, December 2, 1873, and Lowrie to Delano, December 19, 1873, BFM, Letters Sent, K–L, pp. 29, 41; Dudley to Lowrie, November 18, 1873, AIC, M, 285.

36. *Report of the Commissioner of Indian Affairs, 1873,* pp. 9–10.

37. *Report of the Board of Indian Commissioners, 1873,* pp. 24, 31.

38. "Report of the Secretary of the Interior, 1873," *House Executive Documents,* 43 Congress, 1 session, serial 1601, pp. III–IV.

39. Richardson, *Messages and Papers of the Presidents,* 6:4206.

40. Arny to Lowrie, December 11, 1873, AIC, M, 305; Arny to Dudley, December 6, 1873, OIA, T21, Roll 19.

Chapter 7

1. *New York Times,* January 2 and February 21, 1874. Infuriated by the "dishonest course of a portion of the public press," Grant called for a new statute for punishment of lying.

2. *Report of the Board of Indian Commissioners, 1873,* pp. 173–76, 198–200.

3. Truax to Lowrie, March 14, 1874, AIC, O-2, 72; Arny to Dudley, March 25, 1874, OIA, M234, Roll 562.

4. Truax to Lowrie, January 26, 1874, AIC, O-2, 68; Friese to Arny, March 3 and April 1, 1874, OIA, T-21, Roll 22. Friese frankly attributed part of his success in recruiting students to Arny's practice of giving each student a ration ticket at the end of the day.

5. Joseph Gow to Arny, April 30, 1874, and Arny to Smith, May 23, 1874, OIA, M234, Roll 562; H. R. Clum to Arny, June 4, 1874, OIA, M21, Roll 118.

6. Gow to Arny, April 30, 1874, and Arny to Dudley, June 3, 1874, OIA, T21, Roll 22; Friese to Arny, September 14, 1874, AIC, O-2, 99.

7. Stowe to Arny, September 14, 1874, and Arny to Lowrie, September 22, 1874, AIC, O-2, 97, 105.

8. W. B. Truax report, January 30, 1874, in the minutes of the Denver Bible Society, Colorado State Historical Society, Denver, Colorado; Truax to Lowrie, January 26, 1874, AIC, O-2, 68.

9. Arny to Dudley, March 21, 1874, OIA, M234, Roll 562; Truax to Arny, April 1 and April 30, 1874, OIA, T21, Roll 22, Truax to Arny, September 14, 1874, AIC, O-2, 98.

10. Arny to Smith, May 23 and June 15, 1874, OIA, M234, Roll 562; Arny to Dudley, June 3, 1874, OIA, T21, Roll 22; Truax to Arny, September 14, 1874, AIC, O-2, 98.

11. *Annual Report of the Commissioner of Indian Affairs to the Secretary of the Interior, 1874* (Washington, D.C.: Government Printing Office, 1874), p. 290; Arny to Dudley, February 28 and June 15, 1874, OIA, T21, Roll 22.

12. Smith to Dudley, June 16, 1874, OIA, M21, Roll 118; William Breeden, Thomas B. Catron, et al. to the Honorable Commissioner, July 3, 1874, OSI, M750, Roll 12.

13. John Menaul, Sanitary Report, August 31, 1874, OIA, M234, Roll 562; Menaul to Lowrie, January 2 and March 18, 1874, and Truax to Lowrie, September 9, 1874, AIC, N, 25, 68, 152; Menaul to Sheldon Jackson, August 24, 1874, and Menaul to Mrs. M. L. Sheafe, October 26, 1874, Correspondence Relating to Pioneer Presbyterian Missions West of the Mississippi and Missouri Rivers and in Alaska, 1856–1908, PHS, 26 vols., V, pp. 480–81, 521–22. Menaul urged Lowrie to replace Arny with his good Christian friend John

Clum, who later attained a formidable reputation as agent at the San Carlos Apache reservation in Arizona.

14. Arny to Dudley, January 31 and March 28, 1874, and Jacob Hamblin to Navajo Agent, March 7, 1874, OIA, T21, Roll 22; Arny to Dudley, February 16 and May 12, 1874, Arny to Colonel J. Irvine Gregg, June 3, 1874, and Dudley to Smith, June 19, 1874, OIA, M234, Roll 562.

15. *Report of the Commissioner of Indian Affairs, 1874*, pp. 306–7. Arny had no authority to reactivate the police force, but his action apparently received after-the-fact approval. In the report of the Commissioner of Indian Affairs for 1874, Arny's superior described the police as "very efficient in the arrest and punishment of Indian thieves, and in the return of stolen stock to the owner." Ibid., p. 62.

16. Daniels to E. P. Smith, Commissioner of Indian Affairs, August 20, 1874, OIA, M1070, Roll 29.

17. Ibid.; Arny to Dudley, February 16, 1874, OIA, M234, Roll 562; Arny to Dudley, March 21, 1874, OIA, T21, Roll 22.

18. Daniels to Smith, August 20, 1874, OIA, M1070, Roll 29. Responding to Daniels's question about the feeling of the Navajos toward their agents and other white residents at Fort Defiance, John Menaul thought that the Indians were "peaceable and well disposed towards the whites but didn't like the agent."

19. Ibid. The details of the potentially explosive altercation between the Navajos and the rancher are discussed at length in Lawrence Murphy, *Frontier Crusader*, pp. 218–19.

20. Arny to Smith, January 2, 1874, OIA, M234, Roll 562; Arny to Dudley, January 2, 1874, OIA, T21, Roll 22.

21. Dudley to Smith, January 26, 1874, OIA, M234, Roll 562; Smith to Arny, January 26 and 29, 1874, OIA, M21, Roll 116.

22. Smith to Arny, February 16, 1874, and Arny to Smith, March 28 and April 8, 1874, OIA, M234, Roll 562; Columbus Delano to Speaker of House of Representatives, April 30, 1874, OSI, M606, Roll 14; Smith to Arny, August 4, 1874, OIA, M21, Roll 119.

23. Arny to Smith, September 21, 1874, OIA, M234, Roll 562; *Santa Fe New Mexican*, November 16 and 18, 1874. Skillfully woven into the great blanket was the wording "1776-U.S.A.-1876."

24. *Rocky Mountain News* (Denver, Colorado), November 24, 1874.

25. *The Daily Journal of Commerce* (Kansas City, Missouri), November 28, 1874. The cost of transportation from Denver to Kansas City was $538.00. Arny traveled first-class and the Indians had second-class accommodations. Arny to Smith, December 17, 1874, OIA, M234, Roll 562.

26. *St. Louis Dispatch*, November 27, 1874; *St. Louis Daily Globe*, November 28, 1874.

27. *St. Louis Dispatch*, November 28, 1874; *St. Louis Daily Globe*, November 29, 1874. Sherman's position as Commanding General of the Army would

customarily have required his presence in Washington, D.C. However, angry at what he perceived to be lack of cooperation from civilians in the War Department, he arbitrarily transferred his headquarters to St. Louis from 1874 to 1876.

28. *Chicago Journal,* November 30, 1874; *Chicago Daily Tribune,* December 1, 1874; *The Daily Inter-Ocean* (Chicago), December 1, 1874.

29. *New York Times,* December 9, 1874; *Washington Evening Star,* December 1, 1874. The article in the *Times* was written in Washington on December 4 by "an occasional correspondent" to the New York newspaper. In Santa Fe, a commentator sarcastically acknowledged the arrival of the Arny party in Washington by noting that "Governor Arny and his Indians have arrived in Washington and are creating considerable excitement. This is as it should be, for we have seen the time here in New Mexico when that number or less have excited us." *Santa Fe New Mexican,* December 9, 1874.

30. *Washington Evening Star,* December 10, 1874; *Santa Fe New Mexican,* December 19, 1874, citing an article in *The National Republican* (no date). At the same time that the Navajos were in Washington, King Kalakaua of the Hawaiian Islands was visiting the city. After the King called on President Grant, the president and other dignitaries politely returned the call at the King's hotel. Commenting on this display of diplomatic protocol, a writer in the *Santa Fe New Mexican* wondered why a similar courtesy had not been extended to "his Emminence, Manuelito, King of the Navajo nation." *Santa Fe New Mexican,* December 18, 1874.

31. *Santa Fe New Mexican,* December 23, 1874.

32. Arny to Smith, December 12, 1874, and Pope to Smith, January 7, 1875, AIC, O-2, 121, 122.

33. *The Boston Traveller,* December 26, 1874; *Santa Fe New Mexican,* January 6, 1875. While in Washington, Arny asked John Lowrie in New York to secure accommodations for his party during their stopover in that city. He asked for a place where whiskey was not sold and where his Indians could be housed in one large room without beds. As for meals, he indicated that the Navajos required only potatoes, mutton or beef, coffee and bread. Arny to Lowrie, December 8, 1874, AIC, O-2, 117.

34. *Providence Journal,* December 28, 1874; Board of Indian Commissioners, Newspaper Clippings, 1871–1884, RG75, NA unidentified clipping. Reference to the Corliss Steam Engine Company in the latter clipping tied it to Providence, Rhode Island, home of that well-known business enterprise.

35. *New York Sun,* January 1, 1875.

36. Arny to Smith, November 4, 1874, OIA, M234, Roll 562; Truax to Arny, September 14, 1874, AIC, O-2, 98; Truax to Lowrie, March 14, June 11 and September 29, 1874, AIC, O-2, 72, 84 and 106.

37. Menaul to Lowrie, December 2, 1874, AIC, N, 186.

38. Arny to Lowrie, September 22, 1874, AIC, O-2, 105; *The Record of the Presbyterian Church in the United States of America,* 25 (September 1874): 272–

73; "Thirty-seventh Annual Report of the Board of Foreign Missions" in *Minutes of the General Assembly, 1874*, pp. 10–11.

39. *Report of the Commissioner of Indian Affairs, 1874*, pp. 4–5, 13–14.

40. *New York Times*, February 9, June 7 and 8, 1874; Felix Brunot, et al., to the President of the United States, May 27, 1874, BIC, Letters Received, tray 2; *Report of the Board of Indian Commissioners, 1874* (Washington, D.C.: Government Printing Office, 1874), p. 10.

41. "Report of the Secretary of the Interior, 1874," *House Executive Documents*, 43 Congress, 2 session, serial 1639, pp. III–V. Delano also believed that extension of the homestead laws to the Indians would give them property rights which would develop the "habits of industry and economy as are incident to our civilization." Ibid., pp. V–VII.

42. Richardson, *Messages and Papers of the Presidents*, 6:4254. Grant concurred with Columbus Delano's suggestion that Indians receive the same advantages as white settlers under the homestead laws. He also urged the creation of some form of territorial government in the Indian Territory.

Chapter 8

1. *Report of the Board of Indian Commissioners, 1874*, pp. 123, 135, 141–44. Clinton Fisk, who resided at the time in St. Louis, Missouri, had attained the rank of Brevet Major General at the end of the Civil War. In the postwar era he served with distinction with the Freedman's Bureau. Malone, *Dictionary of American Biography*, 3:413–14.

2. *Santa Fe New Mexican*, February 1, 1875; Arny to Commisioner of Indian Affairs Edward Smith, January 4 and February 15, 1875, OIA, M234, Roll 564; Smith to Arny, January 14, 1875, OIA, M21, Roll 122. Referring to Manuelito's impression of the trip, the reporter in the *New Mexican* noted that the chief "thought at first that he would like to live east but finally came to the conclusion that too many people were there already."

3. Truax to Lowrie, January 4 and March 30, 1875, OIC, O-2, 134, 178.

4. Truax to Lowrie, March 23, 1875, AIC, O-2, 176; Lowrie to Arny, May 6, 1875, BFM, Letters Sent, K–L, p. 224; Truax to Lowrie, April 6, 1875, AIC, N, 252. Traux also found fault with Arny's conduct at the agency since his return from the East. According to Traux, the agent "seems to have thrown off the mask and is exhibiting himself in his true character. Two days ago he uttered a *vile oath* at an employee." Truax to Lowrie, April 6, 1875, AIC, N, 252.

5. Arny to Lowrie, May 24, 1875, AIC, N, 278. An influential friend in Santa Fe, who supported Arny in this dispute, insisted that Arny's version of these events was undoubtedly correct because Henry Easton was a notorious liar. T. B. Catron, U.S. Attorney for New Mexico to Honorable E. P. Smith, Commissioner of Indian Affairs, July 12, 1875, AIC, O-2, 284.

6. Arny to Lowrie, February 22, 1875, AIC, O-2, 151. In Santa Fe, Menaul

revealed his bitter feelings toward Arny when he stated that "the disgrace which Gov. Arny has brought on the Presbyterian Church will not be wiped out while the remembrance of his perfidy, hypocrisy, and falsehood remains in the minds of the respectable people of this community." Menaul to Lowrie, February 26, 1875, AIC, O-2, 154.

7. Arny to Lowrie, February 22, 1875, AIC, O-2, 151; Arny to Smith, March 3, 1875, AIC, O-2, 162; Cook to Arny, March 31, 1875, OIA, M234, Roll 564. When Arny relieved William Hall as agent in September 1873, he tried, to no avail, to hire his good friend Whitney, who was employed at the time as a clerk in the Interior Department in Washington, as agency clerk at Fort Defiance. Arny to Smith, September 4, 1873, OIA, M234, Roll 560. The new looms ordered by Arny finally reached Santa Fe and they were shipped from there to Fort Defiance on June 12. *Santa Fe New Mexican*, June 12, 1875.

8. Cecilia Arny to Arny, March 1, 1875, AIC, O-2, 160; Valentine Friese to Arny, February 1, 1875, AIC, O-2, 146; Friese to Arny, March 1, 1875, OIA, M234, Roll 564; Arny to Smith, March 3, 1875, AIC, O-2, 162. In his attack on Arny, William Truax noted that the agent's daughter-in-law Cecilia "in charge of the so-called 'Boarding House and Home' is a Mexican and was brought up in the Romish Church." Truax to Lowrie, March 23, 1875, AIC, O-2, 176. The Commissioner of Indian Affairs rejected the request by Friese for an orrery with the observation that the Navajo children could hardly be sufficiently advanced in their studies to understand astronomy. Smith to Arny, March 30, 1875, OIA, M21, Roll 124.

9. Friese to Lowrie, March 30, 1875, AIC, N, 75.

10. Arny to Smith, February 6, April 2 and June 12, 1875, OIA, M234, Roll 564; Arny to Smith, March 3 and May 31, 1875, AIC, O-2, 162, 199.

11. Smith to the Secretary of the Interior, March 31, 1875, OIA, M348, Roll 26; *Santa Fe New Mexican*, April 12, 1875; Arny to Smith, May 25, 1875, OIA, M234, Roll 564; G. A. Smith, Collector of Internal Revenue, Santa Fe, New Mexico to the Commisisoner of Indian Affairs, July 13, 1875, AIC, O-2, 216 ¹/₂; *Report of the Commissioner of Indian Affairs, 1875* (Washington, D.C.: Government Printing Office, 1875), p. 331.

12. *Report of the Commissioner of Indian Affairs, 1875*, p. 331. In a later case brought before the grand jury in Albuquerque on the question of "certain ill disposed persons living in adultery on the reservation with Navajo women," the jurors decided that there was no current law which said that these persons could be prosecuted. F. W. Clancy, Clerk, U.S. District Court, Second Judicial District of New Mexico to the Commissioner of Indian Affairs, October 19, 1875, OIA, M234, Roll 566.

13. Arny to Smith, September 13, 1873, OIA, T21, Roll 19; H. R. Clum to Arny, October 3, 1873, OIA, M21, Roll 114. Among those perceived by Arny as coconspirators in the plot to remove him were Keams's brother William, Anson Damon, former butcher at the Navajo agency, Daniel Dubois, itinerant trader, and Juan Lorenzo Hubbell, whose trading post, established later on

the Navajo reservation, has now been restored and preserved as a National Historical Site.

14. Arny to Smith, March 3 and May 31, 1875, AIC, O-2, 162, 199. The plan to revise the boundaries of the reservation was rejected because the area contemplated infringed on a grant of land to the Atlantic and Pacific Railroad. Smith to Arny, April 16, 1875, OIA, M21, Roll 114.

15. Keams to Lowrie, June 3 and June 23, 1875, AIC, O-2, 202, 209.

16. Principal Chiefs and Captains of the Navajo Tribe to the Honorable Commissioner of Indian Affairs, May 28, 1875, AIC, O-2, 197. Two of the five witnesses to the marks of the Navajos were Dan Dubois and Anson Damon, longtime cronies of Thomas Keams.

17. Truax to Lowrie, May 12, 1875, AIC, O-2, 191.

18. Lowrie to Arny, June 18, 1875, BFM, Letters Sent, K–L, p. 234; Delano to Lowrie, June 30, 1875 and Smith to Lowrie, July 23, 1875, AIC, O-2, 179.7, 282.

19. Arny to Delano, July 22, 1875, OSI, M750, Roll 14.

20. Navajo Chiefs to Our Great Father, July 15, 1875, OIA, M234, Roll 564. Twelve chiefs, including Manuelito, made their marks on the petition. Juan Lorenzo Hubbell, another of Thomas Keams's close friends, witnessed the signing.

21. Navajo Chiefs to Lowrie, August 13, 1875, AIC, O-2, 237. The marks of Manuelito and Ganado Mucho headed the list of ten chiefs who placed their marks on this document. Once again, Anson Damon and Daniel Dubois witnessed the making of the marks.

22. General W. T. Sherman to the Secretary of War, August 26, 1875, AIC, O-2, unnumbered.

23. Captain J. W. Eckles to Acting Assistant Adjutant General, Department of New Mexico, August 8, 1875, OIA, M234, Roll 565; Whitney to Arny, August 19, 1875, Captain C. A. Hartwell, 8th Cavalry to Whitney, August 21, 1875, W. W. Owens and F. W. Tanner, deposition, September 13, 1875, OIA, M234, Roll 564; *Report of the Commissioner of Indian Affairs, 1875*, pp. 330–31. Tragically, the only casualty associated with these events was Professor Valentine Friese, who became ill and died while staying at Fort Wingate.

24. Arny to Gregg, August 25, 1875, and C. A. Hartwell, Captain, 8th Cavalry to Acting Assistant Adjutant General, District of New Mexico, August 29, 1875, OIA, M234, Roll 564.

25. B. R. Cowen, Acting Secretary of the Interior to Lowrie, August 31, 1875, AIC, O-2, 247¹/₂; Lowrie to Smith, September 7, 1875, OIA, M234, Roll 564.

26. B. R. Cowen to the Secretary of War, August 27, 1875, Arny to Smith, September 25 and October 11, 1875, Arny to Price, September 25, 1875, Price to Lt. J. H. Mahnken, Acting Assistant Adjutant General, District of New Mexico, September 25, 1875, OIA, M234, Roll 564.

27. Price to Mahnken, September 25, 1875, OIA, M234, Roll 564.

28. Deposition by W. F. M. Arny, September 13, 1875, and Price to Mahn-ken, October 9, 1875, OIA, M234, Roll 564.

29. *Report of the Commissioner of Indian Affairs, 1875,* pp. 330–32. In a later letter to the Board of Indian Commissioners, Arny charged that "my experience with the military at that post [Fort Wingate] satisfied me that the soldiers were only kept there to guard their own subsistence. I made various applications for help and was never furnished with it. . . ." *Report of the Board of Indian Commissioners, 1875* (Washington, D.C.: Government Printing Office, 1876), p. 102.

30. Keams to Lowrie, September 7, 1875, AIC, O-2, 252; George Smith to Lowrie, August 23, September 2, and September 18, 1875, AIC, O-2, 241, 247, and 260; Truax to Lowrie, June 28, 1875, AIC, O-2, 212. David McFarland left the Santa Fe church in the spring of 1873 when his health failed. After several unsuccessful attempts to fill the vacancy, George Smith finally accepted the call at the end of 1874.

31. Jonathan K. Cooper to Lowrie, July 31, 1874, AIC, O-2, 88; Smith to Lowrie, September 24, 1875, OIA, M21, Roll 126.

32. *Santa Fe New Mexican,* September 21, 1875; Irvine to Smith, October 3 and 16, 1875, OIA, M234, Roll 564. As Irvine passed through Santa Fe on his way to Fort Defiance, a reporter rather pessimistically wondered how he would fare as he attempted to civilize "a nation of breech clouted brutes." *Santa Fe New Mexican,* September 29, 1875.

33. Irvine to Lowrie, November 15, 1875, AIC, O-2, 272.

34. *Santa Fe New Mexican,* November 17, 1875; P. D. McElroy to Lowrie, November 24, 1875, AIC, N, 356; Irvine to Smith, November 17, 1875, and Irvine to Price, November 18, 1875, OIA, M234, Roll 564.

35. Irvine to Smith, December 6, 1875, OSI, M750, Roll 14; Irvine to Smith, December 6, 1875, OIA, M234, Roll 564. Impressed by the qualities of the new agent, Major Price concluded that "Mr. Irvine seems to be a positive, truthful, and honest man, such a one as need have but little trouble in controlling the Navajos." Price to Lt. Thomas P. Blair, Acting Assistant Adjutant General, District of New Mexico, December 9, 1875, OIA, M234, Roll 569.

36. *Report of the Commissioner of Indian Affairs, 1875,* pp. 3–4, 22–24.

37. Richard Crawford, "Edward Parmelee Smith" and Edward E. Hill, "John Quincy Smith" in Kvasnicka and Viola, *Commissioners of Indian Affairs,* pp. 145, 149–53. Edward Hill concluded that J. Q. Smith was "not among the more illustrious persons to hold this position."

38. Malone, *Dictionary of American Biography,* 2:618 and 3:218. "Report of the Secretary of the Interior, 1875," *House Executive Documents,* 44 Congress, 1 session, serial 1680, pp. V, VIII–IX.

39. *Report of the Board of Indian Commissioners, 1875,* pp. 3–7, 14–15.

40. *New York Times,* November 2, 1875; Richardson, *Messages and Papers of the Presidents,* 6:4307–8. The churchmen who visited him in November may

not have been pleased with one part of the President's annual message. In a very bold statement indeed, Grant called for correction of an evil that could lead to great trouble. Specifically, he pointed to the accumulation in the nation of vast amounts of untaxed church property which should, in all fairness, be taxed equally with all other property. Richardson, 6:4288–89.

41. Kemble to J. Q. Smith, Commissioner of Indian Affairs, January 14, 1876, OIA, M1070, Roll 29.

Chapter 9

1. *New York Times*, July 30, 1876.

2. *Report of the Board of Indian Commissioners, 1875*, pp. 146, 154.

3. Ibid., pp. 154–55, 159–60.

4. Kemble to J. Q. Smith, Commissioner of Indian Affairs, January 14, 1876, OIA, M1070, Roll 29.

5. Ibid. As part of his report, Kemble presented a lengthy evaluation of the issues concerned with Arny's dismissal. He agreed that Arny had certainly been incompetent, but there was no evidence of dishonesty in his conduct of agency affairs. As for the rebellious acts of the Navajos, the inspector concluded that "in their plotting they were encouraged and advised by two white men, brothers named Keams."

6. Smith to Irvine, January 21, 1876, OIA, M21, Roll 128; Irvine to Smith, March 1, 1876, OIA, M234, Roll 567. Average daily attendance figures for the school showed January—13, February—16, and March—20. Irvine to Smith, April 6, 1876, OIA, M234, Roll 567.

7. *Report of the Commissioner of Indian Affairs, 1876* (Washington, D.C.: Government Printing Office, 1876), p. 109.

8. Ibid.

9. William Belknap, Secretary of War, to Zachariah Chandler, Secretary of the Interior, November 10, 1875, OIA, M234, Roll 565; Irvine to Smith, January 16 and October 14, 1876, and Chandler to Smith, May 10, 1876, OIA, M234, Roll 567; *Report of the Commissioner of Indian Affairs, 1876*, p. 110.

10. Irvine to Smith, January 16 and March 1, 1876, OIA, M234, Roll 567.

11. Major William Price to Lt. Thomas P. Blair, Acting Assistant Adjutant General, District of New Mexico, November 25, 1875, OIA, M234, Roll 569; Irvine to Smith, March 1, March 7, and June 3, 1876, OIA, M234, Roll 567; *Report of the Commissioner of Indian Affairs, 1876*, p. 109.

12. Irvine to Smith, March 1, April 13, and June 20, 1876, OIA, M234, Roll 567; *Report of the Commissioner of Indian Affairs, 1876*, p. 110. When Irvine mentioned that one or two chiefs wanted to travel to the East again in the summer to make their case in person, Commissioner Smith quickly and emphatically declared that there was absolutely no need to send another delegation of Navajos to Washington on this matter. Smith to Irvine, May 4, 1876, OIA, M21, Roll 130.

13. Kemble to J. Q. Smith, Commissioner of Indian Affairs, January 14, 1876, OIA, M1070, Roll 29; S. A. Galpin, Acting Commissioner of Indian Affairs to Irvine, May 13, 1876, OIA, M21, Roll 130; Irvine to Smith, June 6, 1876, OIA, M234, Roll 567. Irvine employed Henry Chee Dodge as his Navajo interpreter. Dodge's later service as a leader of his tribe was rewarded by his election as tribal chairman in 1923. Underhill, *The Navajos*, pp. 133, 209, 228.

14. Donald B. Johnson and Kirk H. Porter, eds., *National Party Platforms, 1840–1972* (Urbana: University of Illinois Press, 1973), pp. 49–55. The only references in the party platforms to racial strife in the nation pertained to impassioned pleas from the west coast states to restrict the entry of Chinese laborers into the country. Both parties pledged to support programs that would limit the influx of undesirable "Mongolians."

15. For a thorough and objective analysis of the election of 1876, see Keith I. Polakoff, *The Politics of Inertia: The Election of 1876 and the End of Reconstruction* (Baton Rouge: Louisiana State University Press, 1973).

16. Irvine to Smith, June 21, 1876, OIA, M234, Roll 567.

17. *Report of the Commissioner of Indian Affairs, 1876*, p. 109; Irvine to Smith, September 15 and October 14, 1876, OIA, M234, Roll 567.

18. *Report of the Commissioner of Indian Affairs, 1876*, p. 109; John Pyle, Cimarron Agency to Lowrie, August 31, 1876, AIC, C, 94; Irvine to Smith, April 6 and October 1, 1876, OIA, M234, Roll 567.

19. *Report of the Commissioner of Indian Affairs, 1876*, p. 110; Irvine to Smith, March 1 and November 10, 1876, OIA, M234, Roll 567. In addition to his good rapport with the military, Irvine managed to get along with the "squaw men" who still resided near the reservation. Referring to Thomas Keams and his cronies, Irvine admitted, "Since I have had charge of this agency, I have had no reason to complain of any of these parties." Irvine to Smith, June 6, 1876, OIA, M234, Roll 567.

20. "Report of the Secretary of the Interior, 1876," *House Executive Documents*, 44 Congress, 2 session, serial 1749, pp. III–VII.

21. *Report of the Commissioner of Indian Affairs, 1876*, pp. III–VII. Smith emphatically noted that the salary of an Indian agent was less than the compensation paid to a third-class clerk in Washington or to a village postmaster.

22. *Report of the Board of Indian Commissioners, 1876* (Washington, D.C.: Government Printing Office, 1877), pp. 3–9.

23. Richardson, *Message and Papers of the Presidents*, 6:4355.

24. *Report of the Commissioner of Indian Affairs, 1876*, p. 110.

Chapter 10

1. Lowrie to William Truax, February 15, 1877, AIC, C, 135; *Report of the Board of Indian Commissioners, 1876*, pp. 75, 87–88.

2. *Report of the Board of Indian Commissioners, 1876*, pp. 75–76.

3. *The Record of the Presbyterian Church in the United States of America,* 28 (February 1877): 49.

4. *Inaugural Addresses,* pp. 135–40; Minutes, April 25, 1877, BIC, 1:151. In a statement that invited controversy, J. G. Randall, distinguished Civil War scholar, referred to the settlement of the disputed election as "one of the great compromises of American history, deserving to rank along with the compromises of 1787, 1820 and 1850." J. G. Randall and David Donald, *The Civil War and Reconstruction* (Boston: D. C. Heath, 1961), p. 701. Regarding the new president as someone scarcely suited to lead the liberal movement within the Republican Party, Henry Adams described Hayes as "a third rate nonentity, whose only recommendation is that he is obnoxious to no one." Henry Adams, *Letters, 1858–1891,* edited by W. C. Ford (New York: Houghton Mifflin Co., 1930), p. 288.

5. Malone, *Dictionary of American Biography,* 8:466–70; *New York Times,* May 20, 1877. The *Times* editor wondered why the United States could not govern its Indians with the same kind of humane and civilized method used so successfully by the Canadian government.

6. Irvine to Smith, January 15, 1877, OIA, M234, Roll 572; Irvine to Smith, February 28, 1877, OIA, M234, Roll 570; *Report of the Commissioner of Indian Affairs, 1877* (Washington, D.C.: Government Printing Office, 1877), pp. 158–59.

7. Irvine to Smith, March 9, 1877, OIA, M234, Roll 570; Irvine to Smith, March 19, 1877, OIA, M234, Roll 571.

8. Thomas Blair, 1st Lieutenant, 15th Infantry to Acting Assistant Adjutant General, District of New Mexico, May 2, 1877, OIA, M234, Roll 572.

9. Ibid. Concerned that many of the Navajos would not actually use the items issued, Irvine asked Commissioner Smith if there was any law whereby he could prosecute parties not living on the reservation for trading or buying annuity goods distributed to the Indians. Irvine to Smith, March 1, 1877, OIA, M234, Roll 570.

10. Irvine to Smith, January 20, 1877, OIA, M234, Roll 570; Irvine to Smith, April 21, 1877, OIA, M234, Roll 571. Irvine had hoped to have an officer from Fort Wingate detached for continuous residence at his agency while the Navajos got used to the new requirements on issue days. Commissioner Smith endorsed his request favorably, but next to his endorsement appeared a notation from an official of the War Department asking, "Mr. Commissioner, do you wish to ask for an officer to *remain* at Navajo Agency?" With no evidence to the contrary, it must be concluded that Irvine's petition was quietly pigeonholed. Irvine to Smith, August 20, 1877, OIA, M234, Roll 571.

11. Irvine to Smith, April 19, 1877, OIA, M234, Roll 571; *Report of the Commissioner of Indian Affairs, 1877,* p. 158.

12. Irvine to Smith, March 9, 1877, OIA, M234, Roll 570; Irvine to Smith, April 9, 1877, OIA, M234, Roll 571. *Report of the Commissioner of Indian Affairs, 1877,* p. 159.

13. *Report of the Commissioner of Indian Affairs, 1877,* p. 159; Irvine to Ezra Hayt, Commissioner of Indian Affairs, March 16, 1878, OIA, M234, Roll 573.

14. S. A. Galpin, Acting Commissioner of Indian Affairs to Truax, October 9, 1876, OIA, M21, Roll 132; Irvine to Smith, November 14, 1876, OIA, M234, Roll 567; *Report of the Commissioner of Indian Affairs, 1877,* p. 160.

15. *Report of the Commissioner of Indian Affairs, 1877,* p. 160. Irvine decided that the only thing that the Hopi really needed and, in fact, desired, was a school teacher to educate their children.

16. Smith to Irvine, July 14, 1877, OIA, M21, Roll 136; *Santa Fe New Mexican,* October 29, 1877; *Report of the Commissioner of Indian Affairs, 1877,* pp. 158–59. Irvine believed that the Navajo chiefs objected to his efforts to revise traditional procedures employed in issuing rations and annuity goods because "they consider every pound of supplies and all the annuities as under their control and for their personal benefit." *Report of the Commissioner, 1877,* p. 159.

17. Vandever to the Commissioner of Indian Affairs, October 23, 1877, OIA, M1070, Roll 29. Regarding Irvine's extraordinary declaration that the Navajos produced nine-tenths of their subsistence and clothing, Vandever suggested, "This statement may be exaggerated, I think it is."

18. Ibid.; Carl Schurz to Lowrie, July 12, 1877, Thomas Keams to His Excellency Rutherford B. Hayes, May 1, 1877, J. V. Lauderdale to Lowrie, May 20, 1877, John Pyle to Lowrie, August 15, 1877, AIC, C, 166, 147, 155 and 179.

19. G. R. Russell to Lowrie, January 13, 1873, W. C. Rommel to Lowrie, January 16, 1873, J. C. Walker to Lowrie, February 19, 1873, AIC, C, 3, 4 and 10; S. A. Galpin to Benjamin Thomas, Agent, Pueblo Indians, September 20, 1876, OIA, M21, Roll 132; Edward Kemble to J. Q. Smith, July 31, 1877, OIA, M1070, Roll 29.

20. *Report of the Commissioner of Indian Affairs, 1877,* p. 158. For an analysis of Jackson's definition of his position as mission superintendent, see Norman J. Bender, "Sheldon Jackson's Crusade to Win the West for Christ, 1869–1880," *The Midwest Review,* 4 (Spring 1982): 1–12. After Jackson witnessed the annuity issue in April, he concluded: "It was a sight strangely moving to a Christian heart. 9,000 heathen in the midst of a Christian land. 9,000 immortal souls going down to death unsaved and no man to tell them of a savior." Sheldon Jackson, Diary, 1877 [undated and unpaginated], Presbyterian Historical Society, Philadelphia, Pennsylvania.

21. *The Record of the Presbyterian Church in the United States of America,* 28 (July 1877): 207–8.

22. Irvine to Smith, October 1 and 19, 1877, OIA, M234, Roll 571; Carl Schurz, Secretary of the Interior to the Commissioner of Indian Affairs, December 18, 1877, OIA, M234, Roll 570.

23. *Report of the Commissioner of Indian Affairs, 1877,* p. 159; Irvine to Smith, September 3, 1877, OIA, M234, Roll 571.

24. *Report of the Commissioner of Indian Affairs, 1877*, p. 159; Irvine to Smith, July 26, 1877, OIA, M234, Roll 571.

25. *Minutes of the General Assembly, 1877* (New York: Presbyterian Board of Publications, 1877), pp. 10–11.

26. *Rocky Mountain Presbyterian* (Denver, Colorado), October 1877; James M. Roberts, et al. to the Honorable Commissioner of Indian Affairs [November 1877], Correspondence Relating to Pioneer Presbyterian Missions West of the Mississippi and Missouri Rivers and in Alaska, 1856–1908 (26 vols. in the Presbyterian Historical Society, Philadelphia, Pa.), 7: 168. Jackson published the *Rocky Mountain Presbyterian* from his headquarters in Denver. Describing his tour with Kendall, he contended that the results of that journey would undoubtedly "result in the enlargement of the work in that region."

27. J. M. Roberts, et al., to Lowrie, November 10, 1877, Jackson Correspondence, 7: 173; Lowrie to Roberts, December 18, 1877, BFM, Letters Sent, K–L, pp. 391–92.

28. "Report of the Secretary of the Interior, 1877," *House Executive Documents*, 45 Congress, 2 session, serial 1800, pp. VIII, XIV. A writer in the *New York Times* acknowledged Schurz's good objectives, but he saw nothing really new in the Secretary's "utterly impractical" plans to solve the Indian problem. The skeptical commentator reminded his readers: "Promises are made by the Executive Department of the Government. Congress [then] makes the fulfillment of these promises impossible." *New York Times*, December 5, 1877.

29. Edward E. Hill, "John Q. Smith" and Roy W. Meyer, "Ezra A. Hayt" in Kvasnicka and Viola, *Commissioners of Indian Affairs*, pp. 149–53 and 155–66; *Report of the Commissioner of Indian Affairs, 1877*, pp. 1–5. Alexander Irvine had an angry exchange with Commissioner Hayt near the end of 1877. The Commissioner had apparently suggested to Irvine that the Navajos could surely hunt buffalo to obtain the meat and hides they needed. Irvine carefully explained that there were no buffalo anywhere near the Navajo reservation, and Hayt's letter "contains an insult that my official conduct does not justify. . . ." Irvine to Hayt, November 26, 1877, OIA, M234, Roll 571.

30. *Report of the Board of Indian Commissioners, 1877* (Washington, D.C.: Government Printing Office, 1878), pp. 4–5 and 9.

31. Richardson, *Messages and Papers of the Presidents*, 6:4427–28.

Chapter 11

1. John Lowrie to George G. Smith, June 17, 1878, BFM, Letters Sent, K–L, p. 420.

2. Analyzing the impact of the change of administration on the Peace Policy, Francis Prucha found that "the policy of church appointed agents was clearly on a downhill course." Prucha, *Indian Policy*, p. 60. Henry Fritz saw "a heavy blow to denominational influence" when Hayes selected Carl Schurz, whose favorite cause was civil service reform, as his secretary of the interior.

Henry E. Fritz, *The Movement for Indian Assimilation, 1860–1890* (Philadelphia: University of Pennsylvania Press, 1963), p. 155. Clyde Milner agreed that Schurz and the new Commissioner of Indian Affairs Ezra Hayt "prized bureaucratic competence and routine above religious affiliation." Milner, *With Good Intentions*, p. 187. Roy W. Meyer suggests that Hayt did not officially repudiate the Peace Policy, "but because it lacked statutory force he was able, with the backing of Secretary Schurz, to undermine it by pleading the necessity of speedy appointments and thus not giving the church groups time to suggest candidates." Roy W. Meyer in Kvasnicka and Viola, *The Commissioners of Indian Affairs*, p. 159.

3. *Report of the Board of Indian Commissioners, 1877*, pp. 40–41, 71–74. Reporting on the meeting with President Hayes, a writer in a Presbyterian periodical rejoiced that "nobody could doubt the earnest sympathy of our Chief Magistrate with all friends of the Indians." *The Record of the Presbyterian Church in the United States of America*, 29 (March 1878): 81.

4. *Santa Fe New Mexican*, March 30, 1878; *Report of the Commissioner of Indian Affairs, 1878* (Washington, D.C.: Government Printing Office, 1878), pp. 108–9. The sureties whom Pyle finally secured for his bond were the two men who had the current contract for supplying beef to the Navajo agency. Pyle worried about insinuations of impropriety in this arrangement, but he could find no one else in Santa Fe to take the responsibility. George G. Smith to Lowrie, June 17, 1878, AIC, D, 48½.

5. Sherman to G. W. McCrary, Secretary of War, September 9, 1878, OIA, M234, Roll 575; Pyle to the Commissioner of Indian Affairs, November 8, 1878, OIA, M234, Roll 574. Playing on Commissioner Hayt's presumed antagonism to the War Department and all that it represented, Pyle charged that Sherman had spoken openly about the Office of Indian Affairs as a "weak and contemptible affair."

6. Pyle to Lowrie, January 31 and March 28, 1879, AIC, D, 74, 87; Pyle to Commissioner of Indian Affairs, April 10, 1879, OIA, M234, Roll 576; Senator T. W. Ferry to Schurz, August 29, 1878, and Lowrie to Schurz, March 4, 1879, OSI, M750, Roll 14.

7. Eastman to Commissioner of Indian Affairs, October 18, 1879, OIA, M234, Roll 576; *Report of the Commissioner of Indian Affairs, 1879* (Washington, D.C.: Government Printing Office, 1879), p. 115; Captain Frank Bennett to Acting Assistant Adjutant General, District of New Mexico, April 24, 1880, OIA, M234, Roll 582. A distinguished citizen of Santa Fe, convinced that the Navajos were actually poised to go on the warpath, called for Eastman's removal to avoid a disaster "brought on by the acts of one utterly unfit man, apparently devoid of any vestige of common sense." L. Bradford Prince, Chief Justice, Supreme Court, Territory of New Mexico to President Rutherford B. Hayes, May 7, 1880, OIA, M234, Roll 579.

8. Colonel George P. Buell, 15th Infantry, Ft. Wingate, New Mexico, Special Order 56, June 12, 1880, OIA, M234, Roll 580; E. J. Brooks, Acting Commis-

sioner of Indian Affairs to the Secretary of the Interior, August 14, 1880, OSI, M750, Roll 14.

9. E. S. Stevens, Acting Commissioner of Indian Affairs to the Secretary of the Interior, August 4, 1881, OSI, M750, Roll 14; Eastman to Commissioner of Indian Affairs, June 30, 1881, and Bennett to Commissioner of Indian Affairs, July 1, 1881, Letters Received, Bureau of Indian Affairs [BIA], 1881, NA, RG75, Documents 11736, 11580. Senator Ferry sent a long report defending Eastman's actions as agent to the secretary of the interior. Ferry attributed the tensions at Fort Defiance to "the trader's ring assisted by the military." Senator T. W. Ferry to the Secretary of the Interior, March 10, 1881, OSI, M750, Roll 14.

10. *New York Times*, July 20 and August 12, 1881; J. M. Haworth to Honorable S. J. Kirkwood, Secretary of the Interior, August 9, 1881, Department of the Interior, Indian Division, Inspector's Reports, NA, RG75; Haworth to Kirkwood, August 15, 1881, Letters Received, BIA, 1881, Document 9674.

11. Haworth to Kirkwood, August 9, 1881, Inspector's Reports, NA, RG75; Unidentified and undated clippings in Jackson Scrapbooks, 58: 48, 84 and 122. One of the latter writers, while announcing the arrival of the Donaldson family at Fort Defiance, noted that "like all pagan people, the Navajos are dirty and degraded, yet they are the finest tribe in the Rocky Mountains." Jackson Scrapbooks, 58: 84.

12. Hayt to Lowrie, September 18, 1879 and Donaldson to Lowrie, February 1, 1880, AIC, D, 170, 185; Mrs. A. H. Donaldson to Jackson, April 28, 1880, Jackson Correspondence, X, p. 137; Henry Kendall, Secretary, Board of Home Missions to Commissioner of Indian Affairs, November 11, 1880, OIA, M234, Roll 579; Mrs. J. D. Perkins to Jackson, November 7, 1881, and January 31, 1882, Jackson Correspondence, XI, pp. 298–99 and XII, p. 82. Mrs. Perkins's irascibility may have been attributed to a physical disorder. Her husband told Jackson that she had suffered from ill health since their arrival at Fort Defiance and "now her bowels are troubling her much." J. D. Perkins to Jackson, July 27, 1882, Jackson Correspondence, XII, p. 240.

13. C. H. Howard to Secretary of the Interior Henry Teller, November 29, 1882, Inspector's Reports, NA, RG75; Eastman to Commissioner of Indian Affairs, September 15, 1882, OSI, M750, Roll 14; Riordan to Commissioner of Indian Affairs, January 1, 1883, Letters Received, BIA, Document 368; *The Boston Advertiser*, August 23, 1883, newspaper clipping in Board of Indian Commissioners, Scrapbooks, 1871–1884, NA, RG75; Frank D. Reeve, "The Government and the Navajo, 1883–1888," *New Mexico Historical Review*, 18 (January 1943): 17. In Frank Reeve's opinion, Riordan sought the job as agent at Fort Defiance to investigate recent reports of mineral discoveries on the Navajo reservation.

14. *Report of the Commissioner of Indian Affairs, 1879*, p. III. Secretary of the Interior Carl Schurz dismissed Ezra Hayt as his Commissioner of Indian Affairs early in 1880 after revelation of certain "irregularities" allegedly as-

sociated with Hayt's personal interest in a controversial silver mining venture on the San Carlos Apache reservation in Arizona. Roy W. Meyer, "Ezra A. Hayt" in Kvasnicka and Viola, *Commissioners of Indian Affairs*, pp. 161–62.

15. "Report of the Secretary of the Interior, 1880," *House Executive Documents*, 46 Congress, 3 session, serial 1959, p. XIX.

16. *Report of the Board of Indian Commissioners, 1879* (Washington, D.C.: Government Printing Office, 1880), p. 113.

17. *Report of the Commissioner of Indian Affairs, 1882* (Washington, D.C.: Government Printing Office, 1882), pp. VI–VII.

18. Henry M. Teller, Secretary of the Interior to Rev. Dr. J. M. Reid, Corresponding Secretary of the Missionary Society of the Methodist Episcopal Church, August 5, 1882, in *Report of the Board of Indian Commissioners, 1882* (Washington, D.C.: Government Printing Office, 1883), pp. 53–54. In the annual report of the Commissioner of Indian Affairs for 1882, a change in the wording for the heading of one section conveyed an ominous message to the church mission boards. The caption now read, "List of Indian Agencies *Formerly* [author's emphasis] Assigned to the Several Religious Denominations." *Report of the Commissioner of Indian Affairs, 1882* (Washington, D.C.: Government Printing Office, 1882), p. 367.

19. *Report of the Board of Indian Commissioners, 1882*, p. 54.

20. Forty-sixth Annual Report of the Board of Foreign Missions in *Minutes of the General Assembly, 1883*, p. 14.

21. William Truax to Lowrie, May 27, 1873, AIC, M, 144. Lowrie received many unsolicited recommendations for applicants to agency positions. Of those in the questionable category, he must have wondered why one gentleman should be posted to an Indian agency simply because, while residing earlier in Scotland, he had "kept a very comfortable house [hotel] at which I have known her Majesty repeatedly to lunch in passing to Balmoral Castle." J. H. Burnett, Bart., Crathes Castle, Aberdeen, Scotland, May 24, 1867, enclosed in G. G. Smith to Lowrie, July 23, 1877, AIC, C, 168.

22. *Report of the Commissioner of Indian Affairs, 1871*, pp. 177–78. While admitting that Indian agents under the Peace Policy were underpaid, one writer in an eastern newspaper insisted that their duty "is something more than making as much money as possible." *New York Times*, May 27, 1876.

23. *New York Times*, May 30, 1870.

24. For an excellent study that questions the prevalent attitudes of many historians who always make civilian agents scapegoats in all incidents of white/Indian strife on the frontier, see William E. Unrau, "The Civilian as Indian Agent: Villain or Victim?" *Western Historical Quarterly*, 3 (October 1972): 405–20.

25. *Congressional Globe*, 41 Congress, 3 session, p. 1112.

26. Ibid.

27. Ibid.

28. W. F. M. Arny to Lowrie, September 23, 1873, AIC, M, 249.

29. William Truax to Lowrie, May 27, 1873, AIC, N, 144.

30. *Minutes of the General Assembly, 1883*, p. 14. In his perceptive study of the Grant Peace Policy, Robert Utley concluded that "the cardinal tenets of the Grant Peace Policy were not in the end discarded. They became the vehicles by which the Indian was pacified and civilized." Robert M. Utley, "The Celebrated Peace Policy of General Grant," *North Dakota History*, 20 (July 1953): 142.

Epilogue

1. Blake, "Spanish Speaking Missions," p. 85; Mark T. Banker, "Presbyterian Missionary Activity in the Southwest: The Careers of John and James Menaul," *Journal of the Southwest*, 23 (January 1984): 55–61; Truax to Lowrie, October 12, 1876, AIC, C, 110; Edward H. Roberts, *Biographical Catalogue of the Princeton Theological Seminary, 1815–1932* (Princeton, New Jersey: privately published), 1933, p. 224; *Necrological Reports . . . Princeton Theological Seminary,* III, p. 76.

2. Arny to J. Q. Smith, January 22 and 24, 1876, OIA, M234, Roll 566; Murphy; *Frontier Crusader*, pp. 241–45; E. P. Smith to W. F. Hall, April 12, 1873, OIA, M21, Roll 109; John W. Miller to Edwin Dudley, October 23, 1873, OIA, T21, Roll 21; Winona W. Garbrick, Bedford, Pennsylvania, to author, January 20, 1978.

3. McNitt, *Indian Traders*, p. 199; Jackson to Commissioner of Indian Affairs R. E. Trowbridge, March 24, 1880, OIA, M234, Roll 579; *Menaul School, Seventy-Five Years of Service*, p. 5; *Denver Republican* (Denver, Colorado), May 9, 1909.

4. Alexander Darley, "The Home Board for Home Fields," *The Interior*, February 7, 1878; George G. Smith, "The Foreign Board and the American Indians," *Rocky Mountain Presbyterian*, April 1878; Clifford Drury, *Presbyterian Panorama* (Philadelphia: Board of Christian Education, Presbyterian Church in the United States of America, 1952), p. 191.

5. Senator Henry L. Dawes in *Report of the Board of Indian Commissioners, 1887* (Washington, D.C.: Government Printing Office, 1888), p. 54. The Dawes Act also contained a provision for granting citizenship to Indians who abided by the terms of the legislation. The reservation land still remaining after completion of the allotment process could be sold and the revenues derived from the sale would be held for each tribe in the Treasury of the United States. Unfortunately an amendment to the act in 1891 permitting the Indians to lease their allotments negated much of the original intent of the legislation. For an excellent analysis of the intent and results of this legislation, see D. S. Otis, *The Dawes Act and the Allotment of Indian Lands* (Norman: University of Oklahoma Press, 1973).

6. Charles C. Royce, ed., *Indian Land Cessions in the United States* (New York: *New York Times* and Arny Press, 1971, reprint of edition of 1900), pp. 892, 898; McNitt, *Indian Traders*, p. 140; E. M. Haldeman, *Historical Sketch of Ganado*

Mission (privately published, 1967), p. 1; Edgar W. Moore, "The Bierkempers, Navajos, and the Ganado Presbyterian Mission, 1901–1912," *American Presbyterians*, 64 (Summer 1986): 125–35.

7. Mrs. A. Donaldson to Jackson, May 21, 1880, Jackson Correspondence, X, p. 161.

Bibliography

Government Documents

National Archives
Department of Commerce, Bureau of the Census, Ninth Census, 1870. Town of Neosho, Neosho Township, Neosho County, Missouri.
Department of the Interior. Records of the Indian Division, Office of the Secretary of the Interior, Record Group 48.
    Letters Sent, Indian Division, 1849–1903, Microcopy M606.
    Appointment Papers, New Mexico, 1850–1907, Microcopy M750.
    Applications and Papers Pertaining to Indian Affairs, Letters from Various Churches.
————. Records of the Bureau of Indian Affairs, Record Group 75.
    Board of Indian Commissioners, Letters Received, 1870–1872.
    Board of Indian Commissioners, Letters Received, 1869–1899.
    Board of Indian Commissioners, Letters Sent, 1870–1891, 1893–1909.
    Board of Indian Commissioners, Scrapbooks, 1871–1884.
    Board of Indian Commissioners, Minutes, 1869–1917.
    Office of Indian Affairs, Letters Received, 1824–1880, New Mexico Superintendency, 1849–1880, Microcopy M234.
    Office of Indian Affairs, Letters Received, 1881–1883.
    Office of Indian Affairs, Records of the New Mexico Superintendency, 1849–1880, Microcopy T21.
    Office of Indian Affairs, Letters Sent, 1824–1882, Microcopy M21.
    Office of Indian Affairs, Report Books, 1838–1885, Microcopy M348.
    Office of Indian Affairs, Reports of Inspection of the Field Jurisdiction, 1873–1900, Microcopy M1070.

———. Annual Reports of the Secretary of the Interior.
"Report of the Secretary of the Interior, 1869," *House Executive Documents,*
    41 Congress, 2 session, serial 1414.
"Report of the Secretary of the Interior, 1870," *House Executive Documents,*
    41 Congress, 3 session, serial 1449.
"Report of the Secretary of the Interior, 1871," *House Executive Documents,*
    42 Congress, 2 session, serial 1505.
"Report of the Secretary of the Interior, 1872," *House Executive Documents,*
    42 Congress, 3 session, serial 1560.
"Report of the Secretary of the Interior, 1873," *House Executive Documents,*
    43 Congress, 1 session, serial 1601.
"Report of the Secretary of the Interior, 1874," *House Executive Documents,*
    43 Congress, 2 session, serial 1639.
"Report of the Secretary of the Interior, 1875," *House Executive Documents,*
    44 Congress, 1 session, serial 1680.
"Report of the Secretary of the Interior, 1876," *House Executive Documents,*
    44 Congress, 2 session, serial 1749.
"Report of the Secretary of the Interior, 1877," *House Executive Documents,*
    45 Congress, 2 session, serial 1800.
"Report of the Secretary of the Interior, 1880," *House Executive Documents,*
    46 Congress, 3 session, serial 1959.
———. Annual Reports of the Commissioner of Indian Affairs.
"Report of the Commissioner of Indian Affairs, 1850," *Senate Executive
    Documents,* 31 Congress, 2 session, serial 587.
"Report of the Commissioner of Indian Affairs, 1869," *Senate Executive
    Documents,* 41 Congress, 2 session, serial 1414.
"Report of the Commissioner of Indian Affairs, 1870," *Senate Executive
    Documents,* 41 Congress, 3 session, serial 1449.
Published annually thereafter by the Government Printing Office.
———. Annual Reports of the Board of Indian Commissioners.
"Report of the Board of Indian Commissioners, 1869," *House Executive
    Documents,* 41 Congress, 2 session, serial 1414.
"Report of the Board of Indian Commissioners, 1870," *House Executive
    Documents,* 41 Congress, 3 session, serial 1440.
Published annually thereafter by the Government Printing Office.
Department of War. Office of the Judge Advocate General, Service Records,
    Navy and Old Army Branch, Military Archives Division.

Congressional Documents
"Report of the Joint Committee on the Conduct of War: Massacre of Cheyenne
    Indians," *Senate Report No. 142, Part 3,* 38 Congress, 2 session, serial 1214.
"Proceedings of a Military Commission Convened by Special Orders 23,
    Headquarters District of Colorado, Denver, Colorado Territory, February

1, 1865 in the Case of Colonel J. M. Chivington, First Colorado Cavalry," *Senate Executive Documents No. 26,* 39 Congress, 2 session, serial 1277.
"Condition of the Indian Tribes, Report of the Joint Special Committee Appointed Under Joint Resolution of March 3, 1865, with an appendix," *Senate Report No. 156,* 39 Congress, 2 session, serial 1279.
"Report of the Indian Peace Commissioners," *House Executive Documents, No. 97,* 40 Congress, 2 session, serial 1337.

Other Government Documents
United States Statutes at Large, IV, XIII, XV, XVI.
Congressional Globe, 41 Congress, 3 session.
Inaugural Addresses of the Presidents of the United States, 1789–1969 (Washington, D.C.: Government Printing Office, 1969).

Books

Adams, Henry. *Letters, 1858–1891,* W. C. Ford, ed. New York: Houghton Mifflin Co., 1930.
Amsden, Charles A. *Navajo Weaving: Its Technic and Its History.* Glorieta, New Mexico: The Rio Grande Press, 1971.
The Annual of Washington and Jefferson College, Washington, Pennsylvania. Buffalo, New York: Gies and Co., 1889.
Armstrong, William H. *Warrior in Two Camps: Ely S. Parker, Union General and Seneca Chief.* Syracuse: Syracuse University Press, 1978.
Chavez, Fray Angelico. *But Time and Chance: The Story of Padre Martinez of Taos, 1793–1867.* Santa Fe, New Mexico: Sunstone Press, 1981.
Doyle, Sherman H. *Presbyterian Home Missions.* Philadelphia: Presbyterian Board of Publications and Sabbath School Work, 1902.
Drury, Clifford. *Presbyterian Panorama.* Philadelphia: Presbyterian Board of Christian Education, 1952.
Frink, Maurice. *Fort Defiance and the Navajos.* Boulder, Colorado: Pruett Press, 1968.
Fritz, Henry E. *The Movement for Indian Assimilation, 1860–1890.* Philadelphia: University of Pennsylvania Press, 1963.
Gregg, Josiah. *Commerce of the Prairies,* Max L. Moorhead, ed. Norman: University of Oklahoma Press, 1954; reprint of 1844 edition.
Haldeman, E. M. *Historical Sketch of Ganado Mission.* Privately published, 1967.
Heitman, Francis B. *Historical Register and Dictionary of the United States Army.* Washington, D.C.: Government Printing Office, 1903.
Hill, Edward. *The Office of Indian Affairs, 1824–1880: Historical Sketches.* New York: Clearwater Publishing Co., 1974.
Hoig, Stan. *The Sand Creek Massacre.* Norman: University of Oklahoma Press, 1961.

Bibliography

Horgan, Paul. *Lamy of Santa Fe: His Life and Times.* New York: Farrar, Straus, and Giroux, 1975.

Johnson, Donald B. and Porter, Kirk H., eds. *National Party Platforms 1840–1972.* Urbana: University of Illinois Press, 1973.

Kappler, Charles J., ed. *Indian Treaties, 1778–1883.* New York: Interland Publishing Co., 1972; reprint of 1904 edition.

Keller, Robert H., Jr. *American Protestantism and United States Indian Policy, 1869–82.* Lincoln: University of Nebraska Press, 1983.

Kelsey, Rayner W. *Friends and the Indians, 1655–1917.* Philadelphia: Associated Executive Committee of Friends on Indian Affairs, 1917.

Kvasnicka, Robert M. and Herman J. Viola, eds. *The Commissioners of Indian Affairs, 1824–1977.* Lincoln: University of Nebraska Press, 1979.

Malone, Dumas, ed. *Dictionary of American Biography,* 10 vols. New York: Charles Scribner's Sons, 1933.

Mardock, Robert W. *The Reformers and the American Indian.* Columbia: University of Missouri Press, 1971.

McNitt, Frank. *The Indian Traders.* Norman: University of Oklahoma Press, 1962.

Menaul School, Albuquerque, New Mexico: Seventy-Five Years of Service, 1881–1956. Albuquerque, New Mexico: privately published, 1956.

Milner, Clyde A., II. *With Good Intentions: Quaker Work Among the Pawnees, Otos, and Omahas in the 1870s.* Lincoln: University of Nebraska Press, 1982.

Murphy, Lawrence R. *Frontier Crusader: William F. M. Arny.* Tucson: University of Arizona Press, 1972.

Myres, Sandra L., ed. *Cavalry Wife: The Diary of Eveline M. Alexander, 1866–1867.* College Station: Texas A & M University Press, 1977.

The National Cyclopaedia of American Biography, 58 vols. New York: James T. White and Co., 1897.

Necrological Reports and Annual Proceedings of Princeton Theological Seminary, 4 vols. Princeton, New Jersey: C. S. Robinson and Co., 1891, 1899, 1909, 1919.

The New Mexico, Arizona, and Colorado Missionary Association, Annual Reports bound as *Our Mission Field,* Sheldon Jackson Collection, Presbyterian Historical Society, Philadelphia, Pennsylvania.

Otis, D. S. *The Dawes Act and the Allotment of Indian Lands.* Norman: University of Oklahoma Press, 1973.

Pearce, T. M., ed. with Ina S. Cassidy and Helen S. Pearce. *New Mexico Place Names: A Geographical Dictionary.* Albuquerque: University of New Mexico Press, 1965.

Polakoff, Keith I. *The Politics of Inertia: The Election of 1876 and the End of Reconstruction.* Baton Rouge: Louisiana State University Press, 1973.

Prucha, Francis P. *American Indian Policy in Crisis: Christian Reformers and the Indian, 1865–1900.* Norman: University of Oklahoma Press, 1976.

Bibliography

————. *A Guide to the Military Posts of the United States, 1789–1895*. Madison: The State Historical Society of Wisconsin, 1944.

Rahill, Peter J. *The Catholic Indian Missions and Grant's Peace Policy, 1870–1884*. Washington, D.C.: The Catholic University of America Press, 1953.

Randall, J. G. and David Donald. *The Civil War and Reconstruction*. Boston: D. C. Heath, 1961.

Richardson, James D., ed. *A Compilation of the Messages and Papers of the Presidents*, 11 vols. Washington, D.C.: Bureau of National Literature and Art, 1911.

Roberts, Edward H. *Biographical Catalogue of the Princeton Theological Seminary, 1815–1932*. Princeton, New Jersey: privately publihsed, 1933.

Royce, Charles C., ed. *Indian Land Cessions in the United States*. New York: *New York Times* and Arno Press, 1971 reprint of edition of 1900.

Schroeder, Albert H., ed. *The Changing Ways of Southwestern Indians: A Historic Perspective*. Glorieta, New Mexico: The Rio Grande Press, 1973.

Smith, Duane A., ed. *A Taste of the West: Essays in Honor of Robert G. Atheran*. Boulder, Colorado: Pruett Publishing Co., 1983.

Thompson, Gerald E. *The Army and the Navajo: The Bosque Redondo Reservation Experiment, 1863–68*. Tucson: University of Arizona Press, 1976.

Trennert, Robert A., Jr. *Alternative to Extinction: Federal Indian Policy and the Beginnings of the Reservation System, 1846–1851*. Philadelphia: Temple University Press, 1975.

Underhill, Ruth. *The Navajos*. Norman: University of Oklahoma Press, 1956.

White, Lonnie J., ed. *Chronicle of a Congressional Journey: The Doolittle Committee in the Southwest, 1865*. Boulder, Colorado: Pruett Publishing Co., 1975.

Periodicals

Agnew, Edith J. and Ruth K. Barber, "The Unique Presbyterian School System of New Mexico." *Journal of Presbyterian History*, 49 (Fall 1971): 197–221.

Banker, Mark T. "Presbyterian Missionary Activity in the Southwest: The Careers of John and James Menaul." *Journal of the Southwest*, 23 (January 1984): 55–61.

Baxter, John O. "Restocking the Navajo Reservation after Bosque Redondo." *New Mexico Historical Review*, 58 (October 1983): 325–45.

Bender, Norman J. "Sheldon Jackson's Crusade to Win the West for Christ, 1869–1880." *The Midwest Review*, 4 (Spring 1982): 1–12.

Chaput, Donald. "Generals, Indian Agents, Politicians: The Doolittle Survey of 1865." *Western Historical Quarterly*, 3 (July 1972): 269–82.

Jones, Oakah L., Jr. "The Origins of the Navajo Indian Police, 1872–1873." *Arizona and the West*, 8 (Autumn 1966): 225–38.

Kelly, Lawrence C. "Where Was Fort Canby?" *New Mexico Historical Review*, 42 (January 1967): 49–62.

Bibliography

Kelsey, Harry. "The Doolittle Report of 1867: Its Preparation and Shortcomings." *Arizona and the West*, 17 (Summer 1975): 107–20.

MacCormac, Earl R. "The Development of Presbyterian Missionary Organizations, 1790–1870." *Journal of Presbyterian History*, 43 (September 1965): 149–73.

Moore, Edgar W. "The Bierkempers, Navajos, and the Ganado Presbyterian Mission, 1901–1912." *American Presbyterians*, 64 (Summer 1986): 125–35.

The Record of the Presbyterian Church in the United States of America (1868–1878).

Reeve, Frank D. "The Federal Indian Policy in New Mexico, 1858–1880." *New Mexico Historical Review*, 12 (July 1937): 218–69 and 13 (April 1938): 146–91.

———. "The Government and the Navaho, 1883–1888." *New Mexico Historical Review*, 18 (January 1943): 17.

Unrau, William E. "The Civilian as Indian Agent: Villain or Victim?" *Western Historical Quarterly*, 3 (October 1972): 405–20.

Utley, Robert M. "The Celebrated Peace Policy of General Grant." *North Dakota History*, 20 (July 1953): 121–42.

Waltmann, Henry G. "Circumstantial Reformer: President Grant and the Indian Problem." *Arizona and the West*, 13 (Winter 1971): 323–42.

———. "John C. Lowrie and Presbyterian Indian Administration, 1870–1882." *Journal of Presbyterian History*, 54 (Summer 1976): 259–76.

Miscellaneous

Newspapers
Boston Traveller, December 26, 1874.
Chicago Daily Tribune, December 1, 1874.
Chicago Journal, November 30, 1874.
The Daily Inter-Ocean (Chicago, Illinois), December 1, 1874.
The Daily Journal of Commerce (Kansas City, Missouri), November 28, 1874.
Denver Republican, May 9, 1909.
Herald and Presbyter (Cincinnati, Ohio), February 13, 1873.
The Interior (Chicago, Illinois), February 7, 1878.
New York Sun, January 1, 1875.
New York Times, 1871–1881.
The Presbyterian (Philadelphia, Pennsylvania), September 3, 1870.
The Presbyterian Banner (Pittsburgh, Pennsylvania), 1867–1877.
Providence Journal, December 28, 1874.
Rocky Mountain News (Denver, Colorado), November 24, 1874.
Rocky Mountain Presbyterian (Denver, Colorado), October 1877, and April 1878.
Santa Fe New Mexican, 1867–1877.
St. Louis Daily Globe, November 28 and 29, 1874.
St. Louis Dispatch, November 27 and 28, 1874.
Washington Evening Star, December 1 and 10, 1874.

Bibliography

Dissertations

Benge, Reba. "Benjamin M. Thomas: Career in the Southwest, 1870–1892." Ph.D. Dissertation, University of New Mexico, Albuquerque, New Mexico, 1979.

Warner, Michael J. "Protestant Missionary Work with the Navajo Indians from 1846 to 1912." Ph.D. Dissertation, University of New Mexico, Albuquerque, New Mexico, 1977.

Minutes, Agencies of the Presbyterian Church

Minutes, Synod of Colorado, 1871–1888, Presbyterian Historical Society, Philadelphia, Pennsylvania.

Minutes, Board of Foreign Missions, Presbyterian Church, Presbyterian Historical Society, Philadelphia, Pennsylvania.

Minutes of the General Assembly of the Presbyterian Church in the United States of America. New York: Presbyterian Board of Publications. Published annually.

Correspondence

American Indian Correspondence, Letters Received, Record Group MsIn25, Presbyterian Historical Society, Philadelphia, Pennsylvania.

Board of Foreign Missions, Letterpress Copies of Letters Sent, Presbyterian Historical Society, Philadelphia, Pennsylvania.

Correspondence Relating to Pioneer Presbyterian Missions West of the Mississippi and Missouri Rivers and in Alaska, 1856–1908, 26 volumes, Presbyterian Historical Society, Philadelphia, Pennsylvania.

Garbrick, Winona W., Bedford, Pennsylvania, to author, January 20, 1978.

Other Unpublished Documents

Blake, Alice. "Spanish Speaking Missions in New Mexico." Manuscript, Presbyterian Historical Society, Philadelphia, Pennsylvania.

Jackson, Sheldon. Diary, 1877. Presbyterian Historical Society, Philadelphia, Pennsylvania.

Minutes, Denver Bible Society, Colorado State Historical Society, Denver, Colorado.

The Scrapbooks of Sheldon Jackson, 64 volumes. Presbyterian Historical Society, Philadelphia, Pennsylvania.

Index

Agencies: accommodations at, 106–7; bureaucratic authority over, 3, 128, 149, 194; conditions at, *see* Fort Defiance, Arizona, conditions at; conduct of, 46; employees of, *see* Employees, agency; politics within, *see* Politics, at agencies

Agents, Indian: authority of, 31, 106, 169–70; dismissal of, 99–101; military officers as, *see* Soldiers, as agents; morality of, 29, 30–31, 108; as peacekeepers, 54, 117, 160; protection of, 80, 146; qualifications of, 45–46, 190–91; relations with missionaries, 17, 29, 47–48, 192; salaries of, 112, 161, 191; selection of, xi–xii, 5–8, 21, 27–28, 36–37, 58–59, 108, 142–43, 145, 164–65, 172–73, 177, 181, 183–84, 187, 189, 196; success of, 97, 161; supervision of, 102–3, 116

Agriculture: competence for, 119; conditions for, 94; degree of success of, 23, 53, 115, 127, 159, 165–66, 170, 191; funding for, 34–35; land for, 1–2, 79, 156–57; and Navajos, 12; training for, 18, 25, 55, 103, 115, 191–92, *see also* Mission farm; and weather, 136

Aiken, James, 55

Alcohol, 133, 136, 143, 152, 174–75, 191

Alexander, Andrew J., 9–10

Alexander, Eveline, 9–10

Allotment in severalty, 188, 189, 199–200

Alviso, Jesus, 102, 116; photo of, 62; and Washington trip, 121

Animals: agency-owned, 155–56; as annuity goods, 23, 53; theft of, 17, 35–36, 143

Annuity goods, 14, 195; delays in, 105; distribution of, 20–21, 166–67; makeup of, 23, 166; as pay, 58, 117; sheep as, 53; shortages of, 156; theft of, 138–39, 141, 143; *see also* Rations

Apaches, Mescalero, 13

Armijo, 55

Arny, W. F. M., 99, 198; dismissal of, 138–40, 142–45, 152; goals of, 112, 196; photo of, 62; success of, 109–10; and Washington trip,

119–20, 122, 123, 124–25, *see also* Washington trip
Arny, William, 102, 108, 121
Arthur, Chester, 189
Auburn Female Bible Society, 10

Barboncito, 55
Beef, 105
Bennett, Frank T., 21–22, 30, 48, 49, 184–85
Bishop, Nathan, 29
Blair, Thomas, 166–67
Blankets, 154, 178; centennial, 121
Board of Foreign Missions, 175–77, 186, 193, 199
Board of Home Missions, 173, 175–77, 186, 193, 199
Board of Indian Commissioners, 6, 7, 29, 58; politics on, 128
Boarding schools, 21, 53, 77–78, 103, 113, 198
Bosque Redondo, 11–13
Bozeman Trail, 4
Brown, John, 125
Brunot, Felix R., 6, 27, 58, 73, 89, 93, 108
Bureau of Catholic Indian Missions, 30

Carleton, James H., 11; photo of, 64
Carson, Christopher "Kit," 11, 15
Catholic Church, 15, 17–18, 86, 87, 152; missionary work of, 30; in Santa Fe, 9–11
Census, 36
Chandler, Zachariah, 148, 160–61
Chapin, Seward, 102
Children, civilization of, 90
Chivington, John, 1
Churches: agent nominations from, xi–xii, 5–6, 27–30, 36–37, 108, 129, 188–89, 196; civilization as product of, 89, 131, 151; founding, 10, 104; membership

of, 162; and moral standards on frontier, 9–10, 192; respect for, 107; *see also* Catholic Church *and* Presbyterian Church
Chusca Valley, 159–60
Civil service, appointments to, 164–65
Clinton, William, 22, 31, 33, 41
Clothing: enforced standards for, 178; fashions in, 23; and winter, 105
Clum, Henry R., 57
Cohabitation, 47–48, 54–55, 82, 102, 137, 144, 172
Cole, John, 85
College of Ganado, 200
Colyer, Vincent, 18, 27, 31, 75
Congress, agency appropriations from, *see* Funding, for agencies; and agent appointments, *see* Patronage; attitude toward Indians, 4; and Sand Creek massacre, 2–3
Cook, Harriet, 132, 135
Corruption, 1, 5–6, *see also* Patronage
Cox, Jacob D., 7, 28, 42
Cree, Thomas, 108
Crothers, Williamson, 83, 98
Custer, George Armstrong, 151, 160

Damon, Anson C., 54, 102
Daniels, J. W., 118
Dawes, Henry L., 199–200
Dawes Severalty Act, 199–200
Defrees, William, 106–7, 116
Delano, Columbus, 42, 45, 57–58, 73–74, 89–90, 109, 124, 129; resignation of, 148
Delph, Callie, 104
Dine, *see* Navajos
Dodd, Theodore H., 16
Donaldson, Alexander, 70, 186, 200
Doolittle, James R., 3

Doolittle committee, 3–4, 9, 12
Drought, 53
Dudley, L. Edwin, 86–87, 99;
    agency funding efforts of, 96–97,
    115; departure of, 116; relations
    with W. F. M. Arny, 102–4, 107–8,
    113, 120

Eastman, Galen, 184–87
Easton, Henry W., 102; photo of,
    62; and Washington trip, 121,
    122, 126, 133
Education, 192; compulsory, 58;
    Indians' desire for, 40; and
    missionary work, 19–21; on-going
    support for, 200; success of, 32,
    51, 86, 103, 112, 113–14, 153, 159,
    169, 171, 176, 182; *see also* Schools
Elections, 158
Employees, agency: morality of, 30–
    31, 47–48, 54, 82, 102, 137;
    politics of, *see* Politics, at
    agencies; recruitment of, 153, 157;
    salaries of, 76, 132; supervision
    of, 106
English language, 16, 124; teaching,
    32

Families: composition of Navajo,
    167–68; and morality, 87, 96; *see
    also* Marriage
Ferry, Thomas W., 184, 185
Fisk, Clinton B., 131
Flatt, Jennie, 85
Food: expenses for, 19; and peace,
    126–27; self-sufficiency in, *see*
    Self-sufficiency; *see also* Rations
Fort Defiance, Arizona, 15–16;
    conditions at, 22, 40, 47, 83, 101–
    2, 118, 146, 150, 152–53, 155, 169,
    182, 191; photo of, 67; plans to
    abandon, 94
Fort Wingate, 15; morality at, 136
French, James C., 16–17

Friese, Valentine, 112–13, 118;
    relations with W. F. M. Arny,
    135–36
Funding, xii; for agencies, 34–35,
    42, 53, 59, 74–76, 194; for
    agriculture, 34–35; borrowing to
    supplement, 33, 34, 49, 74, 115;
    conflicts over, 46; for medical
    treatment, 157; for missions, 13,
    15, 19, 25, 33, 41, 182; for
    schools, 84, 103, 113, 186

Gambling, 23, 102
Ganado Mucho, 55, 81, 184; and
    Washington trip, 121
Garfield, James, 189
Gaston, Charity Ann, *see* Menaul,
    Charity Ann (Gaston)
Goats, 192
Gold, 162
Gould, James L., 106
Gow, Joseph, 113
Grant, Ulysses S., 5–6, 28, 43, 59,
    90, 109, 111, 124, 129, 149, 158,
    162; photo of, 63; sketch of, 61
Grant Peace Policy, xi, 7;
    administration of, 193–94;
    continuation of, 163–64, 178–79;
    disintegration of, 181, 188–90;
    goals of, 43; reassessment of, 177;
    success of, 45, 57, 73–74, 88–90,
    93–94, 108–9, 111–12, 128–30, 131,
    147–49, 151–52, 160–61, 175–76,
    178
Gregg, J. Irwin, 141, 142
Guns, Indian access to, 80, 82

Hall, William F., 82–83, 94;
    dismissal of, 99–101
Hamblin, Jacob, 117
Haworth, J. M., 185
Hayes, Rutherford B., 158, 164–65,
    178–79, 181–82, 188–89, 200
Hayt, Ezra A., 177–78, 183, 186, 188

Hazen, William, 93
Health: in Arizona, 41; of Navajos, 78; *see also* Medical treatment
Hides, 174
Hogans, 155
Hopi Indians, 107, 132, 169–70
Horses, 168
Howard, C. H., 187
Howard, Oliver O., 81, 82; photo of, 68
Hunting, 107, 115, 170

Incentive programs, 58
Indian Rights Association, 199
Indians, agents for, *see* Agents, Indian; attitudes toward labor of, 89–90; cultures of, xii, 190; languages of, *see* Navajos, language of; populations of, 3–4, 12; western vs. eastern attitudes toward, xii, 2, 111; *see also individual tribes*
Indian Territory, relocation to, 73–74, 94, 109
Insects, 115
Inspections, 101–2, 118, 150, 171, 187; and agent selection, 185; by Doolittle committee, 3; of goods for Indians, 6
Interior Department, 3, 128, 149, 194
Irvine, Alexander, 145, 146–47, 153–57; resignation of, 170–73, 182; success of, 158–59
Irvine, Kate, 154

Jackson, Sheldon, 173, 176, 186, 198–99, 200; photo of, 64
Joseph, Chief, 179

Keams, Thomas V., 54, 198; as acting agent, 80–82; as agent candidate, 142–43, 145, 172, 183; relations with W. F. M. Arny, 137;

relations with William Hall, 88, 98; and Washington trip, 144
Keams, William, 137
Kemble, Edward C., 150, 152, 173
Kendall, Henry, 176

Lake Mohonk Conference of the Friends of the Indian, 199
Laundry, 40
Lea, Luke, 1
Letters, personal, as information source, xiii
Little Big Horn, 151, 160
Long Walk, 11
Lowrie, John C., 9, 11, 14, 28, 193, 197–98; assessment of Peace Policy, 73, 93, 112, 131, 152, 163, 181–82, 188; and Board of Home Missions, 176–77; and disintegration of Peace Policy, 190; as government advisor, 42; male chauvinism of, 94–95; and Navajo police force, 81; photo of, 65; relations with James Roberts, 78–79, 84–85; relations with Thomas Keams, 98–99, 142–43, 145, 172; relations with W. F. M. Arny, 103–4, 107, 117, 133, 138–39; relations with William Hall, 99–100
Lumber, 155, 166, 168–69

McFarland, David F., 10, 14, 19–20; and agent selection, 36–37, 100; and missionary selection, 83–84; photo of, 65
Manuelito, 55, 81, 119, 171, 183, 184, 195, 200; and Navajo police force, 81–82, 87; and Navajo uprising, 141–42; photo of, 62; and Washington trip, 121, 122, 123, 126, 137–38, 144
Marriage, 30–31, 47–48, 54–55, 137;

Navajo customs of, 82; *see also* Cohabitation

Martin, Cornelia, 9–10, 11

Medical treatment, 39–40, 192; funding for, 157; limitations on, 95, 118–19; traditional Navajo, 87; *see also* Physicians

Menaul, Charity Ann (Gaston), 20, 51, 77, 197; departures of, 80, 86, 103; marriage of, 48; photo of, 69; relations with James Roberts, 32; return of, 94

Menaul, John, 39–40, 197; goals of, 56, 127; marriage of, 48; photo of, 69; as physician, 76, 118–19; relations with James Roberts, 79; relations with W. F. M. Arny, 100, 107, 116–17, 135

Miller, James H., 39, 74, 198; death of, 79–80, 97–98, 109; relations with James Roberts, 46–47, 49

Missionaries, xi–xii; motives of, 56; recruitment of, 174; relations with agents, 17, 29, 30–32, 47–48, 192; relations among, 48–49; relations with mission boards, 46, 94–95; relations with Navajos, 78; salaries of, 19, 33, 41, 52; selection of, 14–15, 83–84, 186; similarity to Puritans, 196; as teachers, 19–20

Mission farm, 17–18, 21, 23, 32–33, 50–51

Missions: and agent nomination privileges, 29–30; authority over, *see* Presbyterian Church, organization of; and churches' power, 26; funding for, *see* Funding, for missions; legal status of, 17; locations of, 50–51; need for, 11; receptions of, 16–17; success of, 46–47, 52, 127–28, 154, 173–74, 193

Mitchell, Robert B., 22

Morality, 9–10, 29; of agency employees, 47–48, 54–55, 82, 102, 137; of agents, 30–31, 108; and families, 87, 96; inflexibility of, 192; of soldiers, 125, 136, 144; on Washington trip, 133, 144

Mormons, 36, 54, 117; influence of, 154

Names, 36; and ration issues, 168, 171, 175

Navajos, 11; barrenness of land of, 94; characteristics of, 18; crafts of, 121, 122, 123, *see also* Blankets *and* Weaving; dress of, 124; family structure of, 167–68; as forced laborers, 33–34; language of, 21, 32, 51, 56, 112, 174, 190; leaders of, 55, 119, 137–38, 171, 184; marriage with whites, 30–31; names of, 175, *see also* Names; as outlaws, 22–23; police force for, 81–82, 87, 105–6, 117; press descriptions of, 121, 122, 123, 124; relations with neighbors, 35, 54, 74, 117, 119, 124, 162, 191; response to Peace Policy, 195–96; treaty with, 13; uprisings by, 141–42

New Mexico, Arizona, and Colorado Missionary Association, 10, 14, 20

Nez Perce Indians, 179

Ouray, Chief, 90

Painter, Amanda C., 104

Paperwork, *see* Recordkeeping

Parker, Ely S., 7, 20, 22, 31, 33, 45, 57; photo of, 63

Patronage, 27, 100, 148, 177, 183–84

Peace Commission, 4–5; and Navajos, 13

Peace Policy, *see* Grant Peace Policy

Performance bonds, 46, 173
Perkins, J. D., 186–87
Physicians, 25, 55, 76, 116; selection of, 132, 135, 157; *see also* Medical treatment
Pile, William A., 35
Piper, Orlando F., 88
Police, Indians as, 81–82, 87, 105–6, 117–18
Politics: at agencies, 78–79, 97–98, 99–100, 106, 115–16, 133, 135, 146, 183; on Board of Indian Commissioners, 128; in Presbyterian Church, *see* Presbyterian Church, organization of
Pomeroy, Samuel, 194
Pope, John, 42, 125, 141
Pope, Nathaniel, 41–42, 54, 74–75, 77, 83
Posses, 35–36, *see also* Theft
Presbyterian Church, 9–10, 28; organization of, 25–26, 175–77, 186, 193, 199; relations with Catholics, 15, 17–18, 86, 87; territorial claims of, 29–30
Price, Hiram, 189
Price, William Redwood, 143, 198
Prostitution, 31, 133
Prucha, Francis Paul, 2
Public opinion, 1–3
Pueblos, 40; conditions at, 106–7; schools at, 85–86
Pyle, John, 172, 182–83

Quakers, 5–6, 7

Rabbits, 170
Rations, 195; composition of, 174; dissatisfaction with, 146; distribution procedures for, 167; labor as price of, 178; need for, 118; opposition to, 165–66; shortages of, 23, 34, 42, 49, 53, 74–75, 80–81, 96–97, 104–5, 115, 136, 156; storage of, 153; *see also* Annuity goods
Reading, 113–14, *see also* Education
Recordkeeping: for agencies, 39, 46, 146; and assessment of success, 147, 149, 153, 161–62, 178; and Board of Indian Commissioners, 58; and names, *see* Names; supplies for, 155
Red Cloud, 58
Repairs, 41, *see also* Fort Defiance, Arizona, conditions at
Reservations, 1–2, 4–5, 8; attractiveness of to Indians, 57; boundaries of, 22, 120, 156–57; as burial grounds for Indian race, 12; drive toward, 109; facilities on, 13–14; fertility of, 94; individual ownership of, *see* Allotment in severalty
Riordan, D. M., 187
Roberts, James Madison, 14, 19, 176, 192, 197; as agent candidate, 38; departure of, 77–78; funding difficulties of, 23, 25, 33, 46; moral attitudes of, 30–32, 47–48, 54; photo of, 67; return of, 84–85; teaching skills of, 32, 56
Roberts, Mary E. (Koons), 14
Rocky Mountain Bill, *see* Taylor, William F.

Sand Creek massacre, 1–3
San Felipe Pueblo, 85
San Juan River subagency, 79, 83, 88, 98, 106, 140–41, 157, 166, 171, 200
Santa Fe, 9–10; photo of, 67
Santa Fe Association, *see* New Mexico, Arizona, and Colorado Missionary Assoc.
Santo Domingo Pueblo, 85
Sawmills, 155, 166, 168–69

Schools: attendance at, 21, 23, 51, 56, 77, 86, 94, 113, 118, 154, 161–62; boarding, *see* Boarding schools; facilities for, 41, 47, 114, 159–60; funding for, 84, 103, 186; need for, 52–53; as part of missions, 16, 17; on reservations, 13–14; supplies for, 94, 112–13
Schurz, Carl, 165, 172, 177, 184, 188
Seeds, 115, 156
Self-sufficiency, 34, 114, 118, 146, 159, 170, 171; and success of Peace Policy, 147; *see also* Annuity goods *and* Rations
Sepoys, 81
Sheep, 53, 83, 192; as annuity goods, 168; Navajos' success with, 146; and weaving, 76, 154
Sherman, John, 148
Sherman, William T., 123, 141, 183
Sioux Indians, 58, 160–61
Slavery, 33–34
Smallpox, 39
Smith, Edward P., 96–97, 108, 124; assessment of Peace Policy, 128; relations with W. F. M. Arny, 120, 125; resignation of, 147–48
Smith, George G., 145, 199
Smith, John Quincy, 148, 161, 177, 198
Society of Friends, *see* Quakers
Soldiers: as agents, 6, 7–8, 21, 27, 143, 149, 184–85; alcohol sold by, 174–75; morality of, 125, 136, 144; and Navajo uprising, 142; and supply issues, 166–68
Squaw men, *see* Cohabitation
Stewart, William, 194–95
Stowe, Catherine, 113
Syphilis, 31, 95, 125, 133, 136, *see also* Cohabitation *and* Morality

Taos Pueblo, 86
Taylor, Nathaniel G., 4

Taylor, William F.: photo of, 62; and Washington trip, 121, 122, 126
Teachers: funding for, 51–52, 113; recruitment of, 24–25, 88, 103–4, 152; relations with agents, 185–86; salaries of, 19–20; skills of, 32
Teller, Henry, 189
Theft, 19; by agents, 141, 143; of animals, 17; control of, 35; murder during, 79–80; and Navajo police force, *see* Police; and rations, 49–50, 74, 126
Thomas, Benjamin M., 55, 79, 80, 88
Tilden, Samuel J., 158, 164
Tobacco, 166
Treaties, 4–5; violations of, 17, 18, 179, 193
Truax, William B., 83–84, 88, 94, 190–91, 197; as agency farmer, 112–15, 119, 127; departure of, 95–96; relations with Thomas Keams, 145; relations with W. F. M. Arny, 132–33, 139; relations with William Hall, 99–100

Uprisings: along Bozeman Trail, 4; causes of, 151–52, 162, 179; at Cimarron agency, 146; at Little Big Horn, 151; by Navajos, 141–42
Ute Indians, 80, 90, 98, 141, 157, 162

Vandever, William, 101–2, 171

Walker, Francis A., 57, 73, 88
War Department, 3, 128, 149, 194
Washington trip, 119–26; benefits from, 132; morality on, 133, 144; photo during, 62
Weaving, 49, 76–77, 121; equipment for, 132, 135, 160; success of, 154

Index

Welsh, William, 6
Whitney, Walter, 132, 135; and
    Navajo uprising, 142
Wild Hank, *see* Easton, Henry W.
Williamson, Samuel D., 38
Winter: and clothing, 105; rations
    during, 34, 74, 96–97, 104–5, 156

Winthrop, John, 196
Women: dismissal of, 94–95; duties
    of, 41

Young, Brigham, 117

Zuñi Pueblo, 40, 48